2/14/85

Tony.

HAPPY VALENTINES DAY!

I hope someday we can have "a place in the country" of our own. Ti amo Tanto!

Julie

A Place in the Country

JOHN BROOKES

A Place in the Country

with 264 illustrations, 98 in colour

THAMES AND HUDSON

Acknowledgments

I am greatly indebted to a wide range of individuals and institutions for stimulating ideas and useful illustrations. My general debts will be apparent from the Bibliography (p. 237). For specific illustration material not my own, my thanks go to the following: Joseph Barrère 18c, 19f; Bibliothèque Nationale, Paris 32; courtesy P.G. Browning/The National Trust 199 below; University of Cambridge Collection, copyright reserved 20 centre and bottom; courtesy The Caravan Club 54; Trustees of the Chatsworth Settlement 37; courtesy Concrete Quarterly 67 above; courtesy Julian Cooper, WMP Landscape Consultants (photo Derek Balmer) 192 above; courtesy Mr and Mrs Adrian Cowell 200; copyright Country Life 45; Croome Estate Trust 30 below; John Ellis 34, 163a; Essex County Record Office 200 top; Ipswich Borough Council 31 above; E.A. Janes, Nature Photographers Ltd 158c; John Kaine 26d, 27f 162; Emily Lane 18d, 19g, 26c 88, 122, 130d, 147 below, 183e, 187d; Michael Laurie 52 below; courtesy Machin Designs Ltd 108, 114 left; after Adrian Martinez 111 centre and bottom; copyright Patrick Matthews 53; National Portrait Gallery, London 30 above; The National Trust 199 above right and below; Ordnance Survey, Crown copyright 60 top; Photo Library International 22; Edwin Smith 11, 20 top, 28, 47, 74 above, 135 below; Colette Thorn 19h, 27h; Jean Tufts 164, 165; Anthony Wickham 175; Valerie Winter 63; Christopher Wood Gallery, London 31 below. Drawings on pp. 126 and 208 are based on illustrations in J.W. Caborn, Shelter Belts and Windbreaks (1965); on pp. 184, 209, 210 and 211, on Charles Coles (ed.), The Complete Book of Game Conservation (1975); on pp. 191 and 197, on Thomas Wright, Large Gardens and Parks: Maintenance, Management and Design (1982).

Finally, I would like to thank my secretary, Hilary Bryan-Brown, without whose assistance and stoic endurance over the interpretation of my appalling handwriting this book would never have come into being.

J.B.
Clock House, Denmans, West Sussex

Printed and bound in Japan
by Dai Nippon

Contents

Introduction: the Way Ahead

Gardens have always had a style, which evolved according to the time when they were created, the status of their owner and the property they adjoined, their location, and their use. The materials and plants in a garden and the manner of their disposition are as revealing of its date as are the material and style of a garment, or the wood and detailing of a piece of period furniture. It is the scale of a garden, both horizontally and vertically, that makes its analysis more difficult, and the picture is made more complex by the fact that British gardens, like British buildings, often show a mixture of periods, with that rich jumbled effect characteristic of our market towns.

But over the last fifty years or so we have had a standardization of the materials available for gardens, and a standardization, if not a paucity, of ideas on how to use them. It must be wrong that the average garden near Edinburgh looks much like one in Wales, the West Country or the south-east, and that all are based on a pre-war ideal of the Surrey country garden, reduced or enlarged according to the land available for its realization. The standardization of materials can be explained by the fact that garden centres have largely taken over horticultural trading from the traditional nurserymen, and that they are supplied by a limited number of companies. Where the nurseryman still exists, he now grows a smaller range of plants which he can be sure will sell, either retail or, more likely, wholesale. And as for the ubiquitous Home Counties aesthetic, it cannot be pure coincidence that the Royal Horticultural Society, from which stems so much worthy literature on plants and planting, has its garden at Wisley in Surrey. The public presentation of our lives, too, has become standardized, dominated by advertisements' portrayal of normal life as a suburban utopia. It is arguable that in retrospect this will produce the style of today's garden – but surely it is wrong that such a mishmash is universal, in town gardens, in the suburbs, and in the country too, with *Cupressocyparis leylandii* everywhere, alongside alien eucalyptus, and all underplanted with heathers!

There is increasing interest now in local habitats, local ways, preservation of the countryside, and also in greater self-sufficiency by the production of one's own vegetables and fruit – and it is all of this that the country gardener must consider, for to push out a foreign boundary round one's site and to create within it an alien world of wholly cultivated species cannot be right, in maintenance terms alone: one is pushing water uphill! Somewhere within this very real interest in nature, and current economic pressures, a new form of garden should emerge, more of its time and – even more imperative – more related to its conditions and setting. The 1930s garden ideal, packaged in 1970s garden centre terms, must give way to the vernacular garden, tailored to the maintenance capabilities of today.

'Most of man's efforts', it was remarked by Francis Bacon four centuries ago, are 'too busie and full of work'. Our task is to rationalize and refine the garden; and to do this we need to look more closely at nature at work. The best time to see the bones of a landscape is in winter, when the trees and hedges are bare. Pure shape reads clearer still when the land is under snow. For, like an abstract sculpture, a landscape's character lies in the massing of forms and proportions, and in winter these can be perceived with no green fuzz to blur them and no bright incidents of colour to distract the eye.

Look then at the shapes created by field patterns. See how the local hills or downs roll and fold, note the placing of trees in a valley bottom, and the way they thin out as they grow up the hill, observe the flow of water – the run of a fast stream compared to the gentle meander of a brook on chalky levels. Experience the enclosed feeling of being between hedges or totally enveloped in a wood, and then emerging into open fields. Moving from enclosure into shade and then into light, you will be conscious of form. It is to the form of a landscape, or of a garden, that one instinctively reacts, feeling that the place is an interesting one, or on the contrary that it is . . . just unsatisfactory.

Strictly formal classical gardens, imposed on the landscape, when maturely backed with trees become equally strict classical outdoor rooms. They express man's domination of his surroundings. We are interested in them more for their decoration, their balustrading and steps, than for their pure form. The eighteenth-century landscape park has a form created from natural elements that reads loud and clear: when driving through a piece of old parkland one is immediately aware of the massing of trees, gentle undulations of the landform, and, perhaps, a quiet stretch of water. These are man-made forms, realized in somewhat contrived natural terms.

The countryside too, of course, is superficially man-made. It appears as open grassland or cultivated spaces interspersed with tree groups and, in many areas, traversed by hedges, which are a more noticeably man-made feature. It is in this tradition of openness surrounded by woodland that the European garden tradition developed, and how, at its most basic, we start a garden: by clearing, levelling, and seeding a lawn. That this is not in fact natural soon appears: such clearings are only maintained by cultivation or by grazing. On a small scale, witness the wilderness (note the word) outside the living room window after only two weeks' holiday. For a garden to be really natural what is needed is not a series of vertical layers (grass, herbs, flowers, shrubs, then trees) but a mosaic of different ones, as might be found in a woodland glade.

Broadly speaking, the taller the 'layer' the more resistant it is to change and to invasion by the next layer. The process of invasion is progressive, starting from the lowest stages. What we choose to call weeds – i.e., our native species – generate very quickly in open ground, and take over grass much more quickly than, say, shrubs do. The earlier the stage in this succession the more difficult it is to maintain horticulturally: mown grass is more difficult than rough, and flowers more difficult than shrubs. Just as with animals, Nan Fairbrother pointed out in *The Nature of Landscape Design*, the smaller and more ubiquitous they are, the harder they are to control: we dealt with wolves and bears centuries ago, but rats and mice are still very much with us. To try to prevent vegetation from growing in open ground in a fertile climate such as England's is to defy nature's basic rules. Many garden plants are not indigenous, and need to be protected from the natives, so clearly we should try not to keep the ground bare but to cover it with suitable native plants of our own choosing. Again, Nan Fairbrother found a descriptive analogy: weeds are squatters, and if you don't want them, don't leave the place empty as an invitation. Ground cover plants have been advocated to this end, but if they are not real tough guys the locals will take them over too. We will never substitute our own designs for nature's except by the sweat of our brow. All we can do is reduce the effort needed by planning for the greatest effect within the natural processes of change.

The planting of native vegetation in a correct habitat would contribute greatly to the health of the countryside, for native species on the whole support a much larger and more diverse population of birds and insects than do exotic species. Intelligently planned gardens can compensate, even if only in a small way, for the loss of wildlife habitats due to the removal of hedgerows.

Look analytically at a particular piece of countryside: consider the broad massings of vegetation which frame the view, noting also their relationship to the open spaces in between. Seldom can one pick out individual species, for they naturally tend to blend together. Exceptions are the stand of beech trees, or the coniferous wood, which is often the result of deliberate planning. Our current garden philosophy tends to be still too concerned with the *content* of the masses, rather than their balance and interrelationship with open spaces.

So, while in the new country garden the choice of plants will ultimately be important, our concern will first be for its design. Addison in the early eighteenth century advocated 'humouring the Genius of the place', and that is what we too should do – to identify this essence and allow it to determine the flavour of the garden. This involves finding out all one can about the conditions of the site, and the mood and feel of the adjoining countryside. One will examine local building materials, hedgerows and fence types – which will often be related; then the local vegetation, on which the wild life is dependent. The vegetation will in turn tell you broadly about the soil (see p. 12) – its acidity or alkalinity, and the underlying rock. You will be concerned about the climate, in winter as well as summer; prevailing winds, frost pockets, the water table. Armed with this information gleaned from your locale (not that your local isn't a mine of information too), you have become your own ecologist, and are ready to proceed to the next stage.

Working from the outside in – which is, incidentally, how other people see your place – consider the 'gardened' part of your land as the meeting area between the natural world outside and the household functions within. Le Corbusier tried to deal with this transitional area by letting the garden flow under the house, but that is impractical. What we seek is far less radical and far more liveable. To use a metaphor, we are designing a garment made of native cloth; however apt the cloth may be to the style the owner wants, it still needs cutting to fit!

The ideal of a garden in which the emphasis is on the natural is obviously more suited to a place in the country, since that is set within the wider landscape. That we should wish to create such a garden is due to the influence of generations of writers, painters and botanists, and it is to the nature and history of the English scene, and the story of changing attitudes to gardening, that we must turn before considering how to create, within a natural framework, the new country garden ideal.

The Look of the Land

There must be few square miles of countryside in Britain that have not been altered by man through the ages, and little of the remote, peaceful landscape that the Romantics so craved and sought out was as untouched as they supposed. Almost more than anywhere else in Europe, the country here has been intensively manipulated to conform to man's requirements – for his current form of agriculture, then for his living and even for his defence. The form these manipulations take depends on the climate and on the underlying geology of the area, and in no country does it change more quickly, resulting in a great variety of landscape types, of vegetation, and of traditional buildings, constructed of local materials before easier transport led to standardization. If we now insert gardens and buildings of the wrong materials and the wrong mood into a setting, the reason must be that we do not understand it.

THE SOIL AND WHAT IT SUPPORTS

Geology is about mud, clay and sand, how these are made into rocks, and how rocks are transformed by great pressures within the earth and shaped by ice, rain and wind. On the fertile residue of this process – soil – our agriculture, our gardens, our food and ultimately we ourselves depend.

Compared with the pace at which the surface of the countryside has been modified by man, the evolutionary stages of our geological makeup are extremely slow. So a landscape exists in time as well as space – a product of the type and form of the rocks, of the climate which determines the agents that attack them, and of the length of time during which the various erosion agents have been at work. Rocks are basically of two types – igneous, formed as a result of volcanic activity, and sedimentary, laid down through the action of the sea. The earth's bed is not stable, and is affected by continual small movements, as well as the more spectacular ones like earthquakes and volcanoes. These constant smaller movements cause the earth's surface slowly to rise and fall, and there is lateral movement as well, which at its most extreme pushes the layers of rock up to form mountain ranges. Where stresses and strains occur locally, cracks appear as faults, the beds on one side of the fault moving in relation to those on the other. In a few cases faults occur on either side of a block which is itself pushed up or down. In the latter case a rift valley is formed, such as that through the centre of Scotland.

The continuous rise and fall accounts for Britain's present position as a group of islands on the edge of a great continental shelf, above the shallow seas which separate us from the rest of Europe. The continental shelf is composed of ancient igneous rock, which through the seas' coming and going has become covered with a sedimentary layer. In places where the two were pushed upward, above sea level, the softer sedimentary coating was gradually worn away, the ragged peaks becoming rounded through the action of

opposite Man and nature at one. The buildings and field walls of this farm in Derbyshire are made of the local stone; on the hill grows a native ash tree.

glaciers, rain, and subsequent river flow. Britain, therefore, consists broadly of two different elements: the exposed igneous rocks of the uplands, running from the Highlands of Scotland down through the Pennines, the Lake District and Wales to Cornwall, and the newer sedimentary formations of the Lowlands. Between these two areas is an intermediate region, at what was the southern end of the comparatively recent ice sheet, which is covered in glacial debris of all sizes from boulders down to finely powdered dust from the glacial clay. Weather acts constantly on all these formations, accentuating the geological differences. Broadly, our weather comes from the south-west on wet Atlantic winds, which meet the range of hills running roughly north-south to give a higher rainfall in the west. This rainfall in turn impoverishes the upland soils by run-off.

Since the Ice Age ended, some twelve thousand years ago, our climate has changed considerably, producing differing types of vegetation which we know from pollen that has been preserved in peat (itself decayed vegetation). The natural vegetation for the present climate in England is deciduous forest, overlapping with a coniferous zone in Scotland. As the altitude gets higher, above 600 m. or so, the conifers peter out to leave bare upland moors.

Our soil, therefore – which we tend to take for granted unless we have a heavy one to dig – reflects the geological formation and the effects of climate, and supports a particular natural vegetation. It consists of mineral material derived from the parent rock, in the form of more or less fine particles of sand, silt or clay, and of decomposed organic debris, forming humus. Air and water are the other two essential elements, their passage assisted by the soil constituency. Air is necessary to the beneficial bacteria and micro-organisms that break down organic matter, and water serves to dissolve and carry vital chemical foods, holding them in solution in the soil so that they support plant and animal life. The flow of water through the soil is affected by the character of the underlying rock, whether hard and impervious, like granite, or soft and porous, like limestone, and the nature of this flow affects the interaction between the humus topsoil and the transitional layer below it. The operative factor is not the amount of rainfall but its effective distribution: a poor soil cannot retain moisture, while a good loam will. These different layers of the

---

Some plants growing naturally in a temperate zone which help to indicate the soil conditions

Canterbury bell (*Campanula glomerata*)	chalky or limy soil
chickweed (*Stellaria media*)	potentially fertile soil
foxglove (*Digitalis purpurea*)	dry sandy or gravelly soil
gorse/furze, common (*Ulex europaeus*)	poor, infertile soil
heat bedstraw (*Galium saxatile*)	dry, light, acid soil
heather and ling (*Erica* and *Calluna* spp.)	dry, acid soil
plantain, hoary (*Plantago media*)	dry, hard, stony alkaline soil
rushes and reeds (*Juncus* and *Carex* spp.)	wet, poor soil
silverweed (*Potentilla anserina*)	damp places, probably on clay
sphagnum moss	wet, acid, peaty soil
strawberry, barren (*Potentilla sterilis*) or wild (*Fragaria vesca*)	dry, stony, barren soil
thistle (*Cardus* spp.)	poor, light, dry acid soil

surface of the earth's crust, from the humus down to the parent rock, are called the soil profile. It is the variation in soil components from place to place, up and down the country, that basically accounts for regional differences in vegetation.

Sand grains are chemically inert and allow water to flow easily through them. A sandy soil is open, allowing easy penetration of air, water and plant roots, but also equally easy leaching out of materials in solution. When calcium is leached out, the soil becomes acid. (Acidity and alkalinity are expressed in terms of pH values, which are the measurement of the hydrogen ion concentration of a suspension of soil in distilled water. A reading lower than 7 pH indicates acidity (earthworms are unhappy when it gets below 4.5); higher than 7, the soil is alkaline. The ideal reading for a garden is 6.5 pH.) Sandy soil was traditionally called a hungry soil, but a warm one, drying out quickly in spring. Constant manuring is necessary to increase its fertility and water-holding capacity. An old method of improving such a soil was by 'marling' – spreading and ploughing in large amounts of clay, where available.

When a sandy soil is not cultivated or grazed, the natural vegetation cycle starts with heath (*Erica*) and heather (*Calluna*). These are replaced by fine, short, tufted grasses; then by brooms and gorse; and finally by sessile oaks (*Quercus petraea*) and Scots pine (*Pinus sylvestris*).

Clay soil has a high proportion of small chemically active grains in its composition, which restrict the content of air and water. When wet, the particles swell, producing the characteristic sticky mass. Clay soils can therefore puddle in wet weather, sealing the surface so that it can be neither grazed nor worked. On drying out the particles contract, and the soil cracks, and may become rock-hard. Such a soil is, however, rich in minerals, and with good drainage, together with applications of organic manure, lime and/or artificial chemical fertilizers, can become very fertile.

The old description of a clay soil being 'cold' and 'late' refers to its slow drying out in spring. In the days of horse-drawn ploughs, the difficulty of cultivating it was indicated by such terms as 'two-horse' or 'eight-horse' land. (The Suffolk Punch horse was specially bred with sleek, short-haired legs to ease its progress through the sticky clay soil.) When undrained, its natural cover was a forest of oak (*Quercus robur*) – which covered much of central England – with some ash and thorn, and willow in the wettest parts.

Silty soil contains a good proportion of medium-size particles and falls between the two extremes of sandy and clay soil. It has less tendency to leach and to puddle and break, and will support a wide range of natural vegetation.

Loamy soil has an ideal proportion of sand, clay and silt, and good aeration; though it cannot be worked when wet, excess moisture dries out quickly. It is the best working soil, and fosters the widest range of natural plant life. Where a good rich soil is not cultivated, the 'climax' vegetation is deciduous mixed forest, for lower-growing species are blanketed out.

Chalky soil is that which overlies limestone. Since the underlying layers are porous, and calcium carbonate dissolves in water, the surface layer may actually show a calcium deficiency, and even give an acid reading. The colour varies from white to grey on pure chalk, and from brown to reddish over other limestones. Open, chalky uplands are the habitat of many of our native herbs, and of a scrub cover of viburnum species, juniper, box, yew, holly and whitebeam. Woodlands on chalk tend to be mainly of beech, with the native wild white cherry on their perimeter.

Water-logged soils comprise swamp, marshland, and peat bog. In a swamp the earth is under water, and tall grasses, sedges and rushes appear above the water in summer. In marshland, the water-table is roughly at ground level. Gradually the level of the soil rises, through the deposit of reeds and rushes and their retention of alluvium, and marshland becomes water-meadow; eventually, a further rise in the level of this grassland due to accumulated humus allows the growth of natural damp oakwoods. Marshland does still exist, notably on Sedgemoor in Somerset, where it is controlled by ditches as in earliest times and farmed in a distinctive way.

Organic soils which are water-logged are known as peat bogs. They form in areas of high rainfall, where practically decayed plant remains are saturated and continue to build up in the absence of air. Succeeding generations of plants grow on top of the compressed remains, reaching a considerable thickness. Peat bogs are usually extremely acid, and support various rushes, sedges, cotton- and deer-grass, heather and bilberry. Fen peat is found where the water entering the peat is alkaline. The vegetation depends on the depth of water. It might include creeping, white and crack willow, alder, buckthorn and bog myrtle, followed by common buckthorn, guelder rose and hawthorn.

THE HAND OF MAN

Northumberland, with its moors and wild beaches, Gloucestershire with its generous hills, Sussex's broad downs, the rolling wolds of Leicestershire and the rich flats of Lincolnshire – everywhere, the character of the land, whether flat or hilly, wet or woody, has affected not only the cattle and cultivations upon its back but the shape of the fields, the substance of their boundaries, the outline of remaining woodlands, whether the lanes or roads are wide or narrow, and, most obviously, of what the houses are made, and how they are constructed.

Over the generations man has bred particular strains of cattle, sheep and horses tailored for specific regions and for the functions he wished them to perform. Most of these have vanished from the fields because they are no longer needed (the Suffolk Punch no longer pulls a plough), or because they have been replaced by more recent 'improved' breeds on an unprecedentedly broad scale (the ubiquitous Friesian dairy cow, for instance). There is a move to preserve these old strains, and animals can be seen in such collections as that of the Rare Breeds Survival Trust at Guiting Power, in Gloucestershire. Traditional buildings, too, can be seen in similar artificial collections, for instance in the Weald and Downland Open Air Museum at Singleton in Sussex, but by the very nature of things, old houses, cottages and farms do survive all over the country, and still stand in the settings that explain them.

The man-made pattern of our landscape began to develop in pre-Roman times, and in some remote areas has changed little since. The earliest farmers worked the land which was the most fertile and driest, and where the native forest was thinnest – the light, dry soil of the limestone hills of the south and south-east. The general flow of peoples coming into Britain was from the south-east too, from the Continent, so that slowly forest clearance spread out from this area across the land. Much of the country was marshy, a fact already recorded by the Romans, and so it remained until the hedge-and-ditch policy of the Agricultural Revolution and Victorian tile-pipe draining largely dried it out, particularly the heavy Midland clays. (The coastal marshlands of England are another story, the land having been reclaimed from the sea since the tenth century by sea banks, the construction of which was a communal effort by several villages.)

Farms and villages were the nerve-centres from which the land was managed. In the flat lowland areas, roughly in the east of the country, farmers gathered together in villages to cultivate and crop the soil, sharing oxen and ploughs, for few could afford their own. In Anglo-Saxon times the village land was divided into vast open fields, within which each villager owned long narrow strips, commonly about 20 m. broad and 200 m. (a furlong, or furrow long) in length. Before the days of fertilizers, the land was allowed to lie fallow periodically to recover, and a 'three-field' rotation system developed, under which parcels of land were sown one year with one crop, the next with another, and the third year lay fallow. The strips are not to be confused with the ridges built up by concentric ploughing in ridge-and-furrow cultivation, that corduroy-like pattern that appears so clearly in aerial photographs and sometimes on the ground, particularly in Leicestershire and other Midland counties where farmland was transformed into sheep pasture in the Middle Ages or Tudor times, before deep ploughing had erased the pattern. Each strip comprised a number of such ridges. Beyond the cultivated fields was common land, on which the villagers grazed their cattle. Virtually everything belonged to the lord, and to him the villagers owed services and goods.

In the damper, hillier south-west of the country, older Celtic ways survived, with isolated farms set among small fields. As opposed to the open-field landscape, properties were enclosed, from very early times, with walls and hedges. The stone walls that shelter the little fields around Zennor, at the tip of Cornwall, go back as far as the Bronze Age. The same pattern occurred at the other end of southern England, in Kent, where farmsteads rather than villages were the rule, and where hedges can be found that are almost as ancient as the thousand-year-old hedges of the west. (The Nature Conservancy estimates that for each different species that goes to make up a hedge over a given length there can be reckoned a hundred years of age.)

The higher, harsher landscape of northern England, much of Scotland and Wales remained relatively poor and primitive, with little change in farming methods through the centuries. Cultivation was restricted to the valley soils, and reached up and down the hillsides as farming prospered or declined. Stones, the great hazard, were cleared from the fields and piled up to form boundary walls. The remainder of the land was grazed, a process hostile to the regrowth of trees, so it gradually became denuded and further impoverished. Eventually, great landowners took over most of these areas for sheep, and the population declined or vanished altogether – most notoriously in the famous Highland Clearances.

The same process of replacing crops by sheep happened much earlier in parts of the agricultural Midlands and north, spurred by the catastrophic visitation of the Black Death in 1348–49 and by succeeding epidemics of bubonic plague. On the whole, the reduction in population meant that the survivors were better off, for their labour was more urgently needed, but in some areas labour-intensive farming was given up altogether in favour of the profitable sheep, which became the chief source of England's wealth. Their marketing and the spinning and weaving of their wool formed the economic nucleus of many of the small market towns which cover the country.

Grazing sheep restrict forest regeneration, and so too do rabbits, aliens introduced as early as Norman times. Gradually, as woodlands shrank, predators such as wolves which would have checked nibbling wild animals were reduced or exterminated. In the late Middle Ages and Tudor period the shortage of good timber became an ever more pressing problem, and time and time again responsible people tried in vain to prevent the wholesale loss of timber stands. So serious was the wood shortage that by the seventeenth century, when England was a naval power protecting herself by her 'wooden walls', she had to rely almost wholly on imported timber. John Evelyn, observing that 'the waste and destruction of our woods has been universal', was moved in 1664 to publish *Sylva – Or A Discourse of Forest Trees*, in which he tried to rally landowners to plant trees for the good of the nation.

In some parts of the country, a system of coppice with standard woodland was developed to replace the lost forest. Twelve standard oaks were allowed to remain on each acre of land, underplanted with hazel, chestnut or ash. These lower trees were coppiced, or cut back in rotation, to shoot again and provide a steady supply of timber for fuel, while the oaks matured to provide wood for building and shipping. This type of woodland still exists, mainly in south-east England, where the younger whip wood is used for fencing.

Towards the end of the seventeenth century, farming methods rapidly improved, with better cultivation, crop-rotation and fertilizers, and new crops of winter fodder. This was revolution indeed, for one was now able to keep one's stock through the winter rather than having to kill it off and salt the meat. This in turn led to the improvement of strains of cattle. With the possibility of fresh meat in the winter, and better vegetables and grain, diet as a whole improved.

Obviously, the system of landholding whereby a farmer held strips in two or more fields, and a further share in the commons, needed rationalization. The process of exchanging or redistributing land to make consolidated holdings had actually begun in the fifteenth century. By the end of the eighteenth century, what with agrarian redistribution and the conversion of land to sheep-pasture, half the farmlands of England and Wales were already enclosed. Then the rationalization became government policy, and Parliamentary Enclosure proceeded with a pace and thoroughness that shocked some observers. Broadly within a belt running between Northumberland in the north-east and Dorset in the south-west, nearly $2\frac{1}{4}$ million acres of land were affected, with a further 2 million acres of common land and 'waste' also being enclosed. All was replanned by surveyors, lawyers and local gentry, and accurate maps were drawn up to show every detail of strips, headlands (where the plough turned), and old trackways of the previous thousand years, with a view to analysing and re-allocating the land. Within this revised landscape there developed a new road system.

Each owner was required to enclose his land in a specified time, often as little as a year, or to pay a heavy penalty. The type of boundary required by Parliament called for a ditch, $4\frac{1}{2}$ ft (1.4 m.) wide at the top and 3 ft (900 mm.) deep, from which the excavated earth would be piled up to form a bank, which would in turn be planted with thorn quicks. While they were growing up to form an impenetrable hedge, the hawthorn plants would be protected from animals by a dead hedge of brushwood or a post-and-rail fence. To compensate for the wood felled to provide this fencing, trees chosen for their timber value were to be planted within the new hedge at regular 6–9 m. intervals. Oak was obviously prized for shipping, and was used on the heavier Midland soil with ash, which is tough and fast-growing. Elm too was planted, which lasts under water and was therefore used for ship keels and harbour construction. In the north sycamore, which is not indigenous, was chosen to withstand the harsher winds and provide shelter for exposed farmhouses.

After making his perimeter boundary, the owner could then subdivide his new farm into whatever small units he chose. In pastoral farming, a field of ten acres was reckoned to be best for stock control. It is this standardization of the landscape which caused a literary outcry at the time, and which accounts for much of the dreary regularity of our Midland scene, broken only by artificial fox coverts.

Even before Parliamentary Enclosure, many small farmers, sharecroppers and smallholders could not, or would not, conform to such reorganization, and left the land, selling up the property that had been in their family for generations to land-hungry country squires. Thus began the migration to the cities and the further enlargement of the great estates with, in the course of the eighteenth century, their landscaped parks. Around 1800, the countryside over vast areas must have looked odd indeed, strewn with miles of straggly hedges and punctuated by newly planted acres of landscape woodland. This revolution was far greater than anything which the modern farmer has yet conceived, and set the landscape pattern which we now enjoy in its full maturity.

Into this matrix the burgeoning townships of the Industrial Revolution crept insidiously, but without basically affecting it: the countryside remained as a pure antidote, to be enjoyed at first by a few Romantics, then increasingly by many as roads and then railways made access easier. Here and there industrial activity left excavated scars – coal mines in the north-east, the Midlands and south Wales, tin mines in Cornwall, lead mines and quarries – but now, with land-shaping and planting, some of these abandoned workings have been transformed into fine recreational landscapes.

In the present century the speed of change has accelerated, and the traditional farming community is being squeezed by the greater pressure of a mobile industrial society, and machinery and economics have joined forces to start changing the face of the land again. Combine harvesters do not get on happily with hedged fields in small units, or with the great barns in which farmers have stored their grain for a thousand years or more.

Faces of the landscape

a Border country near Peebles. Trees in the valley shelter arable farmland. Higher up the ground is open moorland, with new forestry plantations.
b Flat land at the base of the Sussex Downs, planted with oil-seed rape.
c Wicken Fen in Norfolk.
d Wild moorland in Northumberland; on the skyline, the Roman wall.
e A new pattern on the Berkshire Downs – wide open arable fields, interrupted only by shelter belts.
f Acid-loving vegetation of the East Anglian Brecklands.
g An orchard below the Black Mountains of Breconshire. Note the coursed dry-stone walling.
h Moorland with rock outcrops tumbling down to the Langdale valley

a

b

c

d

e

f

g

h

Open and enclosed fields

left An ancient hedged landscape in Kent, on the Pilgrims' Way to Canterbury.

centre The strip pattern of medieval open fields preserved at Laxton in Nottinghamshire. Very rare in England since Enclosure, this pattern is still common on the Continent. At the top are conventional enclosed fields.

below Enclosed fields at Padbury, Buckinghamshire. Used for grazing, they still show the outline of the old open fields cultivated in ridge-and-furrow, crossed relentlessly by hedges.

Boundary walls, hedges and fences

The patchwork quality of the typical English landscape, as we have seen, was far from being a sudden thing of eighteenth-century enclosures, for it had always been necessary to enclose one's stock and mark one's territory. Hoskins tells us that boundaries are one of the most ancient and permanent features in England. At their simplest, divisions were marked by natural features – the edge of a woodland, a particular tree or boulder mass; more substantially, they might take the form of ditches and earth mounding, or hedges, or stone walls. The private estate and large native farm enclosed their land to define a hunting park, a status symbol which required a licence from the king.

The earliest walls were generally in areas where stones had to be cleared from the fields anyway – areas of glacial drift or mountain erosion – and such walls can be seen running almost vertically up valley sides and onto the open moorland in our upland areas. Where a softer freestone was available, and used for house construction, it served for boundary walls too, so that villages in the Cotswolds, for instance, or in Northamptonshire or Derbyshire seem all of a piece, and fields may be separated by dry-stone walls made of irregular fragments ingeniously fitted together like three-dimensional jigsaws.

In the south-west many of the boundaries to the little fields, particularly those bordering deep lanes, are constructed of granite walling, which is then earthed over and planted. Another combination of stone wall and hedge, popular in Scotland, is the 'Galloway hedge', which was developed about 1730. In this arrangement the hedge plants are grown through from the back and up the front face of a massive wall.

The word 'fence' is related to 'defence' – because the first fences were used to enclose land and bar intruders, or to keep livestock in check, and provide another boundary element in the form of paling or hurdles. The type of fence, like the type of house or wall, will depend on what grows locally. Ash, they say, is queen of trees: it makes very good gates and hurdles, because it splits easily along the grain, though its tendency to rot when damp makes it a poor choice for fencing posts. Birch, well seasoned and well creosoted, makes excellent fencing material. Particularly in the Highlands (as in Scandinavia), it is used for virtually everything. Chestnut is the most useful wood of all for the farmer, gardener and estate manager. It does not rot in the ground when used as poles or gateposts, needs no treatment, and cleaves very easily. Sweet chestnut is managed in coppice form, especially in hop-growing areas of the south-east, where it is used for hop poles; and it is also good for the stakes in pole-and-wire fencing, that sort of temporary fencing that can be rolled up and easily moved. Hazel also used to be coppiced, to provide long and pliable wands for thatching and for weaving into hurdles, to protect young quickthorn hedges and sheep, but post-and-barbed-wire fencing now does the latter job far better. Oak is undisputed king, for when kept dry its extremely hard heartwood is practically everlasting. It cleaves well, and is stronger when split than when sawn. Usually too good for fencing, oak makes a handsome gate that needs no painting, and is ideal for gateposts as well.

Boundaries

left Walls of local stone stretch out from Bainbridge in Yorkshire into the frosty landscape.

top Stones picked from the fields form a boundary in the Borders.

above A beautifully laid hedge in the Midlands.

below A granite wall in Devon has become a natural rockery.

Before the advent of easy transport, the type of house one built depended on the natural materials available – timber where trees were plentiful and good, stone in hilly areas, for that is what the hills are made of, and brick in low-lying areas, for clay was easy to excavate for the kiln. The type of timber and the type of stone – hard or soft, available in any size or only in small pieces – affected the structure too. Larger country houses reflected their location as much as humble cottages, though after the introduction of classicism in the seventeenth century their designs became less regionally distinctive and more cosmopolitan, leaving cottages to express the 'spirit of the place'.

To the average city-dweller the country cottage remains an ideal, and no matter how dilapidated, without drainage or mains water, and with awkward internal stairs, rising damp and several kinds of rot, these 'desirable properties' fetch enormous prices, far higher than a new dwelling complying with every byelaw. The Romantic dream is still very much with us: why else does one inflict such a state of affairs on one's family and one's self, if not to achieve some sort of rural idyll?

Our early forebears probably lived in dwellings not very different from the primitive huts that can be seen in Africa today, made of a circle of stakes forced into the ground, with an infill of mud or cowdung, and roofed with a conical frame of sticks thatched with grass. Where loose stones were available, walls plastered with mud replaced the stakes. Another ancient walling material was cob – a mixture of sticky mud with straw to bind it, built up slowly into thick walls with characteristic rounded corners. Coated with a thin layer of plaster or limewash, and protected from rain by a heavy overhanging thatched roof, such walls will last for centuries. They are still found in many parts of the country, but are perhaps easiest to spot in Somerset and Devon.

Until the late Middle Ages, most English houses were made of timber, even in stone-rich areas, for wood is more easily worked and handled. A frame of heavy timbers was filled with panels made of woven twigs (willow in East Anglia, split hazel elsewhere) which were then covered with a plaster made of lime and mud, or just mud, mixed with combings from horses to bind it. The walls would be limewashed, probably in colour – earthy ochres, pinkish madder, blue – and the beams not blackened (a nineteenth-century innovation) but, it seems, left plain or painted with ox-blood. As time went on and large trees got scarcer, the beams became slimmer and more closely spaced, and by the seventeenth century they were usually completely rendered over, giving a smooth façade, which in East Anglia might be decorated with shallow plaster ornaments in the technique known as pargeting. An exception to this general trend is the West Midlands, where timber was plentiful until quite a late date, and a particularly showy style of exposed timber-framing developed.

Where trees had always been scarce, and where they became depleted, builders had to turn to other materials. The most obvious is stone, which comes in two basic types that affect the nature of the structure. Sedimentary rocks – chiefly limestone and sandstone – are known as 'freestone' ('good stone'). Having been deposited in layers, they split quite easily and can then be dressed into regular blocks. Such are the oolitic limestone of the great belt that runs in a gentle curve from Dorset up the centre of England to the Tees (think of dazzling white Portland stone, the honey-coloured or grey stone of the Cotswolds, and the ironstone of Northamptonshire, brown as gingerbread), and the sandstones scattered across Britain (red in Devon and Breconshire, for instance, creamy grey in the north Midlands and north, warm cream and red again in Edinburgh). Freestone can be worked into beautiful smooth ashlar, but in vernacular buildings it is often less finely finished, and laid as coursed rubble.

The second type of building stone is the igneous rocks that crop up in Cornwall, Wales, Lakeland and the Highlands of Scotland. This is extremely hard to work, and whenever possible existing stones and boulders – formed by weathering or streams – are used, giving a characteristically massive walling of random rubble.

Where good stone was not plentiful there were other options. In areas with a chalky subsoil flints are used, but they are not an easy material, being comparatively small and irregular in shape. Corners have to be made of brick or stone blocks, which are often incorporated as a strengthening pattern in the wall as well. Flint can also be knapped, or cracked, to give it at least a smooth face and sometimes a complete cubic shape, and such knapped flints may be intermixed with freestone to form patterns known as flushwork.

Where the subsoil is clay, it was dug and fired locally to make bricks. Known in England in Roman times, bricks seem to have been forgotten until they were reintroduced from the Low Countries – as early as the Middle Ages around Hull in Yorkshire, but in most stoneless areas of the centre and east in the sixteenth and especially the seventeenth century. Sometimes in the Tudor period brick was used instead of wattle and daub to infill a timber frame. Because of the small-scale, localized nature of the brick industry, this material varied in colour and texture from place to place as much as stone. It was only in the later nineteenth century that large-scale production around such places as Fletton in Bedfordshire and Ruabon in north Wales combined with a vast railway network to send standardized bricks at low cost throughout the country.

In the Home Counties, timber-framed buildings went on being built in the eighteenth and nineteenth centuries, covered not just with plaster now but with tiles (some, 'mathematical tiles', made to fit tight together and look like a more expensive brick façade), or with weatherboarding. Softwood planking was cheap, coming from the Baltic on ships that put into many of the small ports lining the coasts of Essex and Kent.

When it comes to roofing, the most common early type was thatch, and its craft has changed little. It does not need sawn timber to support it, and it provides excellent insulation. Reed thatch (the best of it from Norfolk) can last up to fifty years, while the life-span of wheat or rye straw is only a little over twenty, but the latter is cheaper and so more frequently used. In areas of poor, inhospitable soil gorse or heather may be used. Thatch is laid in bundles, which are fixed to the roof timbers by means of iron hooks and to one another by bent hazel sticks, or sways. At the ridge, which is the most vulnerable point, an extra layer of thatch is usually provided, anchored by rows of hazel twigs or spars, which are also used at the sides and bottom edge of the roof.

a

b   d

a An early timber-framed 'Wealden house', with central double-height hall, at Singleton in Sussex. In the background, hurdle fencing.
b An East Anglian timber-framed house with a colour-washed clay bat finish and decorative thatched roof.
c Brick and thatch – Thomas Hardy's birthplace at Higher Bockhampton, Dorset.
d Houses cased in clapboard and tile-hanging at Hawkhurst, Kent.
e A Sussex flint cottage with brick stitching at corners and openings.

e

c

f

f Cotswold stone can be split into neat
rectangles for walls, and further fractured to
provide roofing 'slates' of graduated size. This
house is at Middle Lypiatt, Gloucestershire.
g A robust four-square Northumbrian house
of ashlar below a slate roof.
h A Lakeland house at Grasmere, built of
large rubble stones under a stone roof. Note
the circular chimneys.

g

h

Thatchers have distinctive regional styles: in East Anglia, for instance, thatched roofs are usually steep in pitch, whereas in Devon they are lower, chunky, and with a rounded end often topped by a little peak.

A pitched roof supported on solid oak beams was a more prestigious structure, and timber was transported laboriously for miles. A surprising number of such roofs survive today, and where they do not the reason is more often a change in fashion than failure of the material. Traditionally they were covered with stone slabs in the limestone belt and the Lake District, and elsewhere, particularly from the seventeenth century onwards, with tiles, either small and flat or of the curved pantile type seen in Suffolk. Tiles need a steep roof; thin, smooth slates, on the other hand, do not, and their use affected the shape of roofs not only in those parts where they occurred naturally but, with the greater ease and cheapness of transport from the early nineteenth century onwards, throughout the country.

In their basic form, cottages also varied somewhat from region to region, according to climate and the materials from which they were made. They evolved with time, too, echoing the more elaborate evolution of grander houses. Very broadly, they started as simple structures, with a hall open to the roof and perhaps a screened sleeping area at one end; then the sleeping end would become two-storeyed, providing a bedroom above and perhaps a parlour below; a balancing wing might develop at the other end; and the hall part was subdivided horizontally, making the house two-storeyed throughout. All these designs would be asymmetrical, since the front door led into one end of the hall. As classicism filtered down the social scale, cottages too became symmetrical, presenting an image like a child's drawing of an ideal house. By the later eighteenth century, such symmetry seemed boring to designers in the Picturesque mode like Humphry Repton and John Nash: the former's landscapes included pretty *cottages ornés*, and the little houses of Blaise Hamlet near Bristol, designed by the latter, are self-consciously irregular in form and quaint in their mixture of materials. To the Gothic Revivalists who followed, asymmetry was preferable as a truer reflection of a building's contents. They started a reappraisal of traditional vernacular methods of construction and materials, and put cottage design back on course. But with them we leave the world of the local craftsman-builder, and move to the world of sophisticated design.

Pargetting – ornamental plasterwork – on Bishop Bonner's Cottages at East Dereham, Norfolk, built in 1502.

'Nature still, but Nature methodiz'd'

The idea of designing a garden in order to give aesthetic pleasure has a long history in China and Japan, and was familiar in Persia and in ancient Rome. The source of the European garden as we know it seems to have been the world of Islam, and in particular those areas that were in closest contact with the West – Spain and Sicily. The mystical, almost religious, significance which the Arabs found in the garden was ignored, but its prime symbol, water, was not. Water, essential in a hot climate for irrigation and for cooling the air, was canalized, shaped into pools and set in motion through fountains in a myriad different ways.

In medieval Europe a garden meant an enclosure, a sanctuary from the wilderness of nature, connected as much with the production of food and medicinal herbs as with enjoyment. Within its protective walls the layout was strict. A typical arrangement might be a division into four squares, with a fountain in the middle. The squares would be planted with flowers – some, such as the lily and the rose, grown for their beauty alone – and surrounded by low hedges of herbs. There might be seats, faced with stone and cushioned with turf. A large garden could be subdivided by trellising into various open-air rooms, some devoted to the growing of fruit.

Little is in fact known about medieval gardens before the fifteenth century, but it is certain that the number of different plants in cultivation gradually increased, from fewer than a hundred around the year 900; and that monasteries improved the land by large-scale operations such as the planting of hedges and trees – something the country gardener of today may be called upon to do. John Harvey has traced two traditions of gardening in the Middle Ages: the sort practised in monasteries, where the emphasis was on the cultivation of plants for their usefulness, and on scientific study; and the sort favoured by kings and high officials, interested in a deer park for hunting and a garden for aesthetic enjoyment. Smaller gardens combined features from both traditions. The whole subsequent history of gardens in England was to be marked by these phenomena: the introduction and development of new plants; and the alternative views of the garden as collection of plants and as artistic composition.

Side by side with the feeling for artifice in medieval gardens was a profound love of nature, expressed by Chaucer in his fourteenth-century translation of the French *Romance of the Rose*:

> Ther sprang the violet al newe
> And fresshe pervinke rich of hewe,
> And floures yelowe, whyte and rede:
> Swich plentee grew ther never in mede,
> Ful fay was al the ground and queynt
> And poudred, as men had it peynt,
> With many a fresh and sondry flour
> That casten up a ful savour.

Gardens seen through the painter's eye

left The Stuart formal garden: Little Hadham, Hertfordshire, *c*.1639, from a painting by Cornelius Johnson. An up-to-the-minute design, it includes terracing, urns, steps, fountains, statues, and a wall punctuated by a classical doorway and gazebo.

below The Picturesque ideal: Croome Court, Worcestershire, set in its landscaped park by Capability Brown, with Chinese bridge, church and temple. Richard Wilson's painting, of 1758, perfectly embodies the pastoral vision inspired by Claude Lorrain (cp. p. 37).

above Early nineteenth-century circular flower bed and shrub border: John Constable's loving record of his father's garden at East Bergholt, 1815. Walled at the side, the garden opens out at the end to the rolling Suffolk landscape.

right The 'cottage muddle' beloved at the turn of the century. This is at Haseley in Oxfordshire.

A medieval garden screened from the world (from a fifteenth-century French manuscript).

Around these much-loved flowers grew up a whole folklore of symbolic meanings, charged with sentiment, association and passion. When poets spoke of love, as late as the seventeenth century, they did so in the language of flowers, setting their scenes in the 'pleached bowers' of gardens, away from the bustle of the hall and the parlour.

Only gradually did Western man gain the confidence – or, perhaps, the desire – to break down the protective barriers and look out to the surrounding countryside. As long as gardens were in towns this enclosure was inevitable. But during the Renaissance the idea that the country could be enjoyed, as well as used, began to gain currency. In Italy, especially, princes and merchants (following the example of the younger Pliny, whose works were now being rediscovered by the literate public) built themselves country villas with elaborate gardens. In the hills around Florence and Rome the air was cool, the ground lent itself to ornamental cascades, and the surrounding valleys could form part of a panorama dedicated as much to nature as to art.

Ripples from the Italian Renaissance, in gardens as in architecture, spread to France in the early sixteenth century, and on from France and Flanders to England. The layout of these 'Italian' gardens was still formal, but in design the beds were greatly elaborated into intricate 'knots', outlined with dwarf evergreen plants. Pictures of Henry VIII's gardens at Hampton Court and Whitehall show low beds punctuated by tall painted poles bearing heraldic beasts. Symbolism and allegorical programmes became increasingly popular as the century advanced, and gardens might be divided into several areas, each with a distinct character. Baron Waldstein, a young Moravian nobleman

32

visiting England in 1600, described with fascination the great garden at Nonsuch, which was divided into three parts – the Grove, the Woodland, and the Wilderness – and had, in addition, a circular deerpark. The Grove, embowered in shrubs and trees and reached by a leafy path, was the Grove of Diana, symbolic of the Virgin Queen, Elizabeth. Its centrepiece was a fountain made to look like rocks, among which Diana and her nymphs were bathing, and the peeping Actaeon was beginning to turn into a stag. Elsewhere in the Grove were little structures bearing verses alluding to Diana and to virtue, and a column that sprayed passersby with water – one of those water jokes so popular in sixteenth- and seventeenth-century Europe. In the more formal part of the garden, Waldstein noted representations of the Labours of Hercules and 'other subjects from the poets', and decorative marble obelisks.

'The maner of watering with a Pumpe in a tubbe', from Didymus Mountain's *The Gardener's Labyrinth*, 1577.

This elaboration of garden features and garden types continued up to the Civil War, made more sophisticated by the knowledge of Italian Mannerist gardens, introduced in the reign of James I by Salomon de Caus. The new layouts were characterized by terraces and fountains, summerhouses, statues, flowerbeds in elaborate shapes, and by two new, related ideas concerning layout: the organization of the garden on a system of axes, creating vistas, and the closer integration of the garden with the house. A classic example of such a garden was Wilton, as laid out in 1632–35 by Isaac de Caus for the Earl of Pembroke to complement a new Palladian façade to his house.

At the same time, flowers were not forgotten: the first English book on their cultivation, John Parkinson's *Paradisi in Sole Paradisus Terrestris*, was published in 1629. Among his hundreds of woodcut illustrations with accompanying text (which give particular attention to tulips and carnations), he also includes vegetables and fruit. His title makes punning use of the original meaning of the word 'paradise', which is 'garden' or 'park', to represent his name: 'Park-in-Sun's Earthly Paradise'.

The association between gardens and the earthly paradise had particular significance for the Puritans. To them gardening became a metaphor for spiritual reform, and thus not only a legitimate but a desirable pursuit. When the country was divided by the Civil War, it was also a suitable occupation for noblemen of both parties on their country estates. Lord Fairfax, commander of the Parliamentary forces, withdrew in 1650 to his lands at Nun Appleton in Yorkshire, and there cultivated a garden that was celebrated by the poet Andrew Marvell. With reference to his martial past, he laid it out on the model of a fort, with ditches and five bastions (alluding to the five senses). Marvell mentions woods, a water meadow crossed by a shallow flooding stream, fruit trees, a flower garden in which grew tulips, pinks and roses, and a garden of herbs and flowers laid out to form a sundial.

Elsewhere, in 'The Mower against Gardens', Marvell raised the ancient question of nature versus art, imagining a mower, child of the native grasslands, railing against formal layout and horticultural experiment:

> Luxurious man, to bring his vice in use,
>   Did after him the world seduce,
> And from the fields the flowers and plants allure,
>   Where nature was most plain and pure.

33

He first enclosed within the gardens square
    A dead and standing pool of air,
And a more luscious earth for them did knead,
    Which stupified them while it fed.
The pink grew then as double as his mind;
    The nutriment did change the kind.
With strange perfumes he did the roses taint,
    And flowers themselves were taught to paint.
The tulip, white, did for complexion seek,
    And learned to interline its cheek:
Its onion root they then so high did hold,
    That one was for a meadow sold.
Another world was searched, through oceans new,
    To find the *Marvel of Peru.* . . .

'Tis all enforced, the fountain and the grot,
    While the sweet fields do lie forgot:
Where willing nature does to all dispense
    A wild and fragrant innocence:
And fauns and fairies do the meadows till,
    More by their presence than their skill.
Their statues, polished by some ancient hand,
    May to adorn the gardens stand:
But howsoe'er the figures do excel,
    The gods themselves with us do dwell.

The debate, conventional since the Renaissance, was to have a serious outcome for gardening in the next century, when Capability Brown was to convince landowners that the mower's meadow should stretch right up to the mansion's door.

A classical running scroll in box at Pitmedden in Scotland, *c.*1675.

In the meantime, however, people delighted both in the beauty and picturesque irregularity of the country and in the composed artifice of the formal garden. The seventeenth century saw the beginnings of pure landscape drawing and painting. With the return of the Court from exile at the Restoration in 1660, a new kind of garden was promoted in England: the French. This style, brought to perfection by André Le Nôtre at Vaux-le-Vicomte and Versailles, was still essentially formal but conceived on a larger scale, less intricate and less architectural, and on predominantly flat ground. Most importantly, its entire layout was *house-centred*. It is the visual parallel to an absolute monarchy: just as all France focused on the Sun King, so the garden focused on the house. Perspectives were contrived to extend from each of its four façades. Close to it lay embroidered parterres, symmetrically arranged and elaborately patterned, not only with plants but with coloured gravels. Slightly further away there were *bosquets*, or groves, which might contain little secret open spaces forming green rooms. The axes, sometimes marked by canals, were extended out into the landscape, avenues being planted or straight vistas being cut through surrounding woods.

When the Baroque garden was introduced into England it was always modified in one way or another. Unlike the Ile de France, the little hills of

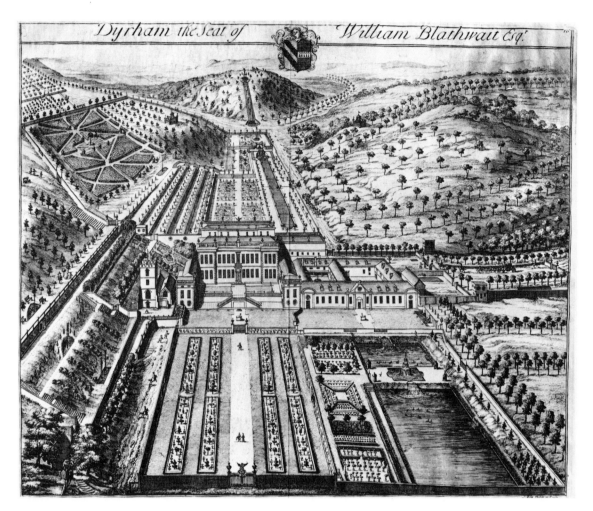

Dyrham the Seat of William Blathwait Esq.

England do not lend themselves to the grand horticultural gesture, and the English temperament seems not to have wanted such total organization. Sometimes the axes were slightly shifted: at Longleat, laid out in the 1680s by London and Wise, the most eminent practitioners of this genre, the main axis ran not through the centre of the house from front to back, but transversely. Elsewhere, it was set off from the house altogether. Radiating avenues were rare, and tended to be planted somewhat later, in response to the general appeal for more timber.

Virtually all these gardens were so thoroughly erased by Brownian grassy swards that it is easy to forget they ever existed, or to think they were a momentary aberration. But engravings of the years around 1700 by Kip and Knyff show dozens of houses surrounded by formalized gardens and parks that often blanket vast areas of country. Dyrham in Gloucestershire, which in its steep hollow seems unimaginable except in landscape garden terms, was surrounded by elaborate patterned plantings which were French in inspiration, though quite un-French in their fragmented grouping. A rare survival of a garden *à la française* is that at Melbourne in Derbyshire, where about 1704 London and Wise laid out a formal parterre near the house and farther away,

By 1712, as shown in Kip's view of Dyrham, the formal garden had somewhat burst its banks, reaching out far into the countryside to become a series of unrelated incidents, held within a strict grid.

35

to one side, a woodland crossed by avenues and paths meeting at *ronds-points* (the sort of Baroque planning that Christopher Wren had proposed for the rebuilding of London after the Great Fire of 1666).

Gradually this area of irregularly patterned woodland was to displace the parterre as the main subject of garden theorists' thinking, until, after centuries of clipping and restraining nature behind garden walls, the old order was reversed and nature allowed to run right up to the house. This informal, natural-looking scene was England's contribution to world gardening, and it is the ancestor of today's informal, easy-maintenance gardens. How did it come about, and what were its historical sources?

Francis Bacon, in his essay 'On Gardens', took up a pose against formality as early as 1597. Knots, he says, 'are but toys: you may see as good sights many times in tarts'. The ideal he sought contained a heath or area of natural wilderness. The word 'wilderness' came into fashion to describe a garden (or more usually a part of a garden) which gave the impression of having been left uncultivated, though of course this was not actually the case. The Nymph in Andrew Marvell's poem had

> a garden of my own
> But so with roses overgrown,
> And lilies, that you would it guess
> To be a little wilderness . . .

It was from such a cultural background that the English concept of the 'landscape' garden emerged, first in the work of William Kent in the early eighteenth century and then, fully formed, in that of Capability Brown. It rested ultimately on a fiction: that the gentleman's park, the setting for his magnificent (now usually classical or Palladian) house, was actually the real countryside untouched by man, a pastoral scene rich with classical allusions and filled with the sublimity which the earliest Romantic poets were beginning to discover in untamed nature.

These parks in fact came about no more naturally than the formal gardens that they replaced. Landowners planned, planted, discussed, visited each other's estates, criticized and theorized to an extent that makes it clear that gardening was as much a conscious art as painting or literature. Moreover – and this is something that one tends to forget – it was for them very much an art of the imagination, since they were planting for the future and never actually saw the mature beauty which they were striving to create.

The visual inspiration of the landscape garden was Italy, but an Italy seen through the eyes of a few painters. Italy was the great goal of English gentlemen on the Grand Tour, primarily to see the remains of ancient Rome, but also to acquire polish, taste and connoisseurship in the land that was in these respects the accepted leader of Europe. They came home with classical sculptures, Italianate plans for their houses, and paintings of the Italian landscape, if possible by Poussin or Claude. What more desirable than to recreate at home the landscape that these artists had recorded, landscape that brought classical mythology, Roman architecture and the Italian countryside vividly before their eyes?

But landowners' tastes and their gardens did not move in one leap from symmetrical parterres to Claudian compositions. We have seen that a new appreciation of the natural landscape developed in the seventeenth century. With the introduction of the ha-ha, a sunken boundary wall, it became possible for the garden and the surrounding landscape to flow together apparently without interruption.

Among the intellectuals who argued for a change were the essayist Joseph Addison and the poet Alexander Pope. As early as 1712, Addison, in *The Spectator*, suggested that 'a whole estate be thrown into a kind of garden':

> A marsh overgrown with willows, or a mountain shaded with oaks, are not only more beautiful but more beneficial, than when they lie bare and unadorned. Fields of corn make a pleasant prospect and, if the walks were a little taken care of that lie between them, if the natural embroidery of the meadows were helped and improved by some small additions of art, and the several rows of hedges set off by trees and flowers that the soil was capable of receiving, a man might make a pretty landskip of his own possessions . . .

With its reference to choosing trees and flowers suitable for the local soil, this seems almost a recipe for the country garden we are advocating today.

It was Addison's idea that by practising his husbandry in this way the small estate owner could combine beauty with necessity. Carried further, this meant that on newly enclosed land ornamental or exotic trees might be planted in preference to native ones, hedgerows were to become draped with jasmine and roses, muddy tracks to be trim walks of sand or gravel, untidy lanes to be carriage rides, and ugly buildings prettied up or disguised as ruins. The idea was attractive: aesthetics and commerce in happy coexistence. The only

Landscape with Mercury and Battus by Claude Lorrain, *c.*1660, a prototype for the English school of landscape: still water, tranquil tree groupings, a classical building, and animals.

37

danger, apart from the cattle being poisoned by exotic vegetation, was of submerging the drudgery of farming beneath a tide of sentiment.

Two famous examples of the *ferme ornée* were The Leasowes, the estate of the poet William Shenstone near Halesowen in Shropshire, and Woburn Farm in Bedfordshire, designed by Philip Southcote in the 1730s. Horace Walpole, the great arbiter of taste, wrote of Woburn: 'the profusion of flowers and the delicacy of keeping betray more wealthy expense that is consistent with the economy of farming or the rusticity of labour – Woburn Farm . . . is the habitation of such nymphs and shepherds as are represented in landscape and novel, but do not exist in nature.'

The gardening style for which the eighteenth century is known to the English, and England is known to the world, started from similar premises but developed rather differently. Pope, following Addison, summed up the new attitude in his *Epistle to the Earl of Burlington* (1731):

> Consult the genius of the place in all:
> That tells the waters or to rise or fall:
> Or helps the ambitious hill the heavens to scale,
> Or scoops in circling theatres the vale:
> Calls in the country, catches opening glades,
> Joins willing woods, and varies shades from shades . . .

The gardener, in other words, should express the underlying spirit of the landscape, not impose an alien ideal. In practical terms, the result was usually a compromise, a natural-seeming landscape sprinkled with the products of learning and artifice. Pope's own garden at Twickenham, which was small in scale and planned (on compositional principles he had learned from the study of history painting) for the delight of the *cognoscenti*, hardly seems to us today to have consulted 'the genius of the place', but its respect for the forms of nature is undoubtedly greater than that expressed in a *parterre de broderie*.

William Kent, who worked for Lord Burlington, seems to have been the first garden designer consciously to apply the principles of landscape painting, positioning clumps and individual trees, creating glades, and designing monuments and follies to satisfy his patrons' imagination. The Roman temples and Gothick ruins in these early picturesque (literally picture-like)

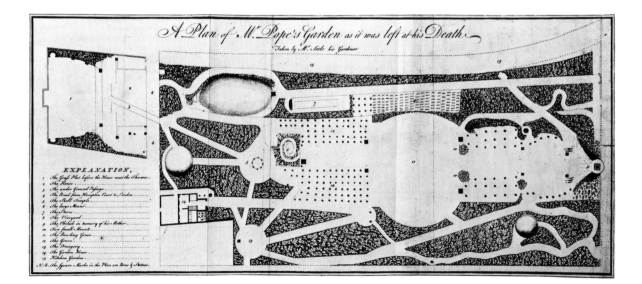

gardens were not purely decorative: they could have individual significance, and they could be so arranged as to form a symbolic programme. The garden at Stowe in Buckinghamshire, for instance, expressed Lord Cobham's disgust at the state of the modern world after his resignation from the government in 1733. Before the middle of the century Kent's style had begun to be replaced by that of Capability Brown. Learned allusions decline; classical temples become less frequent; the natural elements take precedence. Rivers are diverted, lakes dug, groves of trees planted, but all so closely and so sensitively modelled on natural scenery that it is now at times almost impossible to tell one from another.

Horace Walpole was the most persuasive spokesman of the new picturesque movement. It was he who proclaimed that Kent 'first leaped the fence and saw all nature was a garden'. He enthusiastically described the beauties of Stowe, Rousham and Stourhead, and of a view at Wroxton he wrote: 'This scene consists of a beautiful lake entirely shut in with wood; the head falls into a fine cascade, and that into a serpentine river, over which is a little Gothic seat like a round temple, lifted up by a shaggy mount.'

Just as a variety of attitudes to landscape were expressed by painters and writers from the mid-eighteenth to the early nineteenth century – from Stubbs's depictions of the peaceful prosperity of the land-owning squire to Turner's cataclysmic mountain scenes, and from the serene meditations of Collins and Gray to Wordsworth's mystical celebrations of Lakeland – so the attitudes expressed in gardening became correspondingly complex. While wealthier and more avant-garde landowners were (to paraphrase Addison) making a landscape of their own possessions, among the minor gentry the old style persisted throughout much of the eighteenth century. And while Bridgeman's gardens seem not to have included flowers, and Kent and Brown were on the whole concerned to compose with larger elements, flowers did not disappear, and a number of new methods were devised for their use. In the 1730s picturesque irregular areas and circular formal flowerbeds were advocated. Philip Southcote at Old Woburn planned the planting of the outer walks to be triangular in section, from a core of tall beech trees through lower shrubs down to flowers by the path. Joseph Spence in the 1760s advocated what sounds rather like the wild garden of today, writing that 'the most pleasing wild flowers should be supplyd largely; all about the Groves but particularly so toward the walks and margins'. At the same time, he advised formal planting for some areas, and the growing of such flowers as roses, jasmines and honeysuckles in tubs. A famous informal flower garden was created in the 1770s at Nuneham Courtenay in Oxfordshire.

To combine the two modes of gardening – the broad sweeping park devised by Capability Brown and the flower garden of greater horticultural interest, the one found chiefly on great estates and the latter around the houses of the gentry – was the achievement of Humphry Repton. His first landscape commissions date from 1788, five years after Brown's death. Although during his career he designed a number of large estates for great landowners, the majority of his clients were drawn from among the moderately rich, whose income might be derived not from land but from scientific and technical knowhow of benefit to the advancing Industrial Revolution.

We saw that the landscape park initially had strong Italianate overtones, Kent, with his painter's eye, developing views inspired by paintings by Claude. Brown, who was also an architect, simplified this picturesque ideal, but in the process he evolved a pastoral formula that he applied universally in a sometimes rather bland way. Repton – a painter again – had thoroughly observed nature and landscape, and went on to modify the picturesque vision with reference to his observations. For example, Brown had moulded his landscapes with contrived tree groupings (the clump is a sure sign of his work or influence), whereas Repton planted his trees as they would grow if left to themselves. As Dorothy Stroud, his biographer, has written, 'Repton's trees spilled like cream down the slopes to merge in the valleys'. And where Brown would have his client's house sit quite unadorned within his landscape, Repton liked a gentler transition, which he effected by introducing the terrace, often bordered by balustrading and urns. He also planted parterres to join the house to the grounds. Whether intentionally or not, he was beginning to scale down the picturesque to make room for the cosier 'gardenesque'. His designs might perhaps be likened to Constable's landscape paintings, compared with those of the eighteenth century. Writing to his friend, Archdeacon Fisher, Constable expressed the fear that he might be 'doomed never to see the living scenes that inspired the landscapes of . . . Claude', yet concluded: 'But I was born to paint a happier land, my own dear, old England, and when I cease to love her, may I, as Wordsworth says: "Never more hear her green leaves rustle, and her torrents roar".'

Repton's scaling down of the garden also began to change the relationship between the house and its setting. As David Stuart argues in *Georgian Gardens*, by the 1790s the garden was beginning to be designed to be seen from within the house, so contributing to the pleasure of the occupants indoors. (The inside of the house, too, soon began to be designed for comfort and convenience rather than formal show, as the virtues of domesticity were increasingly celebrated.) As the wealth of the country grew, more new small estates were built, with stables, conservatories, and kitchen gardens nearer to the house. And the garden became more clearly defined.

During the eighteenth century there had been an ever-increasing interest in new horticultural species to plant in the wilderness part of the park, and a steady flow of new plant material gradually came into the country as trade and empire extended to far corners of the world. In the reign of George I (David Stuart notes), 182 new species were introduced to gardening. In that of George II the number was 1,770; in that of George III, 6,056. By 1800 more than 150 species were being introduced every year.

This influx of material soon outgrew the wilderness, and a shrubbery became *de rigueur*, followed by an arboretum and then a pinetum. Everyone interested in gardening was anxious to grow as many of these new wonders as possible. This concern for the individual plant was a reflection of the scientific age, and to foster interest and the exchange of horticultural knowledge, gardeners organized themselves into societies – of which the (later Royal) Horticultural Society became the most important – with a resultant swift exchange of new knowledge and plants. Equally important was the rise of a gardening press.

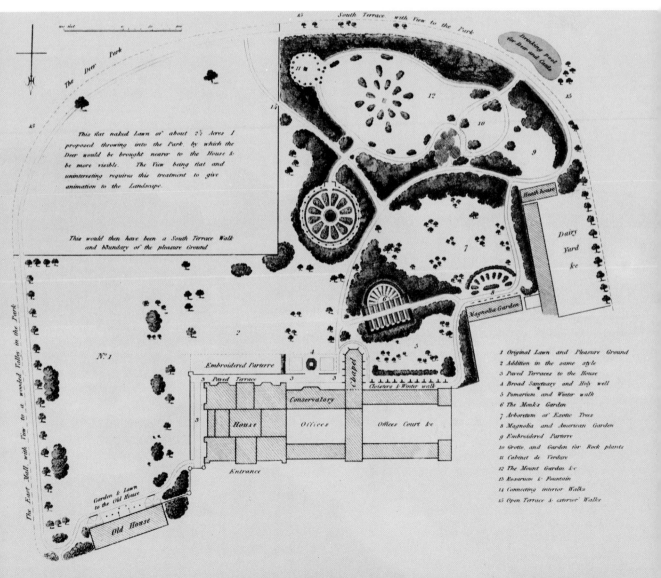

This flat naked Lawn of about 2½ Acres I proposed throwing into the Park by which the Deer would be brought nearer to the House & be more visible. The View being flat and uninteresting requires this treatment to give animation to the Landscape.

This would then have been a South Terrace Walk and boundary of the pleasure Ground

South Terrace with View to the Park

The Deer Park

Drinking Pool for Deer and Cattle

Heath house

Dairy Yard &c

Magnolia Garden

N.º 1

Embroidered Parterre

Paved Terrace

Chapel

Cloisters & Winter walk

Conservatory

House   Offices   Offices Court &c

Entrance

Garden & Lawn to the Old House

Old House

The East Mall with View to a wooded Valley in the Park

1 Original Lawn and Pleasure Ground
2 Addition in the same style
3 Paved Terraces to the House
4 Broad Sanctuary and Holy well
5 Pomarium and Winter walk
6 The Monk's Garden
7 Arboretum or Exotic Trees
8 Magnolia and American Garden
9 Embroidered Parterre
10 Grotto and Garden for Rock plants
11 Cabinet de Verdure
12 The Mount Garden &c
13 Rosarium & Fountain
14 Connecting interior Walks
15 Open Terrace & exterior Walks

John Claudius Loudon now enters this chronology, as the founder in 1826 of *The Gardener's Magazine*. His writing in it, and that of his wife Jane, who continued it after his death in 1843, had enormous influence. Together they wrote and published *The Suburban Gardener and Villa Companion* (1838), directed at the more modest members of the rapidly growing gardening public. Edward Hyams observed of Loudon that he 'contrived to embody the new science of gardening in the old art. He was more of a plantsman than a picture-gardener, but he had the knowledge, the taste, the eye so to use his plants that the pictorial was not smothered.' Loudon defined what he called the 'Gardenesque' style as

> the production of that kind of scenery which is best calculated to display the beauty of trees, shrubs and plants in a 'state of nature'; the smoothness and greenness of lawns, and the smooth surfaces, curved directions, dryness and firmness of gravel walks; in short it is the style best calculated for displaying the art of the gardener.

A garden should be a work of *art*, and it was bad taste to try to deceive the spectator into believing it was anything other. Artifice was necessary, and the garden should not contain native species that might be supposed to have grown there on their own. Loudon distinguished four basic types of design: the Geometric; the Rustic (an imitation of the cottage garden); the Picturesque (an imitation of natural terrain with studied irregularity, allowing nothing merely natural in the composition); and the artful Gardenesque. This diversity was a phenomenon seen also in architecture, where from the later Georgian period onward historic and exotic styles proliferated, reflecting not only men's anxiety at the increasingly industrial world about them (as is so often said) but also, surely, their delight in new areas of study.

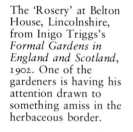

The 'Rosery' at Belton House, Lincolnshire, from Inigo Triggs's *Formal Gardens in England and Scotland*, 1902. One of the gardeners is having his attention drawn to something amiss in the herbaceous border.

To show off the new exotic flowers, new techniques of display were evolved. Bedding-out plants were developed with a longer flowering season than previously, and displayed in beds chiefly of one species each – first pelargoniums, heliotropes and salvias, then petunias and verbenas – in a style which has to some extent survived in the more conservative municipal parks today. To maintain this brilliant display it was necessary to have a battery of frames and glasshouses. Developments in glass technology made these cheaper (sheet glass, produced by rolling, replaced crown glass, made by spinning molten glass), and the repeal of the tax on glass in 1845 made them available to an even wider range of clients. This was the age of heated conservatories, of palm houses, vineries, peach and fig houses, ferneries and stove houses.

Wealthy landowners who had become bored with greensward welcomed a new vogue for formal gardens, exemplified at its grandest by the Italianate garden laid out at Trentham about 1840 by W.A. Nesfield to complement Charles Barry's grand Italianate house for the Duke of Sutherland. Large gardens of this type demanded an enormous amount of labour, so their popularity was always restricted.

The influential gardening writer Shirley Hibberd complained in 1856 that for a massed display of flower colour over a four-month period in summer the garden was wasted for the rest of the year, and gradually improved forms of hardy herbaceous plants were introduced to extend the period of interest. Another solution to the problem was provided by bulbs, which would give interest in the spring before bedding material could be planted out. Daffodils and tulips in a number of forms had already been illustrated in 1629 by John Parkinson, but their breeding was studied in earnest in the 1860s and 1870s.

The nineteenth century was a great age of plant breeding, using the many imports from the Andes, the Himalayas, China and Japan. Roses were improved by the perpetual-flowering *Rosa chinensis*: though it had been available since the 1770s, the earliest hybrid perpetual and tea roses date from the 1830s and 1840s – contemporary, surprisingly perhaps, with most of the 'old-fashioned' roses popular again today. There was intensive work too on the rhododendron, and hybrid rhododendrons eventually became a feature.

Another garden genre inspired by travel was the rock garden planted with alpines. These arrangements could be of monumental proportions, Lady Broughton's at Hoole House actually simulating the Vale of Chamonix! So large gardens were increasingly fragmented, with areas of bedded formality, rockeries of alpines, and wild areas of specimen subjects allowed to develop naturally in order that the beauty of each one could be appreciated. The emphasis was on the plant, with design very much subservient. Hibberd summed this up, agreeing with Loudon:

> a garden is an artificial contrivance, it is not a piece scooped out of a wood, but in some sense a continuation of the house. Since it is a creation of art, not a patch of wild nature, so it should show everywhere the evidence of artistic taste in every one of its gradations, from the vase on the terrace to the 'lovers' walk' in the distant shrubbery.

Hibberd attacked serpentine beds that 'curved like eels in misery', and many designers agreed with him. John Ruskin and William Morris, who were both

43

in love with the Middle Ages, called for rectilinear gardens divided up into compartments, like those seen in medieval manuscripts. As Morris loved the English countryside and the simple (idealized) life of the cottager, he recommended the use of 'good old English flowers' and gardens inspired by those of cottages.

The cottage garden continued as an ideal thereafter, though it was more freely interpreted. William Robinson observed in *The English Flower Garden* (1883): 'one lesson of these little gardens that are so pretty, is that one can get good effects from simple materials . . . Those who look at sea or sky or wood see beauty that no art can show; but among the things made by man nothing is prettier than an English cottage garden.' Robinson prophesied that 'reform must come by letting Nature take her just place in the garden' – not by 'reproducing uncultivated Nature', but by selecting such of nature's material as seemed compatible with the romantic tumbled aspect of the English cottage flower border. He demanded large beds of simple shape, and the use of hardy flowers, which he recommended, together with the abolition of fancy edgings, to simplify the gardener's work.

As early as 1870, in *The Wild Garden*, Robinson had advocated the planting of what best suited a particular soil and situation, commenting: 'the skilful gardener, to whom study and experience have taught these qualities, carefully attends to them in his operations, knowing that thereon depend the health and growth of his plants.' At last a new dawn of commonsense, which when combined with Ruskin's and Morris's love of nature became quite a force in opposition to the demand for a showman's display, achieved by formal bedding out in excessive quantity! Significantly, the gentler watercolours of the end of the century reflected softer and more natural gardening techniques which slowly crystallized into what is now known as the Surrey School.

The new interest in traditional ways and forms was also expressed in the houses of the period. Architects such as Norman Shaw, C.F.A. Voysey and Edwin Lutyens, in England, and Charles Rennie Mackintosh in Scotland, imbued their various designs with the older traditional aesthetic, to produce the prototype of the comfortable modern country home as we know it. The partnership between Lutyens and Gertrude Jekyll, from the 1890s onward, really set the style of the Surrey School, which colours much of our thought on style (indoors as well as out). As she planted the spaces he allowed her within the overall pattern, using hardy herbaceous material, they produced an extraordinarily close-knit total composition, achieving a harmony between structural design, sympathetic use of materials, and strong planting layout which is completely satisfying. It is this mellowing, rounded composition that is still widely regarded as the typical English garden.

Gertrude Jekyll stands out as an important figure at the crossroads in landscape thinking, for she fused tradition with what she saw about her, and composed the blend with a painter's eye. She was very much an educated woman of her time, blessed with enough money to pursue her chosen course. That course was at first chiefly painting (in which she was strongly influenced by the English Impressionist Hercules Brabazon Brabazon), but she was also interested in architecture and in craftsmanship of all kinds, and when in middle age she began to be increasingly short-sighted she turned to gardening,

Miss Jekyll and Lutyens in partnership: the Dutch Garden at Orchards, near Godalming in Surrey (1898–99).

applying what she had learnt as a painter on form, line, light and most particularly colour. Her thoughts were published in a number of books which are enjoying renewed popularity today. She wrote passionately about her native Surrey, which at the time was still largely rural – about buildings, country life and the cottage garden. In *Wood and Garden* (1899) she acknowledged her debt, writing:

> I have learnt much from the little gardens that help make our English waysides the prettiest in the temperate world. One can hardly go into the smallest cottage garden without learning or observing something new. It may be some two plants growing beautifully together by some happy chance, or a pretty mixed tangle of creepers that one always thought must have a south wall doing better on an east one.

William Robinson and Gertrude Jekyll took up the herbaceous border and developed its possibilities artistically. In *Home and Garden* (1900), *Wall and Water Gardens* (1901) and *Some English Gardens* (1904) she wrote at length on the use of plants, drawing the reader's attention to their form, texture and shape in addition to their colour, and continued some of Repton's theories on planting design. In 1908 she published *Colour in the Flower Garden*.

The aesthetic values of colour had not really concerned eighteenth-century gardeners. Kent and his followers had composed with light and shade, using the sombre reds and browns and the golden shades of the Claudian landscapes which they admired so much. When the introduction of new and showy flowers made the subject one for urgent consideration the matter was ignored. At first, those plants which were brightest were considered best, and until their novelty palled geraniums, calceolarias and lobelias, representing the most vivid tones of the three primary colours, were the favourite bedding subjects. The notions of colour blending and colour stimulus in pattern, more familiar to us today, were indirectly fostered by the camera, which recorded effects of light in terms of tonal values. Painters discovered that these effects could be reproduced in painting by judicious combinations of light-reflecting pigments, and the palette was split up into a hundred different shades. Gertrude Jekyll was a horticultural Impressionist, who saw gardening in terms of painting:

> Should it not be remembered that in setting a garden we are painting a picture – a picture of hundreds of feet or yards instead of so many inches, painted with living flowers seen by open daylight – so that to paint it rightly is a debt we owe to the beauty of the flowers and to the light of the sun; that the colours should be placed with careful forethought and deliberation, as a painter employs them on his picture, and not dropped in lifeless dabs, as he has them on his palette.

Christopher Tunnard, in his *Gardens in the Modern Landscape* (1938), compared Gertrude Jekyll with her contemporary, the French Impressionist painter Claude Monet. Both had an almost primitive love of the soil, a passion for gathering from nature the nourishment to sustain burning convictions and long cherished beliefs, and both suffered from failing eyesight. Beyond that, however, Monet in his later years created a painter's garden that was equal to some of his work on canvas, whereas Jekyll the artist was not of the calibre of Jekyll the planter. As a planter, she studied colour effects carefully and experimented with them, observed the tonal gradations in foliage, and realized that the tonal value of pure flower colour is intensified when placed in proximity to white. Systematic colour classification, though not directly of her instigation, derives from her efforts to value each shade and suggest its merited place in the garden scheme. It is interesting that Tunnard slightly knocks Gertrude Jekyll for her lack of theory on light, for he was writing at a time when it was virtually an obsession; but the fact that she evolved any system at all brings her to the forefront of progressive garden thinking, and makes her a bridge between the traditional Surrey values and the avant-garde thought of her time, of which she must have been well aware.

In the twentieth century several schools of gardening evolved, some concerned to break entirely with the past, and others to reinterpret it. As we have said, the somewhat informal mode of gardens that Gertrude Jekyll designed with Lutyens has continued, with modifications, up to the present. But they also worked in a different, much more formal, genre, using terracing, axial planning and compartmentalization in a way that was fashionable for country houses from the early years of the century. Inigo Triggs, in a series of books published between 1902 and 1913 on garden craft in different countries, provided a basis for this formalist movement, echoed by other garden writers of the time. Such a style allowed a diversity of arrangement within individual compartments. Increasingly the garden again became a designed progression from the house, with axes and subdivisions allowing for the development of water gardens, sunken gardens, formal bedded areas, the tennis court (and later the swimming pool) to be contained within green enclosures. The style demanded quite a lot of architectural detailing, with such features as steps, terraces edged by balustrading, formal fountains, gates, and gazebos. After the First World War the changing pattern of labour meant that few of these labour-intensive gardens were maintained in all their details, and fewer still were created. Rare examples of new formal gardens include Bodnant and Blenheim, where the Water Parterre was laid out in the 1920s by Achille Duchêne in the manner of Le Nôtre.

A modified form of garden for the smaller country house, still retaining formal elements, was evolved at two gardens that have since become places of pilgrimage: Hidcote in Gloucestershire, planned by its owner, Lawrence Johnston, and Sissinghurst in Kent, also planned by its owners, Vita Sackville-West and Harold Nicolson. Both consist of small enclosures each devoted to a particular theme or colour. And both were designed to simplify maintenance by favouring hardy plant material.

A different theory of 'rational' gardening grew out of the Modern Movement. As early as 1897 Adolf Loos, the Austrian architect, argued that to find beauty in form, rather than making it depend on ornament, is the goal to which humanity is aspiring. Architects like Frank Lloyd Wright and Le Corbusier thought in terms of unadorned form, painters were content with patterns of line and colour, and sculptors concentrated on the rhythm of plastic form. Tunnard, writing in the late 1930s, argued that the same thinking should apply to gardening. In becoming a science, garden-making had lost sight of its duty to perform an aesthetic function; but it should no more be turned over to the horticulturalist than architecture to the engineer. (That the latter seems to have happened, to a degree, might account for the abysmally low aesthetic standard of many modern buildings – and, dare one say it, landscapes too!) Gardens should be rational, economic, restful and comprehensible.

This doctrine opposed to ornament was a key element in the new architecture. Ivan Chermayeff, F.R.S. Yorke, Maxwell Fry and others rejected traditional materials and forms. Their houses were alien imports in the landscape, but they were designed so as to seem sculptural objects within it, and they incorporated wide areas of glass that opened and allowed outdoors

47

and indoors to flow together. Their structural severity, and their impractical construction and materials, which do not perform very well in our damp islands (despite the designers' proclamation of 'functionalism'), prevented their style from becoming widely popular.

Among garden-makers, the Modern Movement made some headway in isolated groups. Tunnard quotes the following extract from a paper submitted by the President of the Swedish Garden Architects' Association to a congress in Paris in 1937:

> The utilitarian style has strongly influenced the construction of domestic buildings; they are often planned asymmetrically, have large windows exposed to the sun, and if possible, are sufficiently free from screening to permit distant views.
>
> Ordinarily the garden is planned in such a way as to form a direct relationship with the house, access from one to the other being everywhere facilitated. The garden thus becomes a part of the dwelling. Its arrangement is decided more for the activities of people – especially children – than for flowers. It allows for seats and benches resting on paved areas which relate to the house, and lawns as extensive as possible, though not always mown. Paths and walks are reduced to the minimum and often consist only of stepping stones between which grass or creeping plants are allowed to grow, thus conserving a homogeneity between the units of the plan. Pools for the children are much appreciated and, when possible, they are made deep enough to allow for bathing. In general trees are not numerous in these gardens; most people prefer to have flowering shrubs. When herbaceous plants are used they have a definite part of the plan devoted to their culture, and need not, as formerly, be confined to the conventional flower bed. There is little room in gardens now for the bedding plants which for so many years have enjoyed such a wide vogue.
>
> The utilitarian style of building has exercised a profound influence on gardens, which it appears to be ridding of conscious symmetrical planning. The arrangement of gardens is freer and more mobile than formerly. One does not look for axial construction and the monumental planning of former styles, which could never be prevented from looking severe, above all when close to the house, the hard lines of which can be softened by subtle plant arrangements. One strives to create a contrast between the disciplined outlines of terrace walls, paved spaces, pools, etc., and a free and luxuriant vegetation designed to produce a happy decorative effect and to give the impression that it is a work of nature or of chance. It is pleasant to leave an existing gnarled pine in a paved courtyard the aspect of which is otherwise strictly architectural, or to arrange matters so that trees with heads of interesting shape appear to detach themselves from the smooth walls of the house, their rigidity being softened by the foliage. It is admissible that between the paving stones of courtyards space should be left for isolated plants to give the impression that they have grown there spontaneously.

The Romantic notion of landscape had not, clearly, been entirely swept away, and it can prove stultifying to the free development of garden design.

This dichotomy of thought – between a Romantic view of landscape, and utility – appears also in Le Corbusier's writing about his now famous house near Paris, the Villa Savoye (1929–30). The meadows and trees of the estate on which the house was built would be preserved . . . but one's view from ground level is limited, and grass is unhealthily damp to live with, so the garden will be at first-floor level, in the form of a terrace with instant drainage. Extending this principle to a development proposed for Argentina, Le Corbusier wrote:

The Modern Movement in Surrey: St Ann's Hill, Chertsey, 1938. Raymond McGrath's concrete house was set in an eighteenth-century landscape, and Christopher Tunnard effected the transition. To the left, a formal 'architectural garden' is reached through large plate-glass windows and sheltered by an extension of the frame of the house. For the curved swimming pool, see p. 192. (Plan from Tunnard's *Gardens in the Modern Landscape*, 1938)

> I shall place this house on columns in a beautiful corner of the countryside; we shall have twenty houses rising above the long grass of a meadow where cattle will continue to graze. . . . The dwellers in these houses, drawn hence through love of the life of the countryside, will be able to see it maintained intact from their hanging gardens or from their ample windows. Their domestic lives will be set within a Virgilian dream.

This does seem to be going over the top (literally!), for some recognition must be given to normal family functions which cannot be contained in a hanging garden.

A different solution to the integration of a building within natural landscape came from Japan. There had been an interest in Oriental gardens in the West since the eighteenth century, but it had always been somewhat superficial: now Japanese thought and garden layout were looked at more closely, and directly influenced the gardens which were being built in California around the time of the Second World War. Almost all the gardens we have been looking at were conceived as enclosures, based ultimately on fear of the environment – the garden being a space tamed from it, with man as the ringmaster. The Oriental outlook is the opposite: its germ is an attitude of reverence to nature, in which man is only a modest element. His garden is an act of homage to the forces of the cosmos. The Japanese garden developed as an abstract miniature of their island scenery. The house too is a symbol of that accord, being designed with movable screens that allow the inhabitants within to have a sedentary enjoyment of the garden – whereas we choose to perambulate ours. The modest house built of timber was seen as a transitory structure within the landscape. This too was at odds with the substantial nature of the Western house. When with the advent of steel-frame construction it became possible in the West to build houses with a similar aesthetic character, the sliding windows and doors helped to break down the barrier which had always existed between house and garden.

For centuries Japanese artists had rendered the awesome crags of mountains surrounded by swirling mists by a few deft brush-strokes, and found in the curve of rocks or fall of water sensations akin to those aroused by their own spiritual aspirations. Gardeners too were concerned to re-create natural effects with a minimum of fuss, and no illusion as to the merit of their own individuality. The outward manifestation of such a philosophy has many parallels with Modernism in the West, which moved toward the acceptance of the primary importance of form, line and economy of material, rather than colour.

On the West Coast of the United States the two trends met – the Modern Movement, fostered by émigrés from Europe, and the Oriental, many gardeners being Japanese immigrants. The climate was perfectly suited to open-air life, and swimming pools were almost a matter of course: so the Modernist ideal of complete integration between house and garden was achieved almost unconsciously. In the garden, the Japanese influence was directed towards a much more discreet selection of indigenous plant material, with colour used sparingly, and the overall background carefully studied. Simplicity of effect was the aim, and subtlety of grouping and arrangement more important than obvious effect. The same respect for material was

50

This composition in a Japanese temple garden – islands of moss in a gravel sea – could be an abstract painting.

exercised in the grouping of rocks, the placing of stones, the management of contours and the use of water. Eleven centuries of practice in the art had not dulled perception!

The work of Thomas Church epitomizes the California School in the late 1940s, and in his writings he expounded important theories on modern gardening. Writing of small gardens, he said they could not be 'natural' if they were to serve as an extension to the house. Their scale and use called for hard surfaces, screens to separate areas, and design forms that would increase their apparent size. 'Like it or not,' he wrote, 'the function of the house had spilled out into the garden and must be provided for. There was no longer a choice between functional and aesthetic approach.' The use of the garden for outdoor entertaining and play, combined with the need to reduce maintenance, resulted in the widespread introduction of paving materials and groundcover plants used in simple shapes.

Church developed a theory, based on Cubism, that a garden should have no beginning and no end, and that it should be pleasing when seen from any angle. Asymmetrical lines were used to create the effect of greater space. Simplicity of line, form and shape were more restful to look at and easier to maintain. Form and pattern were provided by pavings, walls and espaliered or trained plants. Thus Church developed new visual arrangements in the garden which also satisfied practical criteria. A variety of curvilinear shapes, textured surfaces and walls were combined with a sure sense of proportion, and the gardens incorporated new materials, such as corrugated asbestos and wooden paving blocks. Stylistically they were a very dramatic advance on all previous garden designs, as a combination of numerous different concepts and traditions and a recognition of local conditions.

This new gardening style was taken up on the East Coast of the United States, but modified by the infusion of greater horticultural content, the climate being temperate (as in Britain) rather than subtropical. East Coast gardeners were also influenced for a time by the Brazilian landscape architect Roberto Burle Marx, who was not only a designer but also a painter and a botanist or plantsman. I acknowledge a debt to him in the formation of my own ideas, but question the relevance of drawing too many analogies with plant usage in Brazil. Surely the essential in modern gardening is to use native species whenever possible, to reinforce the basic forms, and to take the existing two-dimensional planning into an equally satisfying three-dimensional composition by firmly controlled designs in abstract shapes.

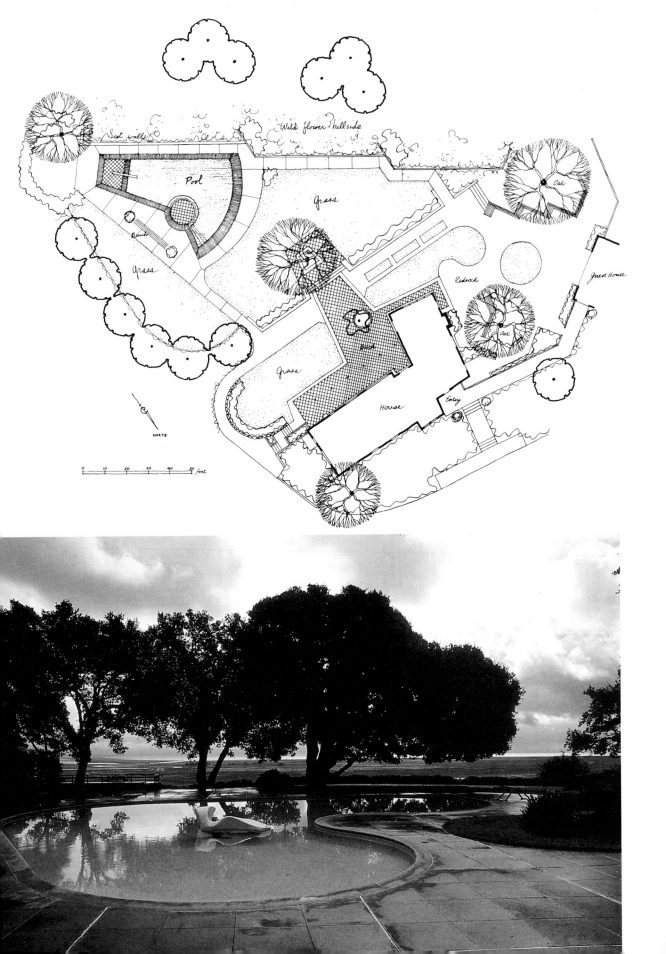

POSTSCRIPT: BACK TO NATURE

William and Dorothy Wordsworth and their friends were among the first to bring a love of simple nature into fashion. It would be untrue to say they created it: there had always been individuals (for instance Gilbert White of Selborne) who loved to observe nature around them. But in the nineteenth century it became common for country ladies to make notes and sketches, recording the cycle of the year, its moods and nuances, and in the literature of the age landscape took on a more prominent role: impossible to think of Jane Austen without her pastoral Hampshire scenery, Sir Walter Scott without the wild country of the Borders, the Brontës without the bleak Yorkshire moors, Hardy without the country that he called Wessex, or Housman without the hills of Shropshire. Nor was this strong attraction to particular localities confined to creative artists. We need only remember Queen Victoria and Prince Albert and their love of the Scottish Highlands, 'the proudest, finest scenery in the world'.

It is surely true that the unspoiled countryside became more deeply loved in the last century because its existence was coming under threat. The spread of the Industrial Revolution provoked an instinctive retreat into the pre-industrial world of nature. Ruskin, Morris, and later members of the Arts and Crafts Movement all preached the same message. Even the industrialists themselves felt the same urge. Unlike their Georgian ancestors, they no longer lived within sight or sound of the landscape they themselves had spoilt: rather, they retreated into fresh countryside, on new estates within striking distance of their wealth but without any risk of seeing the living and working conditions that produced it.

'I can radiate my caravan . . . for at least one hundred miles around, and find England all one sweet, cool, peaceful garden' – Gordon Stables, 1895. This is his land-yacht, 'The Wanderer', of 1886. He is seated on the ground with his children.

In the twentieth century, with the worst of those conditions alleviated and the gap between rich and poor beginning to be bridged, there was still a widespread hunger for the natural life and the open air. 'If thou are worn and hard beset,' wrote Dr Gordon Stables as early as 1895,

> With sorrows that thou wouldst forget,
> If thou wouldst read a lesson, that will keep
> Thy heart from failing and thou from sleep,
> Go to the woods and hills! No tears
> Dim the sweet look that Nature wears.

Dr Stables, known as 'the gentleman gypsy', was a passionate advocate of the touring caravan for holiday use, and named his first purpose-built creation 'The Wanderer'. Walking and rambling became popular; camping gathered its devotees; caravans increased and multiplied; and farmers found their fields invaded by an ever-growing army of townspeople whose interests were often at odds with their own.

After World War II the protection of the countryside became a governmental responsibility; legislation was passed to safeguard 'areas of outstanding natural beauty', and National Parks were established. Membership of the National Trust mushroomed. Such measures, welcome as they were, generated new problems of their own. More car-ownership and more leisure led to an explosion in the demand for outdoor recreation. Managers of National Parks and National Trust properties found themselves faced with the need to provide car-parks, WCs, nature trails, guided walks, and so on, which threatened to undermine the very values they were trying to preserve.

These trends are continuing and are likely to continue for the foreseeable future. The spell of the countryside grows stronger all the time, nourished by reading such writers as Flora Thompson, Laurie Lee and Richard Adams. This, as Margaret Drabble has said, is 'the golden age of remembered youth', and the countryside is, in a sense, its lost paradise. Many dream of bringing up their children in it, or failing that of retiring to it. The fortunate ones have a foot in both camps, living the week in town with a retreat at weekends. With this upsurge in rural interest goes a greater concern than ever for the conservation of rural Britain, its buildings, the landscape of hedges and trees, and the preservation of its wildlife. Much of this mood is reflected in the new country garden. We seem spiritually at least at peace with nature, and seek now only to perpetuate it. Here, perhaps, is the essential purpose, the secret hope, of every modern country gardener.

What Sort of Garden?

Let us now consider the gardener, the gardener's family, and how they see their place in the country. Broadly, country gardeners can be divided into three types:

1. Those who live permanently in the country, and are seeking to create a completely new garden – either because they have a new house on a virgin site (the minority), or because they have an old house which has been restored, and in the restoration the surrounding garden has been laid waste.
2. Those who live permanently in the country, but who seek to modify an existing garden – either to simplify it, or to restore one that has become overgrown.
3. Those who use their house in the country only for weekends or holidays, who may need either to create a new garden or to modify an existing one.

All three categories may want to consider various extra possibilities for their land: planting woodland for shelter, timber, or pheasant rearing; creating a pond for duck; grazing a pony or keeping livestock; and so on. The permutations are legion.

It is at this stage, before starting, that one must think ahead and try to imagine the fullest potential of the site, so as to allow for planned development. Without this thought, the overall effect may in the end reflect a series of ill-related spontaneous ideas, whereas it should appear as a unified conception. Going round the country and looking at large old estates, it becomes clear that a master plan underlies them: hedges are trimmed all of a fashion, fences are of one kind, with their gates in order, and the sense of unity may even carry on through the colour of the paint on the windows and doors of estate cottages. It is this sense of order and identity that we seek to create on the smaller estate.

Think of your family in detail: their ages, aspirations, how they will develop, and – of course – what your financial limitations are. Consider middle age, when the chicks have flown, and then old age. Working towards a satisfactory plan is like programming a computer, feeding in diverse information which will all be taken into account in the solution. If some of the facts are not fed in, the final answer will not be correct.

For a young family, the potential of country living is enormous – indeed, that is probably why the move has been made. It offers a degree of self-sufficiency, impossible in town, and thus a somewhat cheaper way of life: for if one can grow one's own vegetables and herbs, and have a few chickens, and buy timber inexpensively for fuel, some of the basics of life are provided. After a move, a mortgage, and some conversion work, a garden providing more than those basics will have a low priority, but this is the time during which you can study how your place and its immediate surroundings work, so as to evolve an ultimate pattern. It is at this stage that very important decisions will be made concerning the use of the area immediately surrounding the house – decisions which you might not think of under the heading of 'gardening', but which form an important part of the whole. Failure to get the siting of these primary functions correct from the start can cause endless expense later, if piecemeal additions are made over the years and a complete reappraisal is eventually needed.

In the matter of 'useful' planting, consider the siting of the vegetable garden. Generations of villa living seem to have led to the positioning of this important practical item as far away from the house as possible. In a small garden less than ten metres wide one does not wish to entertain on the terrace surrounded by sprouts, but in the country an initial small vegetable plot can often be sited quite usefully close to the house. So too can a herb bed, which will be more decorative. Herbs, which never lost their popularity in most other countries of the world, are undergoing a revival in England, for flavouring (due to new cooking techniques and less use of meat) and even for medicinal use.

In addition to this horticultural powerhouse, useful areas for activity can be designated – at first a drying area, and, for young children, a paved play area and perhaps a sandpit (fewer cats than in town). As children grow older, they will need larger paved areas, for table tennis perhaps, for tinkering with a bike, then a motorcycle, then the first banger. As parents become less pressed, and (on paper at least) more financially viable, the influence of the house will move outwards, with areas for entertaining, perhaps a swimming pool, a tennis court, and so on. These functions, needing a larger area, will be placed in the middle section of the garden. From there the garden should flow easily outward to the boundary where it will merge sympathetically with the surrounding landscape.

Previously, this outer area had been heavily 'gardened', and the boundary between it and the landscape was abrupt. But with sympathetic ground-shaping, the use of wide areas of flower-seeded rough grass, and far greater use of shrubs and small trees which are indigenous to the area, labour can be saved and an attractive natural effect achieved. Where your own pastureland lies beyond the garden, boundaries can be altered to give over more of the garden to grazing.

The lull between the children leaving home and the arrival of the first grandchildren was traditionally the time when the parents took to gardening, with little eye to the future. Fine, if horticulture is your interest: but do not feel obliged to do so! And remember, what is developed when you are forty or fifty has quite a different look when you have to maintain it at sixty. To retire to the country in one's old age is something of a cliché (though many people make the reverse move, taking a flat or small house closer to shops and services). For those who do follow this ideal, enthusiasm and the wish to occupy new-found time on retirement can lead to over-detailing in the garden which will later be regretted. To see a garden which was once your joy deteriorate through lack of maintenance – due to ill-health or incapacity – can be very distressing. Care must be taken when planning ahead to envisage realistically one's eventual disabilities. Before bestowing fifty gold roses for a golden wedding anniversary, the young would do well to think who will not only prune and deadhead them, but manure and cultivate them, remove their suckers, and then trim and edge the bed which holds them.

Having established how the family and its use of the garden will develop, the next stage is to work out the sort of garden that is appropriate – for the site, the surroundings, the type of house, the amount of time you can give to maintenance, and what you can afford to spend now and in the future. Your house style and your lifestyle will give a clue to the type of garden you need. While one might not seek to ape another era precisely, it is sometimes necessary to capture the feel of it in a current practical form. You would presumably prefer a modern kitchen even in a Tudor house: a garden should be more subtle and sympathetic, using brick, perhaps, and stained timber detailing, though in a modern, and certainly not a 'Tudor Tearooms', way!

Any number of styles are possible, depending on how the garden is worked and managed. Each establishes a different mood.

The cottage muddle

This is fairly small-scale, with a little of everything, skilfully woven together to produce a relaxed random effect. The intensity of the horticultural element – which is very much part of this style – prevents it from merging gently into the surrounding countryside. From this very 'gardened' environment you would progress through a gate to an orchard or to the fields beyond.

The detailing of such a garden is tricky. Pavings, plantings and furnishings have to look random, but not haphazard; styling should be considered, but not visibly self-conscious. It is not a style for the weekender, or for a young family.

The cottage garden manqué

This is a similar random style, but without the horticultural element, and therefore ideal for weekenders. While still enclosed, this type of garden is left wildish, with existing characterful trees or shrubs used as points of emphasis in an otherwise clear area, possibly of rough grass with paths mown through. The odd rose grown up a tree, or bulbs in grass, would be manageable, but not too much else: stock might break in during the owner's absence; and there should not be too much to do in the garden when the house is in use.

The country lady's garden

This is the type of garden much favoured by glossy magazines and described as 'charming'. It has rarified horticultural content, and a lot of white and grey, with *Alchemilla mollis* everywhere. The layout is regular, and most viewpoints end in an urn, a white Gothic seat, or a little wire temple. These gardens are the envy of the world, for few other climates allow the growth of such a variety of plant material.

This type of garden has a country feel, though its casual manicured looks are in direct opposition to the surrounding countryside. Its cottage effect is achieved by great sophistication in the flower-arranger's art, and its lush growth and abundant flowers call for a great deal of upkeep. A good basic design for both the layout and the arrangement of individual plants is essential, for the 'country lady's garden' can all too easily become a mess.

57

The closed garden

This is larger that the previous style, but areas of it are in the same idiom, for it is a series of green hedged rooms in the manner of Sissinghurst or Hidcote. Such a garden is a period re-creation several times over, so to speak, with ghosts of the formal gardens of the seventeenth century mingling with those of the Italianate green rooms of Victoria's reign. Its design makes it extremely high on maintenance.

The open landscape garden

The modern version of Capability Brown's park might be called the wild garden, in which the surrounding natural planting is scaled down to domestic dimensions. Once established, it is comparatively maintenance-free, since one is not seeking to repress plants into unnatural hedges or neat borders.

The plantings composing this type of garden will depend upon the soil, whether acid, peaty, chalky or clay. They may not produce many flowers for cutting, but they will be interesting throughout the year for their leaves, berries and bark. They will be extremely attractive to wildlife.

On a larger scale, this style of gardening will suit a small estate, for into it one can fit hedges, fences, and shelters for stock or horses, coverts for game, and domestic amenities such as a tennis court or pool.

This manner can be misapplied, to produce a garden ill suited to a country setting, with dotted conifers, heathery ground cover in areas where it is not native, and other species alien to the local soil type, all fighting with the natural background.

These five categories are broad, but time and time again one sees some aspects of nearly all of them brought together into one garden, with restless and disastrous visual results. The unhappy owner introduces more things in an attempt to improve the effect, but only succeeds in making it worse. The best styling of anything is generally simple and straightforward. So select your style, according to your site and capabilities, and stick with it.

The manner in which you organize your garden, that is the style in which you realize it, very much dictates how you will spend your leisure time. This in turn is governed by how many in the family are prepared to help create the ideal garden. Running a vegetable garden to supply an average family, for instance, will fully occupy one person's leisure time. A weekender, hoping to keep his town kitchen supplied with country vegetables, will find he has little time left to cultivate them after he has mowed the lawn or chopped wood. It is all too easy to fall into the trap of leaving a superbly manicured lawn on Sunday evening which will be waiting for you to restore it again the following Saturday morning. The moral is: if you want a country retreat to relax in, plan it so you can do just that.

If you live in the country all the time and have other hobbies than gardening, do not try to keep up too specialized a garden, but accept that some of it can be left to rough grass or grazing. And the facilities for leisure-time activities can eat into your leisure: swimming pools and tennis courts, particularly the former, can take up an enormous amount of time in maintenance. Above all, don't overreach yourself!

Shaping your Territory

To appraise the long-term possibilities of your site, it is as well to marshal all its parts onto paper – the house and any access points to it, boundaries of both garden and surrounding fields (whether yours or not), existing trees, water runs, and so on. Indicate the sight-lines that give you good views out, and also the bad ones which will need to be masked. Lastly, mark local rights of way, no matter how seldom used. For those unfamiliar with this sort of drawing, the operation can appear mammoth, but approached logically and drawn accurately, with each little wiggle noted, the document becomes invaluable over the years – even if for no other reason than as a record of what your land was like before you started!

To begin with, you will need a base map. You can of course have one prepared by a local surveyor; but there are also other, and cheaper, ways to proceed. If the property has recently changed hands, some record of its boundaries and outline will appear with the deeds; and while the map may be on a small scale, it can always be enlarged. This map may itself have been traced from a local Ordnance Survey sheet, which you can obtain direct. Scales vary according to location and to the date when your area was last surveyed, but whatever the scale such a map will provide a mine of information about neighbouring land.

If all else fails, prepare your own survey. A reasonable scale to use is 1:100. Indicate the scale clearly on the drawing, for it is irritating to come back after a year or so and not remember what it was. Indicate also the north point. Having plotted your house, taking simple running measurements around it, extend lines at 90-degree angles ('offsets') from its walls outward to boundaries and surrounding features. Use your eye to get the right-angle correct. Where there is a tricky angled boundary, take as many offsets as possible to it and then take diagonal measurements as well, as a check. This is known as triangulation.

When locating trees on your drawing, note the girth of the stem and the spread of the canopy. Other factors to check include the fall of the ground, which will give a clue to site drainage. The presence of a clump of reeds or rushes indicates that water stands there at least some time during the year. Investigate any ditches, if you adjoin open fields: do they flow or not, and if so when? You may be fortunate enough to have a running stream throughout the year; but even if the flow is seasonal, a feature can still be made of it. Note what happens outside the boundaries. There may be a splendid view if you opened up a portion of hedge – but before doing so check the direction of the prevailing wind: that hedge may be there for a reason.

Ideally, of course, one should experience a garden for a full season before making major decisions about its future, and the time lag between buying a property, improving it, and moving in often allows this.

Your site plan will now be the basis on which to start thinking and planning. Keep it as a reference, and do not draw any more on it: any ideas you may have should be sketched on sheets of tracing paper laid over the original.

59

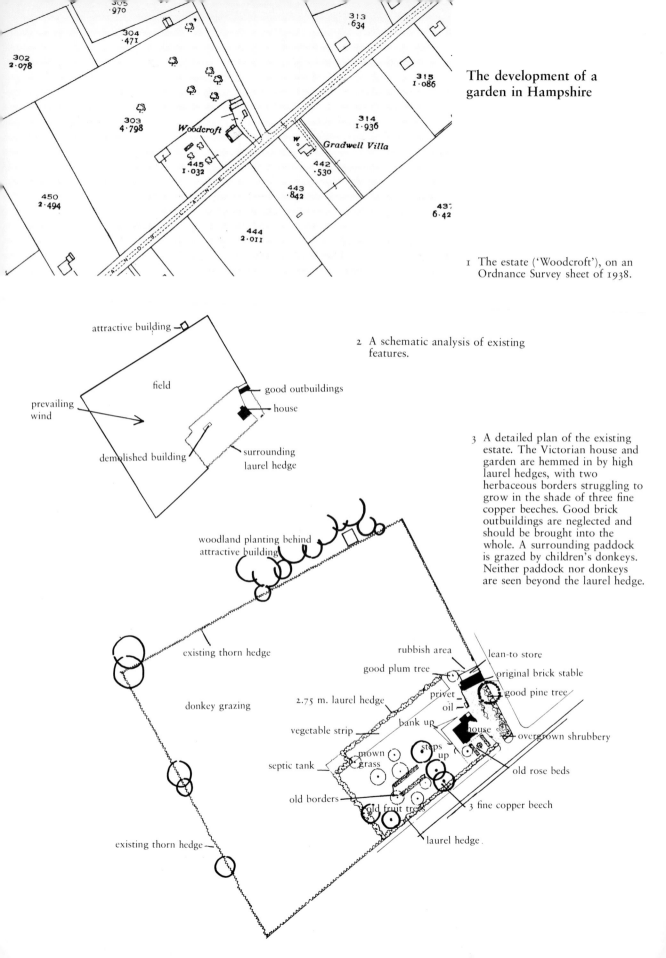

The development of a garden in Hampshire

1 The estate ('Woodcroft'), on an Ordnance Survey sheet of 1938.

2 A schematic analysis of existing features.

3 A detailed plan of the existing estate. The Victorian house and garden are hemmed in by high laurel hedges, with two herbaceous borders struggling to grow in the shade of three fine copper beeches. Good brick outbuildings are neglected and should be brought into the whole. A surrounding paddock is grazed by children's donkeys. Neither paddock nor donkeys are seen beyond the laurel hedge.

Map labels (Figure 1): 302 2·078; 304 ·471; 303 4·798; Woodcroft; 445 1·032; 450 2·494; 444 2·011; 443 ·842; 442 ·530; Gradwell Villa; 314 1·936; 315 1·086; 313 ·634; 437 6·42; THE LANE

Labels (Figure 2): attractive building; field; prevailing wind; good outbuildings; house; demolished building; surrounding laurel hedge

Labels (Figure 3): woodland planting behind attractive building; existing thorn hedge; donkey grazing; 2.75 m. laurel hedge; vegetable strip; septic tank; old borders; existing thorn hedge; rubbish area; good plum tree; privet; oil; bank up; mown grass; steps up; house; old fruit trees; lean-to store; original brick stable; good pine tree; overgrown shrubbery; old rose beds; 3 fine copper beech; laurel hedge

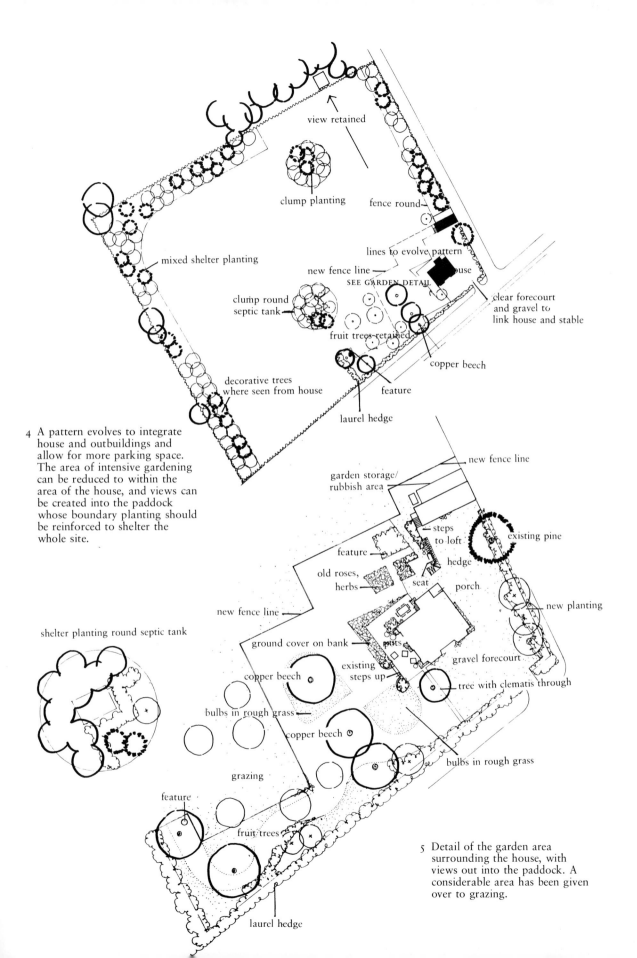

view retained

clump planting

fence round

mixed shelter planting

lines to evolve pattern

new fence line

house

SEE GARDEN DETAIL

clump round septic tank

clear forecourt and gravel to link house and stable

fruit trees retained

copper beech

decorative trees where seen from house

feature

laurel hedge

4 A pattern evolves to integrate house and outbuildings and allow for more parking space. The area of intensive gardening can be reduced to within the area of the house, and views can be created into the paddock whose boundary planting should be reinforced to shelter the whole site.

new fence line

garden storage/ rubbish area

steps to loft

existing pine

feature

hedge

old roses, herbs

seat

porch

new planting

new fence line

ground cover on bank

existing steps up

posts

gravel forecourt

shelter planting round septic tank

copper beech

bulbs in rough grass

tree with clematis through

copper beech

bulbs in rough grass

grazing

feature

fruit trees

5 Detail of the garden area surrounding the house, with views out into the paddock. A considerable area has been given over to grazing.

laurel hedge

PRINCIPLES AND PREPARATION

Few people will be embarking on building a new home, but many will be contemplating an extension, and the same thoughts apply to both. Remember that what you build may become part of everyone's environment, and see that your architect, designing to suit modern living, nevertheless takes into account local scale and materials. Some structures that you might want to erect in your garden – conservatories and greenhouses, garages, summerhouses and pool buildings – will be considered in Chapter 6.

Where at all possible, before allowing any construction work to proceed, move what plants can be re-used to a safe distance, heeling them in and protecting them. If large trees will be near the work, shield them by a stout temporary fence, round not just the trunk but the full extent of the branches' spread. That way bonfires will not be lit underneath them, nor heavy bricks dumped on their root span, nor spoil built up round their stem. It is surprising what a mature tree will stand, but better take no chances.

Before finally agreeing the plans with the architect, if he is providing designs for the garden be sure that they are sensibly detailed, and not too fussy (for he is probably working in a field unknown to him): if there are changes of level, for instance, is there adequate provision for surface water drainage, and are such features as steps and retaining walls satisfactory? If you are using a builder rather than an architect, or have hired your own workmen directly, establish a precise programme on which the estimate will be based, specifying such things as the type of paving selected, for price variations can be enormous. If the budgeting is not correct it is often the finishing touches that have to go, and paradoxically it is they that make all the difference in appearance between a good job and a bad one.

Where heavy machinery is to be used, make provision for foul weather when the ground will be churned up by skidding wheels: ensure a supply of rubble, or have old railway sleepers or the newer type of metal tracking laid. Try to commence a job towards the end of summer, when the ground is dry, completing the heavy work before the winter rains.

If any demolition work is necessary, see that services are carefully sealed off and left in a safe condition, and that old gulleys and manholes are taken up and filled in with clean hardcore. The old building foundations should be excavated – to a depth of at least 150 mm. below ground level if the area will eventually be paved, or at least 450 mm. if there is to be grass or shallow planting.

When there is to be excavation for the footings or foundations of new structures, insist that the topsoil should be moved to one side and kept strictly separate from the excavated subsoil, and that the latter is itself segregated, for it takes a long time to bring subsoil into a fit state for cultivation. When the builder finally leaves, ensure he leaves no rubbish behind.

A new site could be cleared before work commences: try to cut down and kill brambles, nettles and weeds, in preparation for an all-out offensive when the builders depart. Make a note of the weeds, as they are often a clue to your soil type and its fertility (see p.12). Think long and hard, however, before removing any more substantial plants. Hedges, even overgrown, can be laid or trimmed and become exceedingly handsome again. Take the opportunity to clean out any ditches, which often accompany hedges, and repair their banks if you are keeping them.

Think even longer before removing any large trees, for they will give your site instant character. If you think they cast too much shade, are too tall or appear unsafe, have a word with a reputable tree surgeon. It is amazing what can be achieved by reshaping too large a tree, top-guying or bracing an unsafe one, treating hollows and feeding weakly specimens. A tree surgeon will also tell you what is not worth keeping, and will be able to carry out felling without damaging the trees to be retained. He will advise, too, on whether the felled timber has any commercial value, and what will and will not provide good logs for burning. Be sure to employ only skilled men. Unskilled workers can ruin your trees, and eventually involve you in greater expense, either to put things right or to fell the victim. Be sure, too, that the men are covered by third party and public liability insurances.

You may have existing stumps that need to be removed. Depending on the size and height of the stump, this can be done by hand or by machinery, by pushing or pulling, blasting or burning. Digging out is a slow job, which can be speeded up by using a bulldozer or scraper – preferably on the dry ground of late summer, as machines will make a terrible mess of a lawn in wet weather. When the ground is wet, if the stump is long enough it may be pushed out with the blade of a bulldozer; alternatively, it can be pulled out by means of a chain cable or rope attached to a machine or winch. Stumps which are partly rotted and thus difficult to pull out may be burned, but this is a slow job, since there is bound to be a certain amount of sap still present, and it is often easier to dig them out first and then burn them. Blasting out is a complicated and dangerous operation, which calls for a specialist and (not surprisingly) police permission. Other solutions include drilling out the main part of the root bole, and using a caustic substance to destroy the roots. Check the contents of such a substance first, however, in case it is not safe with children and pets about.

EVOLVING A LAYOUT

On your site overlay, start from the house and fix the logical positions of all your working elements, with access to them – areas in which to park cars, locate the oil and septic tanks, put the dustbins, store the wood, hide the cycles, perhaps have another garage, boat store, caravan standing, and so on. All should relate back to the house and its entrances. In thinking of their positioning, particularly the more domestic elements, imagine having to get to them on a wet stormy night in January: are they too far away, is the path hazard-free, could it be covered?

These functional areas will need to be serviced. Someone has to deliver logs; the oil tanker has a long lead, but the handler is not too fussy where he trails it; and the cesspit – which has to be a statutory distance from the house – will occasionally need emptying. (The new fibreglass septic tanks do not need emptying, as they allow for an overflow, but you may find that your local authority makes you have a cesspit instead, if there is any chance of the

Bad and good pruning. The 'lopped' tree grows bushy and shapeless, and will decay; crown-lifting and thinning preserve the natural shape.

63

overflow polluting a well.) The access path or drive will have more logic, and your grounds will look better, if you try to group as many functional areas together as possible, so that from a distance you create a tight, farm-type complex. Avoid creating awkward spaces which it will be difficult to find a use for. Try to get paths and pavings working with the house complex, either at right angles or parallel: the internal logic of rectangular rooms should extend outside to the working area.

Having fixed these key sitings, see whether you can accommodate a herb garden, a vegetable garden, or any other specialized growing area, such as a greenhouse, in a position where it will be convenient to the kitchen door. Work round the complex and fit in your sunbathing and eating-out areas, nestled into a sunny corner if possible to protect them from draughts. Remember that what is sunny in time for breakfast out won't usually still be sunny for an evening drink, so more than one corner will be necessary.

ACCESS

Once you have designated the major functional areas on your block layout, it is time to consider linking them by access routes.

The drive

The point where a drive meets the public highway will be determined by the local authority, or, failing that, by the twin considerations of good visibility when driving out and a meeting as near level as possible. At the other end, the approach to the house or garage will be determined by the layout of the buildings. While the shortest distance between two points is a straight line, we have not yet reached the stage in economizing petrol when a curving drive can be considered frivolous, and a gentle sweep following natural lines can be most attractive. It must always appear to curve for a reason, however: a tree will do, or a slight undulation in the ground. Conversely, a twisting drive would be pretentious where the site is not large enough for the grand gesture, or where it is dead flat. A formal straight approach, possibly lined by trees forming an avenue, lends a tension to the drive – which the property should not disappoint!

It is sometimes worth re-routing an original drive when one is reorientating a property, say by building a new extension. Often a comparatively simple reshaping will radically improve the site. Where the drive will meet the public highway at a different point you will, as for a new drive, need planning permission.

The surfacing of access drives and forecourts deserves careful consideration, weighing up the various factors of durability, cost, and visual effect, and the type of area which is to be surfaced. Where the length of a drive takes on minor road proportions its surfacing can become a civil engineering problem; probably even more difficult to construct is a drive over hilly ground, where it is necessary to engineer water run-off and to prevent icy patches in winter. As a general rule, the smoother the finish of a road surface, the faster the feel of it.

Bituminized or tarmacadam surfacing is smoothest, and while it can appear too urban, when it has been softened by rolling into it local shingle or gravel (washed or quarried), it provides one of the finest settings to any house and garden. It calls for expert laying on a suitable foundation, with curbing at the edges. Where the area to be covered is extensive, some camber will be needed to drain off water. The forms of bituminized surface vary. It can be supplied either hot, as laid on highways, or cold, with a mixture of crushed rock, which is cheaper but not so hard-wearing. The choice of hot or cold will depend on the amount of traffic and its weight; a farm drive, for instance, is likely to have enormously heavy wear daily throughout the year.

Concrete, suitably reinforced to prevent cracking, will be much cheaper. Since concrete expands and contracts according to the temperature, it is laid in sections with expansion joints between them. On motorways these joints are filled with bitumen (giving a characteristic uneven sensation when driving); on a private road, hardwood strips between the sections make a tidier finish. Like bitumen, concrete needs to be well laid on a prepared and consolidated foundation, with falls for water run-off. If water is allowed to stand, the surface will start to crack, and frost will quickly do serious damage. A pure concrete drive over any distance can look rather bald: you might consider laying wheel strips only, with grass up the centre, giving the effect of a minor metalled country road where a central grass path was retained to give horses a better foothold.

Gravel or shingle is probably the cheapest hard surfacing material for an entrance drive. It is of course much harder wearing when rolled into a bituminous surface, but a thin layer consolidated on a firm prepared base is perfectly adequate for normal domestic use. However, such a surface needs annual attention to keep down weeds and generally maintain it looking crisp, for no matter how thin the finished layer, car wheels tend to force out the loose pebbles, which should be raked back into place. Gravel or shingle laid thickly and not consolidated provides a slow, crunchy surface to walk on, which is not suitable for vehicles. The sources and character of shingle and gravel will be discussed in the next chapter.

Paving blocks, though getting more urban in feel, make a very practical and not unsuitable surfacing for country driveways. They are interlocking elements of concrete, made in various thicknesses and finishes. Their virtue is that, being small, they can be laid to follow any ground shape or level, and can be fitted around obstructions, such as a tree trunk by the side of a drive. They will also adjust to movement from roots underground, which would crack other forms of continuous surface.

Nearing the house

A turnabout or forecourt will probably continue the surfacing material of the drive, but greater attention should be given to details such as kerbs. It can also be effective to introduce another material as the drive approaches the house, or where it runs among outbuildings: granite setts, for instance, can be used to create the effect of a yard. Very interesting approaches can be created by routing the entrance drive through a building, by means of an arch; for this you need a spare building – an old barn, perhaps, where a farm complex is being upgraded, and the old yard transformed into a forecourt.

Approaching the house

below left A gravel entrance drive running through an old barn is very compelling, since the view beyond becomes framed and intensified.

left Small iron gates in this Sussex garden are contained between enormously high brick piers, which relate in scale to the house beyond.

below A modern entrance to a traditional flint building, using precast concrete slabs with brick. The false mounting block on the left (which conceals dustbins) is balanced by the steps on the right.

Grouping buildings

opposite, above Bold shapes and a similar black-and-white aesthetic admirably blend a new house (by Diamond, Redfern and Partners) with old farm buildings.

opposite, below The use of sympathetic materials and forms marries the different periods of buildings surrounding this forecourt into a satisfying visual whole. They are further united by the simple gravel surface.

The general shape of the forecourt, parking area or turnabout will have been worked out in your block planning so that it forms an entity with the house or complex of buildings. In deciding its overall size, consider whether you wish to live behind a sea of gravel that will accommodate occasional party requirements, or make do with a smaller space next to the house and a separate area for occasional use. Such a secondary area is likely to be further away, however, which can be awkward at night. The site must dictate the solution. Whatever the number of cars provided for, whether you are after a grand sweep or modest manoeuvred parking, be generous. A parking space will obviously need enough room on either side to get in and out of the vehicle comfortably. A sweeping turn encourages faster driving, so its angles should be easy and flowing. Avoid small islands of grass or planting: they always seem lost. Remember that a large impervious surface will need good drainage to suitably placed soak-aways.

The entrance to the house

Having brought your visitors up the drive, you should lead them naturally to the door you want them to use. This seems obvious, but there are many houses where one arrives and thinks, 'Do I go this way, or that?' Invariably one makes the wrong choice, only to be told, 'Oh, everyone does that' – to which the reply must be, 'Well, do something about it!' A change of surface material, a light fitting, a noticeable bell, or even a group of pots can signpost a door.

Since one tries to present as good a face to the world as possible, it follows that the entrance to one's house is terribly important: even if the rest of the garden is a total wilderness, this small area should have some semblance of organization. If you can provide it, visitors will appreciate the luxury of cover by a porch, canopy, porte cochère or what you will. Consider when designing the treatment of the entrance that this is the point where the style of the garden and the style of the house meet, and try to ensure a harmony of materials and mood.

BOUNDARIES

The wish for some measure of protection at one's boundaries is increasingly strong, and can conflict with the desire for views out, a sense of one's garden flowing into the surrounding countryside. In fact, if your boundary treatment can deter the casual offender, so much the better; but it will not keep out a determined thief, and protecting your stock, sheep, turkeys, game and Christmas trees is an organizational problem. Here we will be considering only boundaries as demarcations: internal divisions, and planting for screening and shelter, will be discussed later.

The boundaries of established properties are likely to be well defined, with a demarcation line backed by planting. The only drawback is that trees along the perimeter may have grown too big, discouraging the growth of lower plants and allowing unwanted views in and out. Slight thinning may be necessary to improve light and allow shrubs to become re-established.

Boundaries may be marked in a number of ways, of which we shall consider hedges, fencing and ha-has.

68

Hedges

Established field-boundary hedges require periodic laying to keep them stock- and vagrant-proof. The natural upright growth is laid at an angle and, traditionally, woven between vertical hazel rods driven in on the line of the hedge; thick young growth is thus continually maintained as the deterrent. The new flay hedgers, which sadly local authorities and farmers are increasingly using, are no substitute for laying: they only give the hedge a short back and sides, so the base becomes thin and penetrable. Used carelessly, they also leave the top of the hedge a splintered mess, and their indiscriminate swathe spares no young trees to regenerate the countryside. (Most of Britain's trees grow not in woods, but in hedgerows.)

An interesting new field hedge may be planted comparatively cheaply by using indigenous species, mixed with decorative forms of viburnum and/or holly. Avoid conifers: their connotation is suburban, and while they are enticingly quick-growing at the start they later need regular maintenance. For an evergreen hedge in acid soils, consider the wild rhododendron (*Rhododendron ponticum*) instead. Hedges of beech and hornbeam can be magnificent, with the odd holly for winter interest. A pyracantha hedge, not too trimmed, can be pleasant in a rural situation, offering flowers and berries for added enjoyment. The permutations of indigenous and cultivated plants which marry well are numerous. When planning such a mixed hedge, look closely at old agricultural hedges and see how they are composed. Before deciding on a hedge of only one species, think how it will relate to your property and to the surrounding countryside when seen from farther away. This is indeed the rule when considering a structural form of boundary too.

For plants suitable for formal and informal hedging, and their management, see Chapter 8 and pp.225–27.

Walls

Few can now afford any length of stone walling; but there are areas where any less substantial boundary would be inadmissible.

Stone wall construction should follow local tradition as much as possible. It will take the form of rubble (thinly bedded stones of irregular shape) or of ashlar (stones dressed with a scabbling hammer or sawn to given dimensions, laid in precise courses). In a chalk area, the stone used might be irregular flints or Kentish rag. Any of these walls should be constructed on a sound base, of concrete or, more traditionally, one or two courses of long stones.

In certain parts of the country, notably the south-west and western Wales, wall and hedge are combined in a distinctive way, which can be copied when building a rural retaining wall. An earth bank is built up and faced with stone, and then planted along the top, grasses and scrub being allowed to grow between the facing walls to bind the whole together.

Brick walling is cheaper than stone and thus more commonly used, but the same rule applies, to choose a type that will be in sympathy with your house. Looking for something cheaper still, one hesitates to mention synthetic materials, but certain kinds of concrete walling and reconstituted stone, provided they correctly follow the idiom of the region, can be extremely

Railway sleepers used for fencing and a bench seat.

Metal bar fencing runs and a painted timber gate at Horsenden Manor, Buckinghamshire.

opposite Picket fencing between high beeches allows a view to fields beyond this Northumbrian garden.

difficult to tell from the real thing, especially when mellowed and overgrown. Concrete blocks need no longer be of coarse breeze-block finish, but are now much finer and available in various colours. Even so, they are probably better suited to modern than to traditional settings. (They are also acceptable for the construction of stabling and other outbuildings.)

Of course, you need not use walls to border your whole site: you might use them only near the house and outbuildings. Most people are looking for the cheapest treatment to extend as far as possible, either to replace an outworn boundary or to establish a new one. And that is where the fence comes into its own.

Fences

When choosing fencing, think whether it can serve any purpose beyond merely bordering your land, how it will relate to the surrounding landscape, the availability of local materials for its construction, and its cost, durability and upkeep.

Of the existing types of *metal fence*, two might be considered: continuous bar fencing, and chain units. Bar fencing is the type that you see in eighteenth-century parks. It consists of uprights through which horizontal rods, either flat or round in section, are threaded and is usually supplied with a suitable flat black finish. Being sophisticated, it is expensive, and you might choose it to border a driveway or provide a boundary near the house.

Chain-link fencing, stretched between posts of timber (preferably), pressed concrete, or mild steel, lies at the opposite end of the metal fencing scale, and is useful for farm or estate work. Well maintained, it provides a fine stock-proof enclosure. It can be obtained with the wire covered in plastic of various colours: black still seems the best, being the least obtrusive. A chain-link fence will also fade into the background if it is allowed to become entangled with weeds, but in time it will inevitably be weakened.

The price of *timber fencing* varies according to its durability. The best woods – chiefly sweet chestnut, larch, oak and western red cedar – need no maintenance. Others need treatment, but are accordingly cheaper: ash, beech, birch, Douglas fir, elm, hornbeam, lime, Austrian, Corsican and Scots pine, silver fir, spruce and sycamore. Whatever is traditionally used in your area will be readily available, and is likely to be relatively better value.

The most suitable type of timber fence for general boundary work is that with two or three horizontal bars, which can be cleft, sawn, or left in a natural state, each of which gives a particular character. Whatever the finish, bark should be stripped off, for it harbours pests and moisture that hasten decay. The vertical posts supporting the bars should be treated with preservative where they will be buried and for about 300 mm. above ground level. Common methods of applying preservative include dipping, which gives little more than surface protection; brushing or spraying, which is equally superficial; application under pressure, which is good, but not practical where the fence is constructed on site; and, best of all, immersion in cold creosote, which is then heated, allowing the timber to absorb it over a period of time. Sweet chestnut, larch and oak resist impregnation, and are treated with coal tar.

The various forms of panel fencing tend to be too dear for extensive use in the country, can deteriorate quickly, and have a suburban feel to them.

Gates

All types of fencing, and most walls, can have a gate of suitable width constructed to suit them. Of the traditional types, the diagonally braced farm gate in oak is by far the strongest. In certain positions, however, particularly at the main entrance, a decorative gateway is called for. Nineteenth-century joiners were masters at making gates in Gothic, Chinese, and all manner of modes, usually of softwood, painted white with black fittings. Such gates are still available, but they need a high standard of maintenance. Like the front door approach, the front gate sets the mood for a visitor on arrival and should be visually inviting. If the gate is too strong for the flanking boundary, the effect will be the reverse.

A traditional crisp white nineteenth-century gate above a cattle grid in Gloucestershire.

Ha-ha ditches

More a decorative treatment than a boundary demarcation, the ha-ha provides a physical barrier without obstructing the view, for it is constructed in such a way that from a distance it becomes invisible. It was much used in the eighteenth century to separate the decorative garden from the surrounding park with its deer and cattle, and still has great relevance where a property enjoys a special view. It can be constructed in various ways, according to the standard of the site. The ditch is usually about 1.2 m. deep, with the inward (garden) side faced with a wall of stone, brick or concrete block, and the outer side grassed on a slope of about 1:3 to permit maintenance. A fence can be concealed in the bottom of the ditch for added stock control.

An eighteenth-century ha-ha ditch intended to deter cattle. Barbed wire has been added to stop sheep jumping the retaining wall.

MOULDING THE SITE

The lessons learnt from the surrounding landscape will have influenced your choice of material for building (where applicable) and for boundaries; the topography of the countryside, its type of undulation and such things as the line of a meandering stream, should have influenced the line of the drive. But it is in the matter of shaping your site – should you need to – that the message of the landscape in which it sits should read clearest.

You may decide to remodel your land surface for visual or practical reasons, creating gentle undulations that will block a bad view, a prevailing wind or the noise from a neighbouring road; or you may be forced to become a land sculptor to get rid of spoil dug from foundations, a new drive or a swimming pool.

In most situations, once it has been planted, the new contouring should look completely natural – part of the landscape, rather than a pile of earth upon it. In some conditions, however, a formal treatment may be more fitting, with geometrical terraces in the manner of those at Dartington Hall.

Before commencing any work, check that what you propose will not interfere with underground service runs, or any existing drainage system, unless you are prepared to relay both. Next, decide whether the work is to be done mechanically or by hand. To many, the cost and complication of employing machinery is a deterrent, but one sensitive driver with a bulldozer or a smaller bucketted digger can do in a day what would take two men with barrows weeks to do. The final determinant will be the scale of the work you propose.

If you decide to use machinery, try to minimize the damage done to surrounding areas of your land by planning the work for the dry end of summer, and arranging access if possible through a neighbouring field. A tracked vehicle will do less harm than one with wheels, since the load is more evenly spread, but neither should be let loose on a newly surfaced driveway. It is vital to programme the work thoroughly and to explain your intentions in detail to the driver. Sections showing the profile of the landform you want are often enough. If you are going to undertake major earth moving, you will need a contour plan, which a surveyor will help you prepare.

The mention of contour lines and levels throws many people into a total flap, but they are really quite easy to understand and to use. Levels are expressed in terms of plus or minus headings in relation to an agreed datum, or zero level. If your house is half way down a hill, for example, you might fix the datum zero at the main entrance step. Readings downhill will be minus one, minus two, and so on, while readings uphill will be plus one, etc. Contour lines are imaginary lines crossing the site, linking points which are at the same level. Where a slope is very gentle, they will be far apart; where it rises steeply, i.e. the levels change rapidly, they will be close together.

A surveyor will need a day or two to take what are known as 'spot levels'. Working on a plan of the site which you have provided, or which he can be commissioned to measure up, he will take readings at fixed intervals: thus he will put a grid with, say, 5 m. squares over the plot and at each intersection give you a plus or minus reading from the datum point. You then link up points with the same reading to produce a contour line. You will get a clearer impression of the contours if you or the surveyor interpolate other lines between these, at perhaps 1.5, 2.5 and 3.5 m. The resulting plan will be a diagram of the modelling of your land.

A contour plan helps not only to work out the revised shaping you require, but also to calculate the mass of earth that will be needed to create height, and it allows the contractor to see how high any retaining wall should be built where the slope is too steep for planting or mowing. You are then working with hard fact rather than a fancy idea, which is important; for what seemed quite clear to you when envisaging your scheme can become lost when the turf has been removed and the digger is wallowing in your site, humping mounds of earth about. The process is further confused by the need to store the topsoil safely to one side while the subsoil is being pushed about. The topsoil will later be replaced, but its storage spot should be agreed on before work begins.

If you are excavating a lake or a pond, or a swimming pool, you will have vast amounts of earth to dispose of, and it is essential that you do not leave yourself with a mountain of subsoil which will not support plant growth. You can, of course, pay someone to take away the excess, and import topsoil if the two have become mixed, but that is an expensive business in man-hours,

The famous grass terraces at Dartington Hall, Devon.

machinery and materials. By using surplus soil on site, you may further gain by transforming a rather dull location into a place of real interest. If you then arrange planting in shapes to complement the contours, you are creating sculptural forms on a grand scale. Some very beautiful contoured and planted forms have been created along motorways and sometimes on traffic islands, while in other parts of the country, over the last twenty years, mining waste has been contoured out and planted to blend perfectly with its surroundings.

If you contemplate this kind of work, which sounds complicated though it isn't – for any capable machine driver knows the process – make sure that you allow for the restoration of grass areas abutting the site (for there is inevitably some overspill), and for making good the ground which the machine will have disturbed on coming and going.

Once the heavy work has been completed by machine, and topsoil has been roughly replaced to give you the broad outline you had envisaged, you will find the soil has been somewhat compacted by the machine, and may even have been panned hard, in which case you will need to break it up, probably by harrowing. Then allow it to settle. If the work is finished in autumn, and the heights created are no more than 2 m. or so, by the following spring, after frost action has helped to break down surface masses of earth, you should be able to start hand raking the topsoil to the required finish as the soil dries out.

Unless you want formal, chiselled terraces, the profile of a bank should not be a straight line, but a very flattened S-bend, starting at the top in a convex curve and melting into the ground in a concave curve. Check the curves and shapes from all angles and correct any irregularities at this stage. Hand raking is vital to achieve a natural effect.

Faceted and flowing contours for banks.

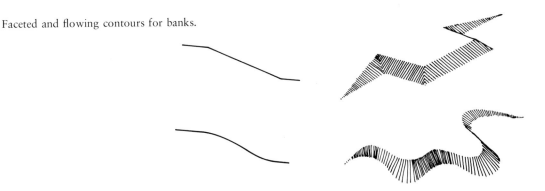

DRAINAGE

During the earth-moving process, in times of rain, you may have become alarmed by pools of standing water on what you had previously considered a dry site. Much of this will be due to compaction of the ground by heavy machinery, which as we have seen will be corrected by harrowing, but some may be collecting at the foot of newly created mounds, and there, if the ground cannot absorb it quickly, you will have to arrange some form of drainage.

The most basic type of drainage to correct standing water, as opposed to a generally wet site, is the digging of soak-aways intermittently at the problem points. The simplest form of soak-away consists of a hole about 1 m. square and 1 m. deep filled with brick rubble, which will rapidly absorb the water run-off and slowly release it into the surrounding earth. Eventually it will become filled with earth that has drained down into it with the water, and you will need to dig a new one. Such a soak-away will deal with surplus water anywhere in the garden, and drainpipes can be run to it if it is not convenient to dig the hole exactly where it is wanted. Soak-aways should not be positioned near the foundations of buildings, where they will cause damp, nor should they be under lawn, for the soil above them will sink noticeably after a time. Try to locate them in an area that will be planted.

A soak-away will only work when the ground in which it is dug is above the general level of the water-table in winter. Some land is waterlogged the year round: there you could create mounds where plants will grow that cannot stand permanently wet roots. Other land is hard, dry and rushy in summer, and sodden in winter when the water-table rises. These conditions are not likely to be suitable for gardening at all, though such land could provide useful seasonal grazing. A different and more common problem is presented by heavy clay soil, which because of its consistency does not allow water to drain away. Before embarking on a general system of drainage, make sure that it is really necessary, for ground which is overdrained becomes impoverished as the mineral elements are leached out and carried away.

General drainage consists of a system of underground pipes, laid in a particular pattern depending on the topography of the ground and the consistency of the soil, along which water flows down to an outlet – preferably a field ditch or stream, or, in a more built up area, the storm water system of the household, but not the sewer, which is the responsibility of the local authority. (The only exception is in areas where storm water systems are allowed to discharge into a sewer via a water-sealed trap.)

Drain runs need to be angled to facilitate water flow and to minimize the risk of blockage. The size of the drains and the gradient will be related to your specific need, as will the spacing. Trenches must be excavated in straight lines (although new flexible pipes allow some curving, for instance around tree roots), at the correct depth, with a firm bottom so that the falls are even.

Land drains are of three basic types. One kind makes use of pipes – traditionally short lengths of porous concrete or clayware, laid butt-jointed in a trench, and more recently perforated pipes made of plastic or pitch fibre. Another, the 'French drain', is an excavated trench filled with selected coarse rubble, with finer rubble on top, left open to the sky. It is chiefly used for temporary drainage relief. The third is 'mole drainage', in which an underground channel is formed by pulling a bullet fixed to a plough through a stiff clay soil. This provides good temporary relief, but gets choked up after a season or two.

We have now considered the broad planning of the site within its setting, blocking out areas for specific uses, access, boundaries, major earth-moving works, and drainage. It is time to get down to the detailed treatment of particular areas.

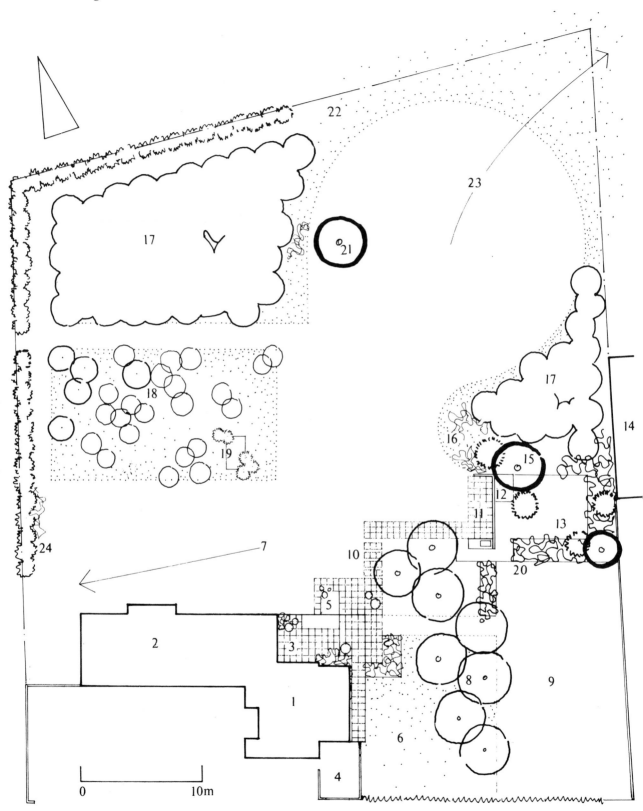

A Midlands garden with a view

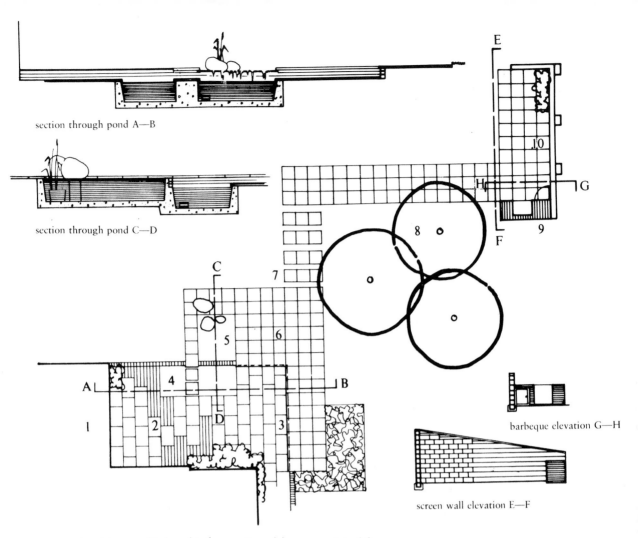

section through pond A—B

section through pond C—D

barbeque elevation G—H

screen wall elevation E—F

A new extension (2) was added to this farm cottage (1) in the Midlands. The garden is dominated on the east by a huge neighbouring barn with a pitched roof (14), but beyond it the view is magnificent, down across wide open fields. To the north and west, to cut out prevailing winds a hedge of *Cupressocyparis leylandii* had been planted (24), striking an alien note on the approach to the house and when seen from the road a quarter of a mile away.

The house, though facing the view, also faces due north, so a way had to be found to sit comfortably in the sun away from the house, while at the same time providing some sort of terrace feature to be seen from it.

An obvious corner of the house seemed the logical point from which to start, with paving steps up to connect to a barbeque terrace (11). The change of level is straddled by two pools with a connecting waterfall (5).

The concrete block wall behind the west-facing barbeque terrace is built with a capping angled to work in apposition to the slope of the roof of the great barn beyond it. The wall usefully hides a garden shed (12) and a rubbish area (13).

Woodland planting, when established on the west side of the garden (17, 18), will allow the surrounding coniferous hedge to be removed. The whole design is for low maintenance by a family with other commitments than the garden.

1 original farm cottage
2 extension
3 terrace paved with concrete slabs
4 service area
5 pond
6 rough grass area
7 mown lawn
8 existing old apple trees
9 vegetable garden
10 stepping-stones through grass
11 paved terrace with barbeque
12 garden shed
13 rubbish area
14 neighbouring barn of black corrugated iron
15 existing screen trees
16 shrub roses in rough grass
17 mixed screen planting of trees
18 silver birch copse
19 septic tank
20 low-growing junipers
21 existing fine horse chestnut
22 rough mown grass
23 mown lawn, with view out to fields
24 conifer hedge, with opening to view from terrace

A contoured garden in Surrey

1 the farmhouse
2 the rear of the farm building
3 a loggia for evening sun, and to block the view to the road
4 enlarged new terrace with raised beds for alpines
5 view into paddock with grazing horses
6 a gravel path runs round to connect to a new summerhouse
7 gravel walk with plants growing in it
8 old tennis court area reshaped to fall to pond
9 existing weeping willow
10 area of rough grass round cherry
11 thickened-up existing screen planting
12 new pond round good willow clump
13 old orchard area
14 view to water meadow through cleaned-up hedge

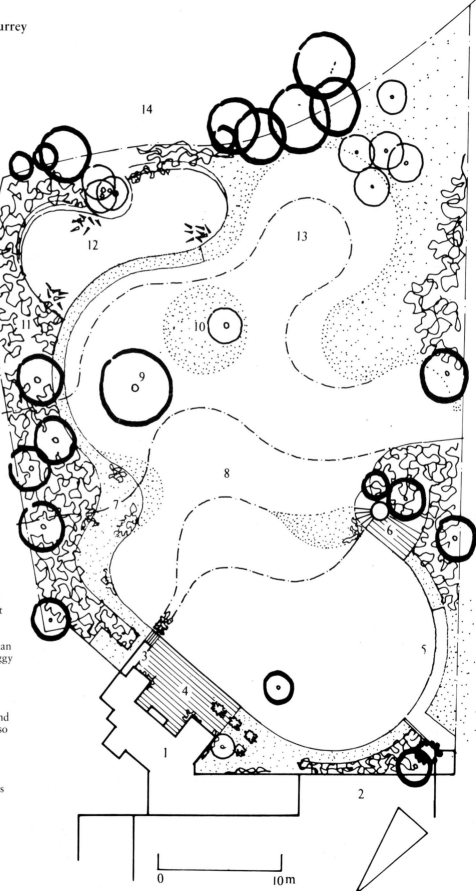

Across an old grass tennis court the land fell away from this Surrey farmhouse to an overgrown formal garden with an orchard (13) beyond. In the boggy low-lying ground to the southwest was a natural pond. The tennis court area was bulldozed away (8) so that the ground sloped down to an enlarged pond (12). The formal garden was also cleared to open the view to the orchard and water meadows beyond. Through the boundary planting of willows the view of fields of buttercups in summer is spectacular.

0   10 m

An awkward site in Hertfordshire

By their very nature, a house tends to be a formal object, while a garden tends to be informal. Where they come together, the garden needs to have some element of the geometry of the house plan. This is illustrated here in a garden laid out on a wedge-shaped site, with some existing large trees.

The total garden layout should relate back to the house and terrace, and not necessarily to the pattern of the site: the difference in shape can be planted out.

The length of this strange-shaped site has been manipulated to create a meandering walk, more visual than strictly functional, since it goes past the septic tanks to the rubbish area!

On the west side of the house, where the view from the sitting-room is to fields, the boundary has been opened up and a wild garden developed to allow the country to flow in (6). In contrast is a small rectilinear herb garden on the north side (4), outside the kitchen window which faces a country road. The photographs show the 'picturesque' garden, looking from the west side of the house toward the tree (9) and meandering path, and the formal herb garden on the other side (4).

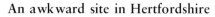

1 garage
2 main access to house
3 kitchen entrance
4 herb garden
5 sitting-room
6 mown strip with rough grass surround linking it to country beyond
7 existing old fruit trees
8 stone-paved terrace
9 ash tree with ground cover under
10 septic tanks
11 mown way leading to rubbish area

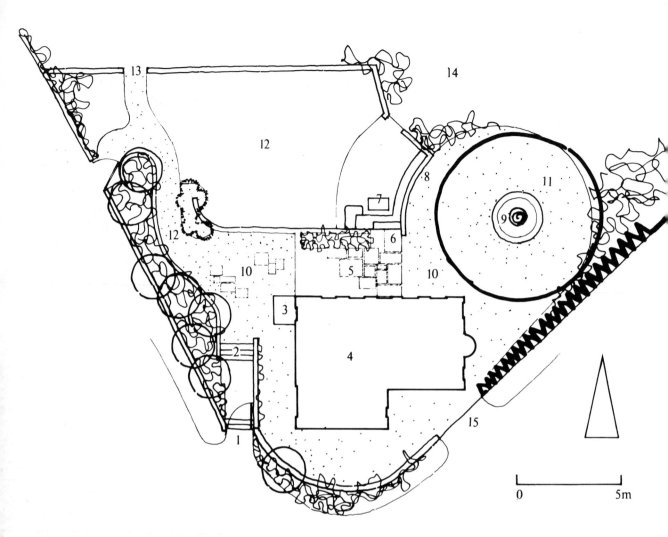

A cottage in the Brecon Beacons

It was important that the garden of this stone cottage on its Breconshire hillside should maintain the feel of the surrounding countryside.

A large sycamore to one side of the house (11) protects it from the fierce prevailing wind, and the garden was created with the tree as its fulcrum. A stone terrace was built along the downhill side of the house (5), with wide stone steps leading to a level lawn held by a retaining wall. The steps are used for seating around a built-in table (7), and the area is sheltered by a massive stone wall.

A circular gravel area, on a level with the top terrace, surrounds the sycamore. Within it, a circular wall (9) serves both as a casual seat and as a retainer to keep the natural level of the soil necessary for a healthy tree.

On the uphill side of the house is a small paved drying area. Outside the front door, a gravel area contains random paving to give visual interest.

Planting is simple, chosen for the climate and for low maintenance.

The photographs show detailing of the steps by the sycamore, a general view of the sycamore and cottage from the lawn, the area by the front porch, and a view from the house to the stone table and hills beyond.

1 entrance from road
2 steps down to garden
3 porch
4 house
5 paved terrace
6 steps down
7 built-in stone table
8 wall shielding terrace from wind
9 stone retaining wall to maintain level
10 gravel areas
11 large existing sycamore
12 raised lawn
13 gate to paddock downhill
14 amazing view up valley
15 car parking

A garden on a tidal estuary in Hampshire

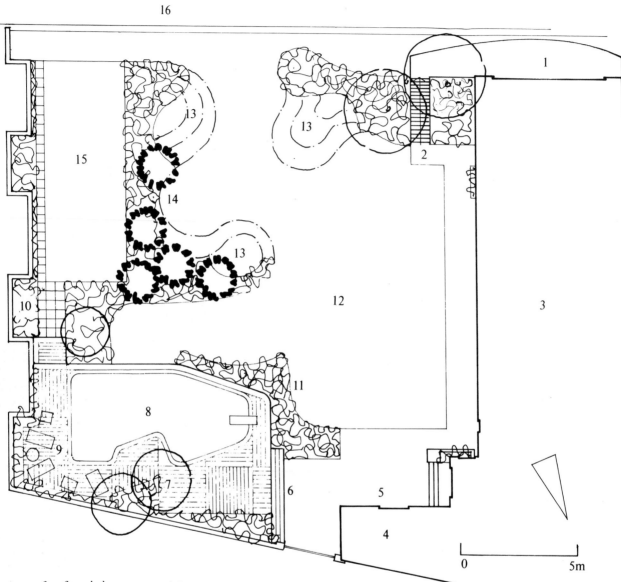

1 first floor balcony over water
2 steps linking balcony and garden
3 house
4 loggia extension for barbeques
5 terrace paved with York stone
6 brick steps up to pool
7 brick paved terrace under shade trees
8 swimming pool
9 sun-bathing
10 fruit in boundary wall recesses
11 decorative planting
12 mown lawn
13 contoured grass mounds
14 planting for salt-laden wind protection
15 vegetables
16 waterfront

Gardens beside navigable water are a never-ending source of
curiosity to those who pass in a boat. People who live by
water thus suffer a peepshow existence, although for many the
reciprocal view of the passing river traffic is adequate
compensation. For this client, professionally connected with
boats, it was not: the problem was to create privacy. Further
problems were the risk of flooding at particularly high tides,
and the salt-laden winds which limited the choice of plants.

A swimming pool (8) was sited in the most sheltered corner,
where the ground level had to be raised since the water table
is so close to the surface.

To screen the brick-paved terrace around the pool
contoured mounds were created, rising to a height of 2 m. On
these a pattern of planting was made of subjects which can
stand the wind, and which by being planted on the mounds
have their roots out of salt water when the garden is flooded.
As well as giving privacy these mounds shelter a small
vegetable garden (15).

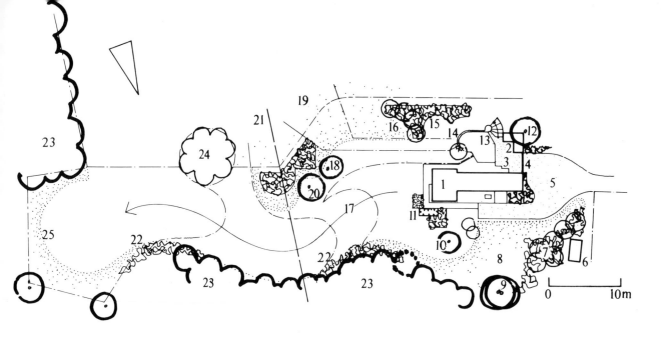

West Sussex *ferme ornée*

This was the *ferme ornée* within a park of a larger house situated across a valley to the east. With the sale of 'the big house' the tables have been turned, and the view has been moulded and shaped to frame the view from the dependency. Additional views have been controlled by new planting in the grazed parkland, which also helps to block out prevailing south and west winds. The detailed plan shows the area around the house (right, in the larger plan).

1 Dairy Cottage
2 original outhouse becomes a loggia and store
3 new gravel courtyard
4 white timber gate
5 forecourt for parking
6 stable
7 screen planting
8 rough mown grass with bulbs
9,10 existing fine ash trees
11 herb beds
12 mown grass bank up
13 steps up round plinth
14 flint retaining wall
15 mixed planting
16 whitebeams
17 grading down
18 existing sycamore
19 view into grazed parkland
20 existing crab apple
21 proposed initial boundary fence
22 decorative planting at edge of wood
23 existing mixed woodland
24 new tree clump fenced round
25 trees felled to open view back to large house across the valley

grass bank

steps up

ELEVATION TO FIELD

existing low wall capped in brick and returned with bank gradient towards house

brick plinth

stone steps down

existing ash

grass bank eventually graded down

catalpa

grass

openings

tub for annuals

almond or winter flowering cherry

gravel

solid white timber gates

stone paving

HOUSE

planting in gravel

parking

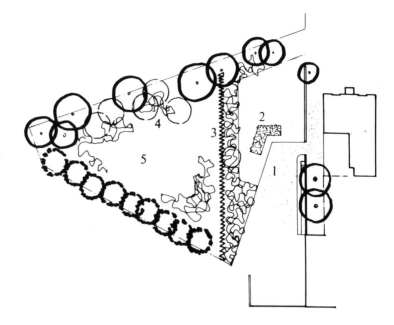

The problem
1 the original bottleneck house
   approach
2 rose bed
3 coniferous hedge with mixed
   border
4 scrub and seedling sycamore
   round fine copper beech
5 overgrown paddock

South coast farmhouse with a drive problem

The surround to the Georgian farmhouse, though flat, had not been gardened for some years. Strong punishing winds come from the east, south and south-west, and the only sheltered part was a lawn with a rose bed (above, 2).

The owners wished to separate the working access to the farmhouse (for Land Rovers, etc.) from the private access, and to elevate the approach generally since what was the back of the house is now the entrance front. They also wanted herbaceous borders and a rose garden.

A private access drive was therefore routed through a derelict paddock (below, 4) and much of the dividing coniferous hedge (above, 3) was removed. The house frontage was paved with brick stepping-stones through gravel. By further clearing trees a view was opened to the surrounding farmland (6).

The old facade of the Georgian house looks out on to a formal lawn surrounded by herbaceous planting and backed with holly hedges (10). From this garden a path leads to a rose garden (11) and into an existing lawn area (12). A series of enclosed and sheltered rooms have thus been developed, making the most of the flat views seawards (14).

The solution
1 Georgian farmhouse
2 garages
3 farm parking
4 new private drive
5 coniferous hedge removed
6 scrub cleared to allow view to
   farmland beyond copper beech
7 new brick paved forecourt
8 two fine evergreen oaks
9 new border and screen hedge
10 herbaceous borders with paved
   edge surround lawn
11 formal gravel paths through new
   rose garden
12 existing sunbathing lawn
13 summerhouse
14 view seawards across open
   farmland

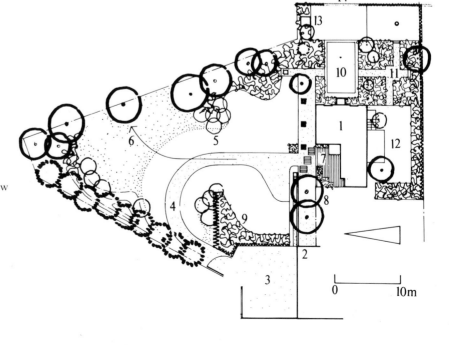

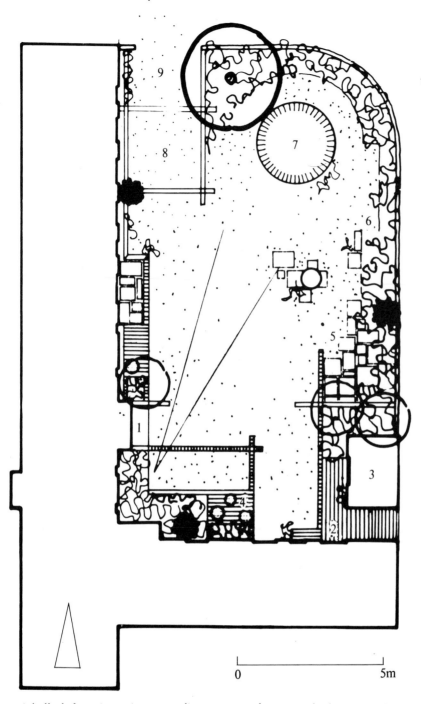

West Sussex
farm building conversion

1 front entrance to house
2 service door to kitchen
3 building containing storage
   space and oil tanks
4 raised brick plinth and bed
   for grouped pots
5 random York stone infill with
   plant backing to form terrace
6 mixed shrubs and climbers
   around perimeter
7 raised brick seat/plinth
8 sealed gravel infill within
   brick pattern
9 entrance to yard
10 multi-stemmed *Catalpa
   bignonioides*

0   5m

A bullock-fattening unit, surrounding a concreted open yard, was made into a marvellous home with farm office included. The yard gives access to both the front and rear entrance to the house (1 and 2). The finished surface had to be able to cope with Land Rovers turning up fairly regularly for tea or lunch breaks. At the same time, the area needed to be decorative since it has a fine view to the Downs on the north, beyond the farm buildings, and to be usable as an occasional place for a drink.

A pattern of brick to match the house was laid into the concrete, and a terrace defined with old York stone (5). The surface of the remainder of the yard was lightly

broken up, and a fine layer of washed gravel laid over it and sealed with a cold bituminous emulsion.

Pockets have been allowed for occasional plantings, marked by the odd half barrel for bulbs and annuals, and the perimeter concrete has been removed to allow for internal planting and for climbers to soften the surrounding flint walls to the yard (6).

A raised brick circle (7) approximately 400 mm. high, infilled with concrete whose surface was brushed, makes a none-too-demanding feature, doubling as occasional seating with space for a drink or coffee tray. This works as a composition in juxtaposition to a large-leafed *Catalpa bignonioides*.

Using the Garden

'The great challenge for a garden maker is not to make the garden look natural, but to make it so that the people in it will feel natural.' So wrote Thomas Church in 1948. Both results are of course possible, but a garden is primarily for use. One does not have that expensive piece of ground for looks alone: as the eighteenth century discovered, it becomes boring after a time, no matter how sublime. The garden is a place to be enjoyed in clement weather by all ages and for any number of reasons; if it is also good to look at, that is a bonus.

The range of users and activities is enormous, for the garden now reflects life styles indoors. And, as indoors, one seeks a discipline or structure for one's activities – a feeling of containment, of being *in* the garden, rather than just on it – which comes from the definition of areas. These areas are no longer framed by hedges, but are characterized, say, by different surface materials. They will follow each other in a logical sequence, of which the starting point will be the house. A gentle transition can be achieved through a conservatory or garden room (see Chapter 6). Beyond that you will need a terrace area, which will become the power house of your garden.

THE TERRACE

If it is conceived correctly, making the most of the sun and cutting out draughts (which are more inhibiting than lack of sun), a terrace will be used many days of the year, not only for sunbathing, entertaining or eating outdoors, but for household chores. It will also be on the route to the herb garden, the fuel store, and so on.

The terrace should, however, be conceived as a static place, from which paths might lead off – an effect you can create by the materials you use in its construction. It should also be big enough comfortably to hold all the furniture and people that will occupy it at its busiest. A great defect of many gardens is that the scale of individual elements within them is too small, visually as well as physically.

If your large terrace looks too bleak in winter, furnish it with pots or tubs on castors, which can be pushed to one side in the summer. Alternatively, you might soften the terrace by random areas of planting within it. For the weekender, or the country gardener who does not want too much work, these areas could quite successfully be the only horticultural elements in a garden which is otherwise allowed to become more wild. Indeed, the country garden terrace can be treated in a much more imaginative and informal way than the hard, paved patio of the sophisticated town garden. It is a place for relaxation, and its design should reflect that – though it must still be well detailed, and not sloppy.

A sympathetic blending of flint walls with stone and brick terracing – Lutyens at Overstrand Hall, Norfolk (1899).

Just as the terrace provides a natural extension for the activities of the house, so too it should be a natural extension of the *feel* of the house – particularly if the two adjoin. The terrace then acts as a setting to the building, and in form and material it should be inseparable from the architecture of the house. There is a current revival of interest in the work of Sir Edwin Lutyens, who set his houses amongst walls and on terraces conceived as a unity. They may have looked somewhat harsh when new, but when planted with a balance of material by Lutyens's colleague, Gertrude Jekyll, the whole quickly became integrated and softened. The Modern Movement in turn conceived of the house more as a sculpture set down upon the landscape. The 1960s reaction to that attitude was to integrate the building organically into the site. There is a movement now which goes further, to bury the house within the site, the surrounding earth providing insulation.

It is a very basic need in all of us to wish to sit against something, not to be completely exposed – no doubt due to a primitive fear of attack from behind. With our backs protected, we wish to face outward to a view, if possible; and most people will want some sun. These conditions, combined with ready access to the house, should begin to suggest a location for the terrace. Few houses are so formal that a terrace has to be placed symmetrically, when the result might in any case be stagey. Remember that you will probably want some measure of seclusion.

Having established the position, decide on the size. If you are working on paper, draw in a few 2-m. lengths to represent people lying down. Then put in a table roughly 1.5 m. across, and allow 2 m. on each side around it, to give space for chairs to be pushed back. In this way you will establish some sort of scale from which to work. Obviously the size will vary according to your lifestyle – whether you are entertainers outside or not.

The shape of the terrace will be partly governed by the material with which you surface it, for it will be a multiple of a basic unit. Both shape and materials should relate back to the building, so that vertical and horizontal surfaces complement each other. To get a rough shape, go back to your big overlay plan and try to work out a pattern around the drawing of the house. First, start from various features of the house – corners, windows, doorways – and extend lines outward at 90 degrees, and see if these produce a rhythm. If they do, use this rhythm to form a gridded pattern to the necessary width and depth. Now fill in the grid with a suitable material (see below). You can use the grid lines to break up the area, for instance by running bricks between stone paving, or concrete slabs through tarmac. Try to make any changes of level coincide with the grid lines.

If no rhythm appears from your plan, begin by selecting your paving material and then work outward from the house, using the size of your paving units to suggest the overall shape (concrete slabs, for instance, are 500 mm. square, and standard metric bricks laid two by two are 250 mm. square). The outer edge of your terrace might echo the pattern of the inner edge where it follows the line of the house.

Some of the materials available can support light wheeled traffic, so long as an adequate foundation is laid.

opposite The flooring of this outside room is of gravel. Sheltering walls are painted ochre, on which the purple *Vitis vinifera purpurea* looks well. Flowers are lemon yellow.

88

Stone must be hard-wearing. A sawn face is more meticulous and formal; a riven or axed finish is better if there is any risk of the surface becoming slippery when wet. Stone varies in thickness from 50 to 75 mm. depending on the type.

Purbeck stone is a hard limestone, which is prohibitively expensive for all but the grandest situations unless you happen to live in the area of Dorset where it is quarried. Portland stone, also from Dorset, is a cheaper and softer limestone, suitable for paving which will not get too heavy use. York stone, though increasingly expensive, is the most widely used: a hard sandstone, it has an open-grained finish which is resistant to skidding. Laid in a systematic pattern of large slabs around smaller key stones, it provides a fine serviceable traditional-looking surface. It is obtainable in random squares and rectangles, so you can lay it with an irregular edge towards any planting areas it adjoins, creating a much softer effect than with a straight line. York stone is also obtainable in broken slabs, which can be laid in a crazy pattern; but the slabs should fit neatly together, as in a jigsaw, and the result should be as tailored as the more regular pattern.

Flagstones of York, Portland or Purbeck stone may be laid on a 75-mm. foundation of dry sand (either directly, or with a mortar dot at each corner and in the centre to assist the levelling process), or over a dry mixture of sand and cement, or even, where necessary, over concrete. They should be laid with a slight slope (1:32), so that water drains off. Joints can either be carefully grouted with a liquid mortar mix or filled with a dry mix of sand and cement which will take up ground moisture and set. When the joints are nearly dry, brush them back some 3 mm. to expose the edges of the paving stones.

Slate is something of a luxury, unless it is local. It has wearing quantities similar to granite, is slow to weather, and can become slippery unless it is riven. It can be laid in the same way as other stone paving; offcuts and slips are also available, which can be used as a decorative infilling within another paving medium or set on edge to form a demarcation line or border.

Setts – oblong blocks of granite – can be had new or second-hand. New ones are usually imported from Portugal, while second-hand ones can sometimes be obtained from a local authority which has taken them up from an old road in a nearby town. Sizes vary, but setts are always fairly small, so the cost of labour for laying them will be proportionately high. They can be laid flat, to form gulleys or infills within another medium, or stood on end, to form the fan patterns that one sees in many Continental streets, when half a sett is used. Such an arrangement would be suitable for a forecourt, to complement a local building stone of a similar colour.

Bricks have for centuries been used for paving, providing a warm, mellow, natural surface that is equally in harmony with stone, with brick buildings, and with plants. Paving bricks need to be resistant to frost and to have a low calcium and magnesium content. Overfired bricks, usually darker in colour, can also be used, since the process reduces the risk of damage due to the action of sulphates within the brick. A cheaper form of surface is now available in the form of brick paviors, which are slightly larger and thinner than normal bricks. Having said all this, one must also say that many old brick paths, which

opposite Stable tiles may be used for paving inside and out.

Slate used to surface both a terrace and steps. Unless obtainable locally, this material is expensive.

A brick path laid in herringbone and straight patterns, retained by bricks on edge.

must have been there for ages and which are pitted and scored, nevertheless look marvellous. The only drawback to their use as a regular route is that they may collect standing water and in winter become icy.

It is traditional to lay bricks in herringbone or basketweave patterns, but straight coursing can also look exceedingly handsome. Do not overcomplicate your ground pattern. Bricks should be laid on a firm foundation of concrete, with the outermost row set on end to stop the paved area creeping outward through use or frost damage.

Concrete paviors, a fairly recent development, come in various interlocking forms. Many have a textured surface, and they make an admirable alternative to brick, being a better match for certain stones and also much cheaper.

Pre-cast concrete slabs now exist to suit nearly all situations, for they come in various sizes, textures, patterns and colours. A selection can be seen at almost any garden centre. Hunt around, however, when making your choice, for a builder's merchant might have more. A building centre in a major city will have a greater selection still. Failing that, write round for manufacturers' catalogues.

Beware of slabs that are too highly textured or, worse, too highly coloured. You are not trying to create a visual feast with your paving. The rest of your garden can do that. In what is, after all, only a serviceable area, keep the paving subdued. With time, most concrete slabs mellow until they can easily be mistaken for stone (only their perfection and crispness giving the game away). Beware too of very cheap slabs, which have not been formed under high pressure: they tend to disintegrate before they come off the lorry, and their softness makes laying difficult. It is possible to saw concrete slabs to fit awkward corners; but again this will be difficult with the softer ones. Something to watch when concrete paving is being laid is that the contractor has the slabs the correct way up: he is inclined to lay the textured surface downwards, leaving a smooth surface on top, and this may not be the manufacturer's intention.

Cobbles may be used for decorative infilling. Large water-worn pebbles, up to 100 mm. or more in size, they come from beaches, riverbeds and gravel pits, and may also be had as surplus wash mill flints from potteries. Some are imported. They are obtainable in sacks through garden centres or builders' merchants. Local authorities tend to use cobbles as a pedestrian deterrent, but in a garden they can make an attractive break in an otherwise flat paving medium and in association with plants. When laid in mortar, they should be up-ended like eggs in a crate and packed tight together, and they will need to be retained by a firm surround to stop them spreading outward. Cobbles can also be laid loose, to create a Japanese or waterside effect.

Quarry tiles can be used in mild areas in sheltered positions and make a good transitional material between indoors and out. They tend to become slippery when wet. Glazed tiles are not frost-resistant and should not be used outside.

92

PATHS AND ACCESS WAYS

When we considered the block planning of a site, in Chapter 4, we suggested locating the main practical features in consecutive order, giving the pathways a logical progression. But access ways need not be linear. If the various units of your site are close together, then the logical arrangement is a paved or gravelled courtyard. Even when the units are further spaced out, try to achieve a feeling of enclosure, linking them by areas of surfacing to create a feeling of place.

Work out these areas in conjunction with the terrace, picking up any existing features to create a modulated grid in which to fit the elements of paving. Only when the hard surface has served its function to connect the garage, the greenhouse, a woodstore or a stable should it become linear and lead one around the remainder of the site.

If the path can be at the edge of the lawn, next to a planted area, it will serve an extra purpose, for shrubs can flop out on to it without getting in the way of the lawnmower. Paths so sited will also have the effect of not splitting up the lawn, leaving large areas which can be mown more easily.

Paths may continue the same paving material as that of the terrace and service area, but usually the quality of the surfacing will drop for reasons of economy. Entrance paths, however, should be of top-class material, non-slip, well lit, and detailed in a very straightforward way.

Materials which might be used, other than those already considered for terraces, include **unsealed gravel or shingle**, which is relatively cheap to lay and maintain and comes in a variety of colours. It is obtainable from a wide range of suppliers; a local source will obviously be cheaper (since transport costs are virtually eliminated) and more suitable to your site. Shingle is rounded, being natural water-worn pebbles from a riverbed or gravel pit, while gravel is sharp, the product of crushed stone in a quarry. Grades vary: coarse material is slower to walk across, and makes a crunching noise which is incidentally something of a burglar deterrent. Sharp-edged chippings should not be used where children might fall on them. **Self-binding gravel**, which when watered and rolled forms a cement-like surface, is also available. It is an economical surfacing material for drives and other areas of light-weight traffic. **Pulverized bark**, where available, provides a very dark-coloured, soft surface for a path, particularly suitable for use through woodland.

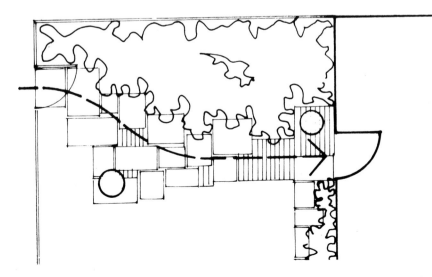

York stone and brick or tile laid together to form a random-looking path. The route over its surface is direct, however: avoid paths which wiggle pointlessly.

a Timber blocks make a
sympathetic paving, though
they can be slippery when
wet.
b Cobbles of two colours
laid in a fishscale pattern.
c A circle of granite setts
laid on end.
d Sandstone slabs and
granite setts in
Dumbartonshire.
e Large pads of timber (a
use for dead elm).
f A brickwork pattern
infilled with brushed
concrete.

above and right A mix of brick, tile, and black stable paver, seen in overall pattern and in detail. Note too how effectively the low brick walls frame the view.

below A characterful grouping of water-worn boulders used for walling, with slate and a timber decking. The strong form of bamboo contrasts well.

opposite A straight path at Castle Drogo, Devon, softened by planting.
a Brick and York stone in a rectilinear pattern.
b Old York stone in a random pattern through consolidated gravel.
c Bricks of different colours harmonize with wood, stone and tile.
d Old York stone, interplanted, at Sissinghurst.
e Large flints used to define a path in gravel.
f Concrete slabs laid in an abstract pattern through grass.
g Railway sleepers used for a path.

Terraces

left In this mill conversion in Surrey a timber bridge over the millrace becomes a terrace. The pattern zig-zags away from the shelter of the house to blend into the surrounding countryside.

below and opposite Two views of a paved area that forms a natural extension to the author's own house in Sussex. For a large part of the year this is as much a room as the kitchen which it adjoins.

KERB TRIM FOR TERRACES AND PATHWAYS

Terracing does not usually need a kerb to prevent the surrounding earth from falling onto it: if that happens, the soil level is too high and should be reduced. Certain surfacing materials, however, need retaining, to prevent them spreading through use or crumbling at the edges due to frost. Brick, as we have seen, can be turned on end to form its own kerb. For gravel and pulverized bark bricks on edge are ideal. A cheaper alternative, coming in longer runs, is a concrete kerb, which looks better laid with the square edge upwards. Cheaper still, but comparatively short-lived, is timber edging. Suitable hardwoods for this are elm, larch and oak; any softwood should be pressure creosoted.

STEPS AND CHANGES OF LEVEL

Changes of level within the new layout may take the form of ramped or graded earth which has been grassed or planted, or retaining walls of brick or stone. The obvious way to cross from one level to another is by means of a straight flight of steps. You might also consider steps that change direction, or a ramp rising in an easier slope.

Movement about a garden is fairly gentle, so any steps must be generous in their proportions – that is, the tread must be wide enough (say 450 mm.) and the riser not too steep (no more than 150 mm.). If you are making each step out of two slabs, allow the tread to overhang the riser by approximately 50 mm.: the shadow thus created makes the steps appear to 'fly' a little.

Steps can of course be constructed in all the materials suggested for paving a terrace, and there are others, too, which fit into the rural idiom. **Timber** may be either temporary or permanent, depending on the wood used, and is relatively inexpensive. The hardest wood for outside use is undoubtedly oak (traditionally used for gates and fences), followed by sweet chestnut and elm. Old railway sleepers are of softwood, heavily impregnated with preservative. They can be used to form whole steps of wood, but have a tendency to be slippery. Alternatively, the risers only may be of timber, with the infill of another material – soil with a high gravel content, or the local soil with small amounts of aggregate mixed in. Compact it well as you lay it, and finish it with a layer of crushed stone or shingle rolled into the surface. **Earth** steps seldom survive heavy winter downpours. In a very rugged area, you might consider carving steps out of **natural rock**, though the nature of the design will depend upon the mason's skill.

Where steps cross a ramped bank, the angle can be tricky. If they stand proud, they interrupt the flow of the bank they cross; if they are set into the bank, which will be either planted or grassed, it will be difficult to retain the planting or to mow the grass on either side of them. The problem can be solved by containing the steps within sensitively designed retaining walls, but that is an added expense.

Flights of steps should never be longer than twelve risers without having a landing for a breather, and it is even pleasanter to have more frequent landings, with space for pots and even informal seating. There is likely to be a

view back in the direction from which you have come, and in winter months, with the right orientation, such a spot might provide a memorable warm perch.

The intermediate solution between a stepped flight and stepped levels is a step treatment which changes direction. The user takes longer to get to the top, but the outline of the flight from a distance becomes all the more attractive.

A ramp serves the same purpose as a flight of steps, but allows the ascent to be taken at a gentler pace. Ramps are usually thought of for the elderly and the infirm, who do indeed find them far easier to use; but remember that the same will be true of anyone pushing a wheelbarrow or a mower. The principal drawback to a ramp is that it needs more space, since the gradient should be no more than 1:12. The surface may be grassed, or covered with a non-slip material, and there must be adequate drainage at the bottom to prevent ponding. If the ramp looks like being too long (you can check its probable length by working out the difference in level between top and bottom and the angle of 1:12), then you may want to break it by intermediate flights of steps, known as perrons.

In this new garden in Jersey steps and changes of level provide an important feature at the entrance, and make a sculptural attraction when seen from the house.

a

Changes of level

a Finely coursed Cotswold stone used for walling and curving steps.

b Wooden steps blend well with a timber gate and fence.

c Brick steps leading to a front door. Note the pattern and brushed concrete infill at the lower level.

d When using a thick tread material, allow plenty of overhang. Plenty of landing space at the top will prevent grass wearing.

opposite Step risers of old railway sleepers with treads of consolidated gravel – a deliciously random approach.

b

c

d

Wind protection in Essex

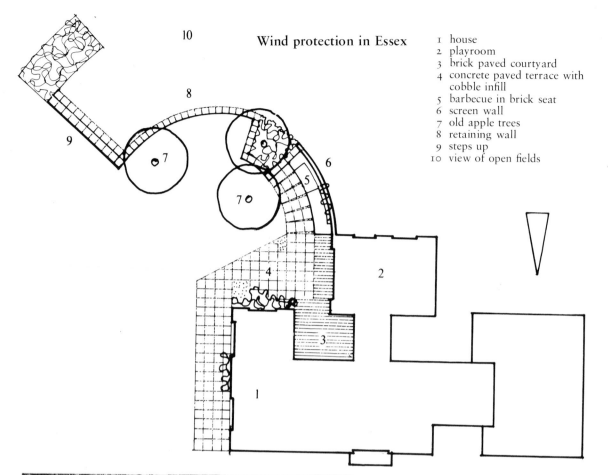

1 house
2 playroom
3 brick paved courtyard
4 concrete paved terrace with cobble infill
5 barbecue in brick seat
6 screen wall
7 old apple trees
8 retaining wall
9 steps up
10 view of open fields

A playroom was added to the rear of the house, with its doors opening eastward to share a terrace with the reception area of the house. A prevailing wind from the south-west made the space unusable at some times of the year, and a solution had to be found which dealt with the wind while retaining the view southward to fields.

By curving a screen wall out from the playroom, wind shelter was instantly provided. Into this wall was built a bench incorporating a barbecue. Its curve then continues in a low retaining wall, which helps to gather the distant view and the randomly placed old apple trees into one cohesive design.

Additional Buildings in the Garden

In an ideal world, if one was starting to build a country house from scratch, integrated with planting, one would include all the outbuildings that any household seems to need. Even then it would be difficult to foresee the emergent interests of everyone – a reason why farmhouses make such excellent country homes, for they are surrounded by all manner of outbuildings, which can be adapted to suit almost any purpose. The rest of us will have to erect additional buildings piecemeal, but with careful thought it is possible to plan them so the result does not look haphazard.

Additional structures that might be needed include glazed areas for domestic use or for cultivation, extra garages or car ports, a 'hide' for the oil tank, summerhouses, and shelters to accompany swimming pools sited at a distance from the house; and, farther away, perhaps kennels or loose boxes (see Chapter 14). Many of the readily available buildings on the market are too small or too characterless to read as a handsome addition to a country garden, and the answer is to shop around: the Chelsea Flower Show is worth visiting for this aspect alone. Well designed, grouped as much as possible, and serviced by a hard approach, these features can at least become a working entity, which with the help of careful planting will not dominate the rest of your property.

With glazed constructions, the closer they are to the house the cheaper they are to service with water, electricity, and if necessary gas. So let's start at the house and work outwards.

GLASS STRUCTURES: CONSERVATORIES, GREENHOUSES AND FRAMES

Conservatories

There is a great revival of interest in the conservatory, as a decorative way of adding an extra room to the house. It is more attractive than a home extension and more useful as a place to grow plants, so that your window-sills are not all cluttered up; but better still is its function during the long winter months when it is not possible to do much in the garden. The idea of pottering about in mid-January surrounded by a warm earthy smell, with hyacinths, paperwhites and mimosa further scenting the air, is powerfully attractive. It is further claimed that the fully-glazed conservatory provides one of the most practical forms of thermal management: in winter it helps to reduce heat loss from the house, while in spring and autumn it can actually warm the house, the heat collected being distributed either by natural convection or by forced ventilation.

opposite A purpose made though modular conservatory, designed by Room Outside Ltd of Chichester, blends modern and traditional styling well together.

right The cool conservatory at Denmans provides a delicious flowery retreat throughout the year. Originally a Victorian greenhouse, it has been adapted to modern domestic use.

below A conservatory designed by Litchfield & Stout adjoining a Sussex cottage. This structure provides an ideal transition from house to garden.

A ready-made Victorian type conservatory by Frances Machin, with ogee roof and PVC glazing. Sides may be single- or double-glazed.

The essence of a conservatory, as opposed to a smaller lean-to structure, is that it should be large enough to sit in, while also having adequate space to grow plants, on staging or directly in the ground. Anything smaller than this becomes impractically cold in winter and unbearably hot in summer. It is important to define for yourself clearly at the outset what the function of the structure is to be: if it is to be chiefly for plants, it will need much watering and spraying down in summer, which in turn will mean hard paving and no upholstered furniture; if on the other hand what you want is a pretty garden room, you will have to make concessions horticulturally, in which case you may not even need a glazed roof.

Before deciding on your structure, obtain information on what is available from as many sources as possible. The price of conservatories is slowly being reduced by the introduction of modular systems, with panels of varying sash designs which can be chosen to suit most forms of architecture. If you can afford it, you can buy or have specially designed for you something with the charm and character of a Victorian conservatory or earlier orangery. Basically, there are three different ways to proceed. First, you can buy the conservatory from a supplier who will take care of the whole operation – foundations, erection and glazing. Second, you can commission your own builder to buy the conservatory from a supplier and do all the necessary construction work. And third, you can do without a supplier: you or your architect will provide the design, and you will commission your own builder, carpenter, roofing contractor, etc. Having made your choice, contact your local planning office to find out first if planning permission is necesary and then what the building regulations are. The building inspector will probably want to see your plans, and will be interested in the materials you intend to use, the foundations and the drainage, and how the work conforms to the current building regulations. If you are buying from a supplier, he should provide you with plans.

What you can grow in your conservatory, and how, will obviously depend on its orientation. A structure getting full sun will need more watering in summer and more attention to ventilation, both of which can be controlled automatically. It is not essential for a conservatory to receive full sun, but if it doesn't you might find that additional heating is needed in winter.

When choosing plants and furnishings, try to establish a particular mood, by a particular colour range in the flowers, for instance. Make the overall impression clear and strong on entering – tropical, say, with lots of spiky-leaved plants or very lush, jungly, large-leaved subjects; or pretty, with pale blue clusters of plumbago and heavy scents of hoya and jasmine; or a shaded, ferny grot!

Greenhouses

From the conservatory, one moves to a more functional form of glasshouse, which is essentially for growing. You will again be concerned with temperature, and again you will find that the smaller the structure the more difficult it is to regulate the climate, and the more limited the range of plants you can grow. A greenhouse is heated naturally by the sun warming the soil, which in turn warms the air. In summer it can become too hot, if not properly ventilated, while in winter, when the sun's rays are weak, it can be too cold, and require more than a minimum of expensive heating. It is therefore important to get as much sunlight as possible: try to orient the greenhouse east-west, see that it is not shaded by house or trees, angle the roof to reflect the minimum of light, and keep the glass clean.

The forms of greenhouse now on the market are legion, in both size and construction. They are made of metal or of timber, the latter either cedar, which needs little maintenance, or softwood, which needs regular painting. Metal structures admit more light, since the glazing bars can be thinner. A house glazed to the ground will also be lighter, but one resting on brick side walls 600–900 mm. high will be warmer.

The permutations of ventilation, watering, and especially heating are complicated, and you may need specialist advice to get them right for your situation. To manipulate the temperature accurately by hand is both difficult and time-consuming, so an automatic ventilation system is probably advisable. Further time can be saved by the use of an automatic watering device – of the trickle irrigation type, perhaps including capillary trays and mats on which the plants stand, or a misting system activated by the strength of the sunlight. The heating will probably be electrical, by fan convection or tubular heaters, depending on the purpose of the greenhouse. You can reduce the bill by having a propagating unit, a small glass case which is heated independently from beneath, allowing you to lower the temperature slightly in the remainder of the house.

left A Gothic garden room at West Dean in Sussex

below This greenhouse was originally used for a vine. It has now been transformed into a summer sitting-room and playroom, linked internally and via the terrace to the main house.

Partially sunken greenhouses in the United States: earth is an insulator, and double glazing further conserves heat. In the design shown in section and plan, solar energy is used to heat the house.

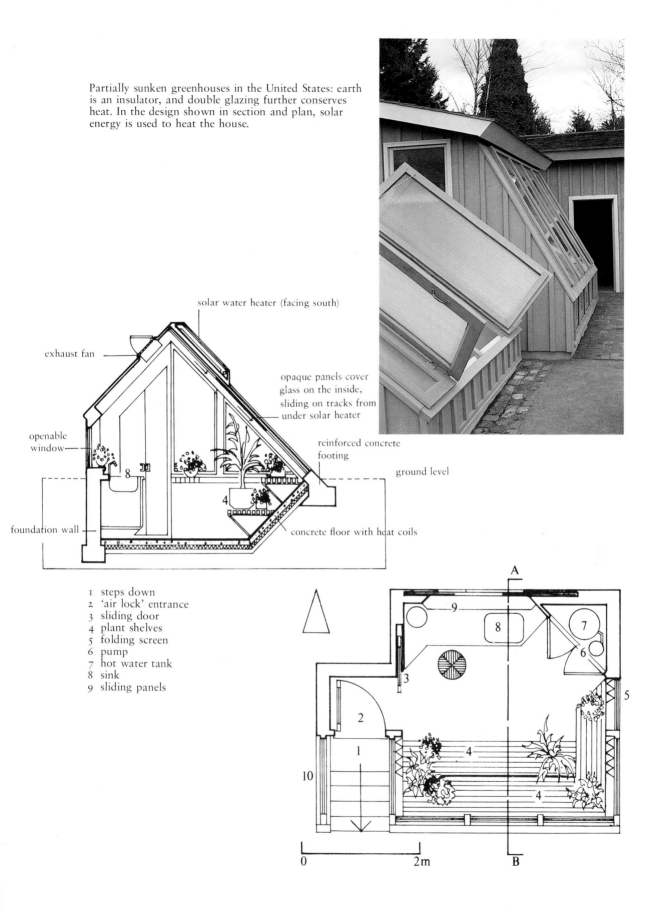

solar water heater (facing south)

exhaust fan

opaque panels cover glass on the inside, sliding on tracks from under solar heater

openable window

reinforced concrete footing

ground level

8

4

foundation wall

concrete floor with heat coils

1 steps down
2 'air lock' entrance
3 sliding door
4 plant shelves
5 folding screen
6 pump
7 hot water tank
8 sink
9 sliding panels

A

9

8

7

6

3

2

5

1

4

4

10

0   2m   B

Various experimental greenhouses have been constructed in the United States which make use of the warmth-conducting properties of earth by being let into the ground. A further innovation is solar panels: water heated by the sun in a reservoir is circulated through floor coils to heat the floor and radiate heat in the greenhouse, and cooled water from the coils is pumped back up to the reservoir. When there is not enough sun, the reservoir can be warmed by an immersion heater. There are various types of layout, depending on the situation. Solar panels are still too expensive in this country for them to be widely used, but where they are installed for another purpose, say to heat a swimming pool in summer, they could be adapted to warm a greenhouse in winter.

Frames

Near the greenhouse you will need some frames, in which to raise seeds and harden off young plants before they are set out. The simplest ones are made of Dutch lights – window-like panels of glass of a standard size (about 1.40 × 0.72 m.) set in wood – supported on a brick base. Other frames are made of metal and glass, and have glass sides: they admit more light, but are colder at night.

Frames can be heated, if you wish, by electric cables in the soil, or by air-warming cables fixed to the sides of the structure.

Near your greenhouse and frames you may want somewhere to store tools and the wheelbarrow, and you can arrange the whole group of structures as a small entity, preferably next to the vegetable garden. Service the complex with hard paving, wide enough to take the wheelbarrow, that will be mud- and frost-free throughout the year.

GARAGES, CAR PORTS AND OIL-TANK HOUSING

Beyond the structure conceived as part of the design of the house, additional shelter may be needed for another car, a boat or a caravan. All will require hard standing and ready access from the drive, and all should be camouflaged as much as possible. For a boat or a caravan, both large structures, you might consider erecting a set of lattice screens which can be detached from their supports when you need to move the vehicle. For a car, whether you want just a shelter or a complete garage it is preferable to build next to an existing garage, since the services for one will then reach the other. You may be lucky and find a ready-made structure that will look well; failing that, use the outer wall of the existing garage as one of the walls for the new one, thereby minimizing its impact and avoiding a draughty no-man's-land between the two. Garages tend to be left open when unoccupied, revealing years of stored junk and old toys – a further reason for screening them.

If you do not already have a hard standing next to the garage where you can wash the car, you could provide one now by increasing the area of concrete being laid as the base of the new structure. Be sure this area drains away from, and not towards, the garages!

A double garage and carport by Peter Aldington. Both are sensitively designed in a low key, with a careful use of natural materials. The area around the garage recalls a traditional stable yard; the open carport is cleverly married to its site by planting.

Where the garaging is at a distance from the house, you might consider siting the oil tank next to the hard standing, making access to it easy. Nothing will grow in oil-sodden earth, and oil drips seep into and stain a flat concrete surface: a good solution is to lay up-ended cobbles beneath the structure and under the drip.

SUMMERHOUSES AND CHANGING ROOMS

There is a fairly large selection of such structures on the market, but one cannot say it is satisfactory. Such a little building will become a focal point of interest, and should have some character, whereas many of the designs on offer seem only one stage removed from a garden shed, though their price is far removed from it. Scale is of course a problem, since the ground area tends to be too small for the height.

Where a period mood is desirable, it is possible to buy pillared structures, and also to get individual columns in stone, concrete or reconstituted stone, with which you could make up your own building, using concrete blockwork which is then painted. Crafty siting and screening can hide the rear of the building, so that only the front need be finished to a high standard, and can also disguise the size. Other styles available in timber or fibreglass (maintenance-free and very durable) include Gothic, which can look very well indeed in stone-coloured fibreglass that soon weathers to a mature appearance, and can be set off by a roof finish in bronze, lead or copper. Structures can also be bought in a Victorian rustic idiom, with thatched or shingled roofs – but beware a nasty outcrop of Swiss Chalet type buildings designed to house saunas and provide poolside amenities. It is perhaps sad that no good modern designs are available to suit such a twentieth-century purpose. In general, poolside buildings will be larger and more complicated. They may need planning permission, and the expertise of an architect to design them.

Summerhouses: a pavilion in eighteenth-century mood by Frances Machin, in which the fibreglass roof is held up by a timber framework; and a similar shape for a more rural setting, in textured stonework with stone tile roofing.

A columned stone poolside summerhouse at Tintinhull in Somerset. There is a relaxed casualness about the placing of pots on the adjoining terrace.

A new poolhouse in West Sussex of brick, flint and tile, the lines of which are continued into a pergola.

Preparing the Ground

CULTIVATION

Before you begin planting, the ground will need to be cultivated, to destroy weeds and to break up the surface layer so that air penetrates, assisting the processes whereby plant food in the soil is liberated. But what sort of cultivation? Gardeners in the old days would double-dig, going two spits or spade-lengths (500 mm.) deep and incorporating a heavy load of manure. It was a long, slow, and back-breaking process; but little mechanical can improve upon it.

What mechanical aids you use will depend upon the site conditions and the final intention. A virgin soil, supporting scrub, rough grass, or any other wild vegetation, will need clearing or burning off and then deep ploughing, which will bury the remains of any vegetation. Even in a relatively small area you can use a fixed tractor plough – much preferable to a rotary tiller, which does not go deep enough for a new soil. Land previously cultivated, but still containing weed, may be turned with a rotary tiller or a disc plough. In both cases, it is then further broken down with a disc harrow. Larger roots and tufted grass not buried should be raked out and burned. Hard compacted ground may need ripping – but be sure to avoid underground pipes or cables, and do not use the machine anywhere under the span of a tree's branches, or you will damage the roots.

Where there is no room for machinery and you are not up to double-digging, prepare the ground by cultivating it one spit deep, burying any remaining weed as you go along. (For mechanical cultivators see below, Chapter 15.)

THE SOIL, AND HOW TO IMPROVE IT

If you have not already analysed your soil, or had it tested for its pH value (see p.12), you can roughly establish its type by working a handful of it between your fingers.

Sand is gritty and does not soil fingers.

Sandy loam is gritty, can be pressed roughly into a ball, and soils fingers.

Clay is sticky, becomes polished by sliding between finger and thumb, and is plastic enough to be rolled into long flexible worms.

Clay loam is sticky, quickly polished, and easily moulded, but not as plastic as pure clay.

Silty loam is not sticky and cannot be polished; it can be moulded into shapes, but they will break apart if handled. It feels silky or soapy.

Medium loam is not gritty, sticky or silty. It smells good.

No additive will change the basic type of your soil. You can alter the pH value slightly, but extreme conditions of heavy, hungry, acid or badly drained soils can only be planted with subjects which will tolerate them. What you can improve, up to a point, is the texture and quality of the soil. As a general rule, for a properly balanced soil-improvement programme bulky organic manures should be incorporated during winter, and fertilizers applied as a top dressing in spring.

Fertilizers

In type these can be either organic or inorganic. The former differ from natural organic material in that the nutrients they contain can be more precisely determined. The amount of nutrient is expressed as a percentage of the total weight. 'Complete fertilizers' contain the three basic elements: nitrogen (N), phosphates (P_2O_5), and potassium (K_2O). 'Compound fertilizers' contain only two of the elements, and 'single fertilizers' only one.

Nitrogen assists plants to make lush growth and well coloured foliage. It should not be applied alone too vigorously, or it upsets the natural balance of the soil.
Organic forms act more slowly but over a longer period than inorganic forms. They include:
— dried blood (12–14% N), which starts acting relatively quickly
— hoof and horn (13% N)
— shoddy (5–12% N)
The inorganic, quicker-acting, forms include:
— nitrate of soda (16% N), not suitable for heavy soils
— nitrate of lime (13–15.5% N), used as a top dressing for dry soils
— sulphate of ammonia (21% N), for chalky or limy soils, slower acting than the others
— ammonium nitrate (33–35% N), the most concentrated and fast-working
Phosphates are essential to the development of growing plants, particularly seedlings. They occur naturally in soils with a pH value of 6–6.5.
The organic forms are:
— bone meal (6–22% P_2O_5, plus 4% N long-term)
— steamed bone flour (25–30% P_2O_5, plus 1% N), similar to bone meal, but more concentrated, since the fat and gelatine are removed
Inorganic phosphatic fertilizers include:
— super phosphate (18–19% P_2O_5), quick-acting
— triple super phosphate (46% P_2O_5), quick acting and longer lasting
— basic slag (10–18% P_2O_5), which also contains calcium compounds, and is thus a good slow-acting food for acid soils deficient in lime
Potassium is important for photosynthesis and the uptake of water in plants. Heavy soils usually contain a sufficient amount, but light sandy soils will have had the potassium leached out.
Organic potassium is provided by wood ash (5–15% K_2O), which may also contain some calcium. It is quickly leached out by rain.
Inorganic potassium may be:
— sulphate of potash (48% K_2O and 12–14% N), the most popular, being quick-acting and water soluble but not washed out by rain

— potassium nitrate or saltpetre (45% K$_2$O and 13% N), which is expensive
— muriate of potash (60% K$_2$O), used mainly in mixtures with chlorine

Bulky organic manures

Decaying animal and vegetable matter is broken down by soil bacteria to form humus. This will help a dry, sandy soil by binding it together (aiding water retention), and is equally good for a clay or chalky soil, breaking it up to improve drainage and aeration. It also supplies plant nutrients. There are a number of types of bulky organic material.

Rotted farm manure provides potash with nitrogen and phosphates.

Poultry manure is very rich in nitrogen, and also includes potash. If used too fresh, however, it can be over-rich.

Leaf mould is a valuable organic material, but it contains calcium carbonate, which makes it unsuitable for areas where lime-hating plants are growing.

Peat is sterile and useful only as a soil conditioner.

Compost provides a wealth of slowly released plant nutrients, and also improves soil structure. The rising cost of chemical fertilizers, the health food movement, and a trend towards self-sufficiency have led to the compost heap rightly resuming its place in the garden.

The best composting method involves 'aerobic' decomposition, where the material is broken down by micro-organisms in the presence of oxygen. They also need warmth and some moisture to do their work quickly. Too much moisture and not enough air, and the material will rot instead. Within a few days, good aerobic composting should achieve a temperature of 60°C (140°F), which will effectively destroy most weeds, seeds, and diseases.

Virtually everything that has once lived will decompose in a compost heap, including lawn mowings, remains of vegetables, the leaves of most trees, and even garden weeds. Evergreens are unsuitable, however, and you shouldn't include more than 10 per cent garden leaves. With persistent weeds such as dock, couch grass, bird weed and ground elder, smash the roots and place the plants in the centre of the heap, where the heat will kill them. From the household you can include not only vegetable peelings, etc., but also moistened shredded newspaper. From the farm would come straw and manure.

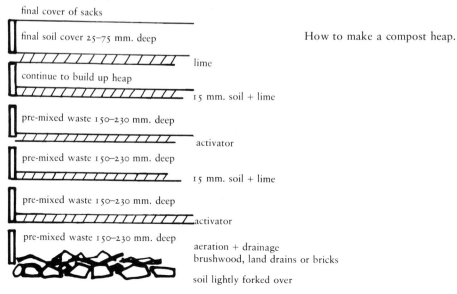

How to make a compost heap.

final cover of sacks
final soil cover 25–75 mm. deep
lime
continue to build up heap
15 mm. soil + lime
pre-mixed waste 150–230 mm. deep
activator
pre-mixed waste 150–230 mm. deep
15 mm. soil + lime
pre-mixed waste 150–230 mm. deep
activator
pre-mixed waste 150–230 mm. deep
aeration + drainage
brushwood, land drains or bricks
soil lightly forked over

A major consideration in compost-making is to achieve a balance between the carbon and nitrogen contents in the waste material: carbon is present in all organic matter, but as plants get older and tougher the carbon is less easily digested by the micro-organisms, and they need nitrogen to help them. In spring and summer there is plenty of nitrogen in grass cuttings, young leaves, and weeds – especially stinging nettles. In autumn and winter, however, when you are using dried leaves or straw, you will need to add an activator. Animal manures are excellent for this purpose, and so too are some organic fertilizers, such as bone meal, hoof and horn, and non-toxic sewage sludge. You can also buy organic activators (mainly based on seaweed). For those not committed to organic cultivation, there are a number of chemical compost-makers on the market, which supply both nitrogen and lime. It is claimed by the organic school that these do not provide the same protection against pests and diseases for the plants they feed.

Compost should be applied as soon as it has cooled, after about six weeks, at the rate of one bucketful per square metre. Used in autumn, it should be left as a surface mulch: lightly fork in the top few centimetres and let the earthworms work it into the soil below.

Lime

Lime is not a plant nutrient. It is applied after manure has been dug in, as a top dressing, to reduce soil acidity. Over-liming should at all costs be avoided, since it is very difficult to rectify. Lime is available in three forms.

Calcium oxide (quicklime or burnt lime) is the most concentrated. It is caustic, however, and should only be used on vacant ground. When exposed to air, it absorbs moisture to become slaked lime.

Calcium hydroxide (slaked or hydrated lime) is similar to quicklime but not so caustic, and therefore safer to use.

Calcium carbonate occurs naturally as limestone or chalk. It is more effective the finer it is ground, but it is always slower-acting than the other two.

Mulching

This is sometimes confused with the process of surface-dressing with organic matter, such as compost, but it does not serve to feed plants. Its purpose is to retain moisture in the soil. A surface layer of peat, bracken, pulverized bark or lawn mowings is applied in spring around the base of young plants – usually shrubs – to protect their roots throughout the drying summer.

There is one final school of thought on cultivation, whose message is quite different from all the rest: 'Don't.' It is argued that in nature plants establish themselves without special attention, and therefore in a garden they may be left with only an annual application of compost around them. Over a period, proponents of this school claim, in an area of intensive production such as a kitchen garden a layer of humus is rapidly built up on the surface, and is carried down to the plant roots without artificial aids, by earthworms and bacterial action.

Structural and Decorative Planting

Various strands will have been woven together to produce a garden plan that sits comfortably in its country setting, but so far the elements of that composition are static. Now, with the introduction of plants, first trees and then groupings of shrubs, we are taking a broadly two-dimensional scheme into a third dimension, and then into the fourth, time. For the great art of garden design is to create an arrangement of subjects which is not only satisfactory (both visually and practically) at the time of planting, but which as it develops and matures over the years actually improves. This needs both foresight and management, together with a knowledge of a specimen's potential, for plants have differing lifespans too. Few now consciously plan for posterity, as in the eighteenth century: we want to see immediate results. So long-term planting has to overlay and be interwoven with the short-term scheme, and the whole be managed, thinned and pruned to achieve a gentle transition from one lifespan to another. Large-scale gardening is something of an act of faith, for few will live to see the full maturity of a tree they have planted. Yet it is this sense of continuity in a garden and its surrounding landscape that is a great source of fascination, as the scene constantly changes, season by season and year by year.

STRUCTURAL PLANTING

The different aims of this kind of planting can be generally summarized as follows: to establish one's domain, to shelter or screen it; to blend the garden with the surrounding landscape; to channel views to or away from the house; to create outdoor spaces, enclosing or breaking up areas and giving them a three-dimensional setting; and to provide contrasts in form, texture or colour with buildings, water or some other feature. Structural planting, composed of trees and shrubs, will be needed as a year-round feature in your landscape, and should therefore contain a good proportion of evergreens. Other than the occasional 'special' acting as an eye-catcher, the selection will probably be bold and simple, for you are creating the bones of your layout, in conjunction with the pattern already established by circulation routes and contouring. Only afterwards will you be concerned with decorative material.

In choosing specimens you will of course have to take into account the soil, their siting, and the local ecology or existing vegetation. But the most important consideration is the final visual effect, for one is seeking to create a working composition which will provide form, colour and interest throughout the year, which will frame the house, and which will fold gently into the surrounding landscape. Each function calls for a different approach in the choice of species, but none can be studied in isolation. Any compromise for quick results must be made in full consciousness of the long-term process. Existing planting that you retain will provide some immediate effect, which you can supplement with newly planted trees. Let us consider trees and shrubs as individuals, then their function as windbreaks and hedges – something which in your actual garden plan you will be concerned to establish first – and finally decorative planting and ground cover.

Trees

Trees will provide fixed points in your layout, remaining while fashion and function may change the garden round their feet. Their scale will of course depend on the scale of the garden. Forest trees can reach a height of some 20 m. and a span almost as great. Next comes a tier of more moderate-sized trees, and then smaller (often flowering) types no taller than a large shrub. (For a list of native trees and their characteristics, see p. 222.) A long-term programme might involve interplanting, a technique suited also to all sizes of shrub, whereby you plant to form an initial pattern, and then modify it over the years by the selective removal of some specimens to allow others the space to grow to full maturity.

Trees occupying key structural positions in your layout will not necessarily be decorative themselves: they may form a background for more decorative shrubs, depending on the effect you want to achieve. Are you interested in a pattern of contrasting shapes, contrasting textures, a greater sense of enclosure, a frame to a view or perspective? Each objective will have a suitable tree or tree types. The more of any one species you use, the stronger the characteristic you achieve. We seem afraid to plant single species in any number, but commercial stands of poplars, for instance, look spectacular, as do avenues of limes or chestnuts and, indeed, orchards of fruit trees. In the wild, think of birchwoods, beechwoods, and pine groves.

As you get closer to the house, or the domesticated part of the garden, you will choose more decorative species – but avoid the spotty arboretum effect unless you particularly want it. The arboretum is for the collector of trees, as others have albums full of stamps. Specimen trees, which are individuals rather than part of a mass, should be selected and placed within the layout to serve a purpose, and when considering them you will be interested in particular features. First, the tree's scale, and how soon it will reach maturity. Then its shape: fastigate (tall and compact, like a Lombardy poplar), conical or tapering, broad-headed, rounded or square; angular or contorted; weeping, spreading or horizontal branching; and so on. Then its foliage: evergreen or deciduous; glossy or matt; how coloured in spring, summer, autumn or winter. And finally the look of bare twigs and bark in winter, and, especially in the north, how it holds snow.

How you position your specimen trees is crucial, for too many points of emphasis within a landscape are disturbing – unless it is a scene of Tuscan hill-towns, punctuated by dark cypresses. Dominant tree forms might be arranged to form a rhythmic sequence within the total picture, the eye moving from one to another. Alternatively, a single tree might act as a foil to the house (think of a massive cedar in the forecourt of a Georgian house) or, on a smaller scale, to

The cedar of Lebanon is thought to have been first introduced into this country about 1650. This specimen (at Lydiard Tregoze, Wiltshire), seen to its best advantage, may be 200–300 years old.

a piece of sculpture. The weeping willow by water is a stock combination, the vertical lines of the tree contrasting with the horizontal of the water. Similarly, you might play your trees off against landscape features such as hills. This is the art of planting design, which governs the positioning of everything from forest trees down to perennials in a border. Once you have developed an eye for analysing planting, you will realize how poor many of our so-called 'good' gardens are. That they contain the most amazing collection of items is not enough: they must also be *composed* – not because this suits a designer's whim, but because it is the way to display all the plants to their best advantage throughout the year.

To give an instant effect of scale and maturity to a very particular situation, 'semi-mature' trees – developed, but not yet mature, between 6 and 15 m. high – are sometimes planted. Specialist suppliers will have the commoner trees, including alder, ash, chestnut, elm, false acacia, lime, maple, plane, poplar, sycamore and willow; other species, like birch, beech, oak and hawthorn are more difficult to establish, with more mature conifers hardest of all. Semi-mature trees need specialist lifting and planting, which is a costly business, and they need special aftercare for up to three years, so they are really to be considered only when an instant dramatic effect is vital. The process of moving will have broken their supportive roots, so they will need to be supported by guying ropes, regularly checked for stress: the minute hair roots, which channel nutrition to the tree, must grow from the root ball undisturbed, without top movement. Along with guying, various top-spraying techniques can be used to inhibit transpiration from the leaves while the roots are recovering. One might draw an analogy between tree planting and human surgery: the older the person undergoing an operation, the greater the shock to their system, while a younger, healthy body will recover far quicker from the ordeal. If you want to speed matters up a little, it is safer and cheaper to buy 'heavy nursery stock'.

Trees from commercial nurseries come in the following sizes:

heavy nursery standard	4–5.5 m. straight stems
tall standard	1.8–2 m. straight stems

standard	1.65–1.82 m. straight stems
half standard	1–1.35 m. straight stems
quarter standard/bush	300–750 mm. on standard tree
weeping standard	1.65 m. minimum stem height

All, with the exception of quarter standard and bush, should have a stem at least 19 mm. thick when measured at a height of 600–900 mm. from the ground. These are British Standard dimensions; you may find nurserymen who take no notice of them.

Unless the tree is container-grown (a more expensive way of buying it), planting should be carried out during the dormant season, which for deciduous trees is from the end of October to the end of March, and for conifers from October to April. Trees planted after February will need watering if there is a dry period in spring and early summer, something one tends to overlook. Evergreens succeed best when planted either in autumn, when the ground is still warm, or in spring, when it is starting to warm up again. This will depend on the particular soil.

Plants are despatched from the nurseryman any time from the end of October through the frost-free periods of winter, whenever they can be lifted. The earlier your order, the earlier the despatch; you will usually be warned when the delivery is likely. On arrival, trees can be planted immediately; if not, they should be unpacked and placed in a trench and the roots well covered with moist soil, which should then be heeled in. Do not plant during periods of frost, when frosted soil may be dug in, causing root damage, or when there is wind or bright sunlight, which can dry out the roots.

For normal site conditions, when standard trees are not being planted in prepared areas of cultivation, they should have special spot holes prepared for them, not less than 750 mm. deep, and wide enough to allow the full splay of their roots. Trim off any damaged roots before planting. This is the time to position the stake that will support the tree, for if you drive it in after planting you may damage the roots. Stakes should be strong enough to support the tree for three years; they should be of larch, spruce, sweet chestnut, or sawn timber, with a pointed end, and coated with preservative for a metre up from the end. With the tree and stake in position, you should have enough space above the roots to backfill with topsoil to a depth of not less than 500 mm., so that the tree can get nourishment. After a light shaking to ensure that all the pockets round the roots are filled with the topsoil, carefully firm down the earth. The tree should then be well watered if the earth is at all dry.

The technique is the same for planting container-grown stock; but, if you are using a contractor with unskilled labour, be sure the containers are removed before planting!

The spacing of trees is governed by the ultimate spread of their canopy and the effect you want. When two or more trees of the same type are planted close together, the general rule is that the distance between them should be half the mature span, so that the group takes on an extended profile of the individual specimen. If you want the effect of a multi-stemmed individual – difficult to obtain from commercial sources – you can plant five or even seven saplings such as birch in one hole, each with an individual stake and tie.

above Boundary trees planted as a windbreak between the garden and neighbouring land. Low junipers screen the drive entrance on the left.

left Multi-stemmed silver birch makes a background to modern sculpture.

opposite A handsome grouping of evergreens at Knightshayes, Devon. When space allows, the gold form of *Cupressocyparis leylandii* called Castlewellan makes a beautiful tree. It is this proportion that the foolhardy try to restrain to domestic hedge height!

below The suckering form of *Populus alba*, the white poplar, is a useful boundary tree, and its white leaves also show up well against darker foliage.

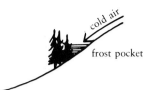

cold air

frost pocket

dense windbreak

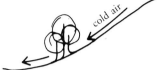

cold air

filtered windbreak
allowing air to flow away

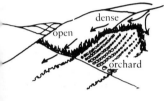

dense

open

orchard

Windbreaks, pleached trees, and hedges

Shelter from wind is second only to shelter from frost in determining what can and cannot be grown. The two must be thought of in conjunction, for too absolute a windbreak can create fatal frost-pockets instead. The frosts most damaging to plants occur on clear nights when the earth that has been warmed during the day suddenly meets freezing air, and radiates its heat very strongly. Sheltered spots tend to suffer most: any circulation of air lessens the risk, so in gardens inclined to be frosty windbreaks should be left open at the base. Strategic planting can be used to give some protection from frost to a garden lying at or near the bottom of a hill, for cool air drains downhill, almost like a river, forming pools of frost in hollows and valley bottoms, and it can be deflected to some extent by walls and planting. In Scotland many old walled gardens at the foot of slopes have higher walls on their uphill side. Unless you have a very high barrier, cold air may still overflow on the chilliest nights, so it is better to guide the stream of cold air away by running planted barriers across the slope. If your garden is not quite at the bottom, leave its lower boundary open enough for the cold air to creep on down the hill. Such measures will not prevent the worst frosts, but they can reduce their effects.

Windbreaks

The advantages of windbreaks are several: horticulturally, because the sheltered soil warms up earlier they allow a greater range of species to be cultivated, and encourage earlier fruiting of orchard trees; domestically, they make the garden more comfortable to use, and they can be dramatically effective in insulating the house. Experiments in the United States with test houses in four separate localities showed that a windbreak on the north side reduced fuel consumption by more than 20 per cent. We in Britain are notoriously bad at insulating our houses, and indeed it is difficult to do so with many old properties; further, we have an over-rated addiction to 'airing' rooms. A good windbreak acts as insulation, trapping air as in a cellular blanket, with the result that it can cost less to heat an old stone house in a sheltered position than a solidly built modern house exposed to the winds.

There is of course no point in exchanging windiness for unwanted shade, spreading tree roots that rob the rest of the garden of moisture and minerals, and an enclosure so dense it gives you claustrophobia. It is a question of finding the worst wind, blocking it, and then building up from that. A very large garden can afford full-scale windbreaks on two or three sides: little direct shading or general loss of light will be felt where the distance between house and trees is four times their height – or five times, if you want to divert a prevailing wind from the south-west, where the best sun is. In a smaller garden, you may choose to have a high windbreak specifically to protect the house, but otherwise a low one is preferable. A mixture of tall and low plants, tender and hardy, interwoven to give mutual protection, can give as much shelter near the ground and be as effective as a tall hedge. Should you be worried by draughts rather than gales, these can be controlled by deploying low hedges or clumps of shrubs and trees, or even alternating high and low crops in the more windy spots of a vegetable garden in such a way as to form natural suntraps.

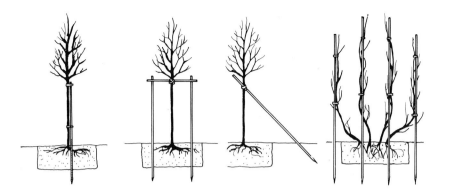

The thicker the belt of trees you can plant, the better they will be in filtering the air, and the greater the microclimatic effect. Where space allows, a multiple-row windbreak is desirable, and you might even plant a broad shelter-belt or a woodland on the edge of your territory which could be developed commercially (see Chapter 14). Otherwise, in most situations a single-row windbreak should be sufficient to dampen winds and provide ample shelter. The only exceptions are in coastal and upland positions, where trees must be able to achieve a root anchorage sufficient to resist the extreme pressure of winter gales, and a single row would not grow to any size. Trees out of tune with their environment cannot give of their best: some will flourish in youth but fail to reach any size in maturity, while others will die off due to mineral deficiencies. The more inhospitable the soil and climate, the hardier the species chosen should be. If in doubt, see what grows well naturally in your area, rather than in the protected world of a garden, and use those species.

Remember when making your choice that your land will be seen against a background of the countryside, where the trees are mostly native species, supplemented by a few foreign elements imported in the past and now established. These trees help form the character of a particular region, and where you are introducing new planting that character should be preserved as much as possible. We know what the Midlands look like without elms, but suppose Buckinghamshire had no beeches, and the north no ash? A list of species suitable for windbreak and shelter-belt planting will be found on pp. 224–25. Observation of your area will suggest which are best.

Single-row windbreaks are in fact likely to consist chiefly of evergreens, among which the fastest-growing are not necessarily the most permanent or the most desirable: the ubiquitous *Cupressocyparis leylandii* tends to be blown over when grown on rich soils, and its suburban associations make it wrong for the country. Thuja and Lawson cypress are suitable in fairly mild climates, and where slow development is acceptable you might use more ornamental species, like cryptomeria. Better for a rural situation, if you have the space, are the larger evergreens – pines, spruces and hemlocks – and deciduous larches. Scots and Austrian pine form good screens when young, though after 7 m. or so they become open at the bottom. Sitka spruce and Norway spruce have the same tendency, but both can be topped successfully. Broadleaved evergreens that might be used include holly, laurel, and the common rhododendron in areas where it has naturalized itself.

Few broadleaved deciduous trees work as single-row windbreaks, though in milder areas limes, planted closely together, make a fine shelter. Poplars are slim, but their eventual height makes them unsuitable for all but a very large garden. Planted and trimmed as loose hedges, you could use hawthorn, beech, hornbeam, alder, mountain ash, field maple and hazel.

It is not easy to mix species of different form and habitat, but possible mixtures of coniferous and broadleaved trees include larches interspersed with coppiced willow, with sycamore or with oak (or, indeed, with a layer of shrubs to fill out the lower area), and pines combined with beech and hornbeam, pruned to keep them low.

Multiple-row windbreaks allow the inclusion of a greater variety of trees, thereby making the landscape more interesting, and they require less attention in the early years. The failure of the occasional tree is no longer a crisis, since it can be replaced temporarily by a quick-growing species, and as the screen develops the poorer specimens can be removed.

The outer, windward, row of trees should be chosen as for a single-row windbreak, but within the 'fortification' there is almost no limit to the type of tree you might use, and with the exception of a quick-growing variety interplanted for temporary effect until the main specimens have grown up, supplementary planting can be largely chosen for decorative effect. Formal gardens may suggest a formal planted arrangement of trees and shrubs, while other situations will call for a less rigid arrangement. Both can be effective.

If you want to be able to use a rotary cultivator to deal with weeds in the early stages, the trees will need to be planted in rows, but this does not mean you cannot group them: the clumps can be arranged so that the rows continue within them. Lines make planting as well as tending easier, and in mixed plantations they soon disappear – but they are by no means obligatory.

Pleaching
Half-way between the windbreak composed of standard trees and the hedge is the row of pleached trees, of which the crowns are trimmed like a hedge. They are an effective solution, for quite a tall screen occupies little space. Where they are used to give added height in conjunction with a wall or fence, that barrier will keep the lower part closed, and their foliage will sieve the wind that is deflected over the top.

Trees 1.5 to 1.8 m. tall are planted 1.8 to 3 m. apart. They are not pruned until they are established, usually between 2.5 and 3.5 m. high. Then they are topped and trimmed front and back, leaving side branches to be trained into a continuous screen. Shorten these too to promote further branching. Annual pruning will be necessary until the trees are about 5 m. tall. Altogether, the training takes considerable time, and the pruning might be an expensive job.

Lime, beech, hornbeam and plane have all been used for pleaching in the once popular *allées* of the formal garden tradition; apples and pears can also be trained in this way to provide a more limited screen, but they will probably need a wire frame to support them until they are established.

Hedges
Hedges can provide useful windbreaks in situations where larger trees would

be unsuitable, and they can also delineate areas within a garden – though one is unlikely now to be able to afford the labour-intensive type of compartmented garden. Today one might use a hedge to extend the architectural influence of the house into the garden in green terms, providing at the same time, perhaps, a windbreak or a fine backdrop to planting.

A hedge is a living barrier, built up of closely-spaced plants set along a defined line – which need not be straight. The type of plants you use will depend on the height you want, on the character of your garden, and on the speed with which you want results. You may choose a formal clipped hedge, or an informal tousled one. Certain general guidelines apply in all cases.

Many of the plants we use for hedging are by nature quite large trees, and although their tops are clipped their roots will go on growing. If individuals are planted too close together some may be choked and die, leaving gaps which are particularly difficult to fill if the hedge is a formal one. Further, if the hedge gets too wide, little water penetrates to the roots, and there is relatively less food in the soil for each plant – and few people ever think of watering and feeding an existing hedge. If you do need a thick hedge, you might plant a staggered double row; but single-row planting is far healthier for the constituents.

Most deciduous hedges will be planted between mid-October and April, while evergreens are planted in late September–October, or between early March and early May. You will be guided by the weather and soil conditions. Whenever possible, choose young plants, which will make healthier long-term growth. Treat them as you would shrubs, setting them in a prepared trench of the required length, 460 mm. wide and 380 mm. deep, with the bottom well broken to a further depth of 150 mm. A new hedge along a wall or fence should be 300–460 mm. or more away from it. The distance between individual plants will depend on the species. Careful maintenance during the early stages is vital, to lay the foundation for healthy, sturdy mature growth. Water the hedge well as you plant it if the weather is dry, to encourage the roots to make contact with the soil. Cultivate the area around it for the first year, to keep down weeds: it is better to eliminate any competition within one metre of the plants than to rely on applications of fertilizer. Mulching will control weeds and conserve moisture, and a mulch of well-rotted stable manure will also boost a poor soil.

Pruning and trimming is part of the aftercare operation. In the first year after planting, the hedge should be cut back to encourage new growth from the base. Thereafter, if your hedge is a formal one, with vertical sides – or preferably sides which taper together at the top, allowing the lower branches more light – you will need to restrain growth at the top so that the hedge remains thick at the bottom. The more reluctant the plants are to adopt this bushy habit, the harder their pruning must be. (See p. 226.)

Informal hedges need less attention. If you use flowering species, however, your pruning cannot be done just any time, or you will destroy next year's flowers (see p. 227). Plants that flower on new wood made during the season should be trimmed in winter or early spring; those that flower on the previous season's wood should be pruned after flowering; those that flower on spurs or sideshoots should be trimmed as little as possible.

a The domestic form of seventeenth-century topiary.
b Holly hedges clipped into a serpentine pattern in front of standard hollies, at West Dean, Sussex. Note the difference in texture.
c Hornbeam being pleached over a framework to create an amusing garden room.
d Pleached limes at Houghton, Norfolk. A simple framework of verticals and wires is needed to establish such a stand.
e The space contained by these yew hedges is strictly articulated, and the timber gate is in keeping.

d

a

b

c

e

Two faces of Dartmoor: the golden conifers (*right*) are visually indigestible – instant suburbia – whereas the composition at Castle Drogo (*below*) uses artifice as a foil to nature. A compelling view is framed by high yew hedges, with beech trees beyond. Simplicity is the essence of the design.

Shrubs

Now comes the time to fill in those cultivated areas between the trees. The range of choice in a nurseryman's list can be totally bewildering if you are not very familiar with plants; but you will solve the problem by going back to your overlay plan.

Try to build up plant masses stage by stage, as with trees, selecting the largest first and then working down to the subjects in the foreground. Visualize the finished effect (complete with trees) in bold masses of a particular shape, form or colour, and then transfer your vision onto the plan. Once you have established the mass, work through the characteristics – the ultimate shape, whether deciduous or evergreen, the colour of leaf and flower – and then try to find the corresponding plant in the nurseryman's catalogue. Catalogues usually also include lists of subjects suitable for particular locations. Then sketch in each plant as a circle on your plan, with the size it will have reached in, say, five years, and add up the total number. You may want to check what the plant actually looks like when established – in a friend's garden, a garden centre, or the Royal Horticultural Society's grounds at Wisley. The whole operation can be a long one, and needs at least as much patience as choosing wallpaper; but since the area to be covered is considerably larger, it is well worth the trouble. And there is a safety net: one of the pleasures of working with shrubs is that if you get your plant associations wrong you can always move things around the following autumn to create a new picture.

Try to envisage the planting in winter as well as summer, for winter is the great testing time for a garden's appearance. If it looks handsome then, it will work in summer too. Evergreen masses should be well disposed to give a balanced result; a mixture of lush winter greens, peppered with the soft colours of winter flowers, is one of the most attractive faces of a good garden.

Bear in mind the mood and character you are trying to create, and use the correct plants. (This is particularly important if you are restoring an old garden, as plants have been introduced at various times over the centuries.) Keep the statement clear and simple, too. A rule of thumb for a beginner might be: select your species, and then eliminate half of them.

When composing in terms of flower colour, keep the strongest in the foreground, and gradually fade back to softer shades which will blend with natural colours in the distance, for nature uses her colour subtly, and there should not be a hiccup at the boundary. The colouring of native flowers in the British Isles is very soft. In winter it is green, lemon or muted white; as the season progresses, it moves through creams into the pinks and pale blues of early summer; then these intensify and mature into deeper yellow, and the copper tones of autumn, before the cycle commences again. High summer itself tends to be fairly dull. Brightly coloured garden flowers are either native species that have been hybridized or alien introductions from sunnier climates where their brilliant hues are in keeping with the quality of the light. And where nature here establishes a mass of a single colour, it is usually soft in the open and only stronger in the shade of trees. Where colours are mixed, as in a meadow or cornfield, they are diffused through a screen of grass.

For a list of wild shrub species native to Britain, see p. 223.

DECORATIVE PLANTING

Once you have established the structure of your garden, decorative planting can take many forms. It can be set against a background of structural planting, with which it should relate; it can consist of a mixture of shrubs; of shrubs mingled with herbaceous plants; of an all-herbaceous mixture of perennials and biennials; of decorative plants treated like wild plants, scattered through grass, with space for a mower between them; or, increasingly, a 'natural' effect may be obtained with true indigenous plants, growing as they would in the wild – not, perhaps, an arrangement for the tidy gardener.

Whatever the type of decorative planting, its scale should relate to its position: a small area near the house might include two of this and three or four of that, followed by larger, more positive groupings of five or six of this and seven or eight of that, until at a distance one has whole stands of a particular species. This then blends with natural groupings, which may be of mixed species but which from afar appear to be all one tone.

So let's start thinking about planting in relation to buildings, and then work outwards. Plants can be used to complement the structure. For this one might use specimens of a strong architectural character, but trying as far as possible to get their period as well as their form right. For instance phormiums, which have a sword-like, tropical feeling, would look wrong against an eighteenth-century house, whereas *Magnolia grandiflora* looks right. Older, beamier properties will be more sympathetically set off by random herb-like plants. Plants can also be used to smother a structure – either to enhance it, with tumbling roses or evergreens, or to conceal it: an unfortunate extension or necessary outbuildings can be camouflaged and the proportions of the original house restored. Further away, massed groupings can be created which will frame a view when one looks out from the house, and will frame the house when one looks back at it.

Whatever the function of your planting, ensure that it earns its keep throughout the year. If not evergreen, it should have an interesting form when the leaves have fallen. Hollyhocks and delphiniums seem to many the epitome of cottagyness, and make a strong impact, but remember that their period of interest is limited.

'Climbers' come into their own in association with buildings. They may cling by themselves, or they may ramble on supports, or a woody species may be trained to give the same effect but to support itself. Where a support is necessary, make sure that it is either not seen – by running wires along the joints between brick courses, for instance – or in keeping with the architectural style and rhythm of the building. (Odd fan shapes of plastic or lattice work, for instance, would be a disruption on a wall pierced by regularly spaced windows.) Remember, too, the full potential growth of the plant, and allow for that at the start rather than adding piecemeal. Wooden lattice will rot long before most climbers reach maturity, and it may also be broken by the weight of the plant. Consider too what maintenance the wall behind will need. Letting down a two-year-old climber rose to whitewash the cottage may be easy enough, but it is another job altogether after ten years.

Framing a view

top The twisted shape of an apple tree enhances the view of Peter Aldington's house and garden in Buckinghamshire. Its scale is reflected in large, bold plant groupings beyond.

left A yew hedge frames a view to the orchard at Sissinghurst in Kent. Ground cover planting in the foreground is contained, but linked visually to the wilder area by narcissus planted in both. Other planting includes

muscari, fritillarias, and various euphorbia species.
above Yew natural and clipped lead the eye through at Tintinhull, Somerset. They are contrasted with softer shrub planting, and the interest is stepped, – top left, mid-right, lower left in sunlight.

A shelter planting of hollies in a Jersey garden not only frames the view out to sea but provides an evergreen background for more exotic foreground planting and detail.

This semi-wild grouping at Highdown, Sussex, makes a lovely transition to pure wildness beyond: *Clematis montana alba* romps through evergreen *Viburnum davidii*.

Moving away from buildings, open planted areas will be composed along the lines we considered for bolder skeletal groupings, when the features of height, form, leaf shape and texture will blend together with colour. If you are working with colour for close-up interest, the process of selection could be made easier by opting for a particular range or blend of shades. You might choose to echo the colour of your house, whether brick or painted; or, if there are large glass windows, to pick up a colour visible through them inside the house. One range might be from orange through yellow to red, with a touch of purple and white; another of blue, with some grey; creamy colours with a little brown; a border of green-flowered plants; and so on. There are pure white borders, which can be seen for instance at Glyndebourne and Sissinghurst. Grey-foliaged plants all need good growing conditions, since most are from hotter climates. With any of these groupings, there must be a proportion of evergreen or ever-grey to maintain interest throughout the year.

left Commonly and wrongly called the Scotch thistle, *Onopordum acanthium* provides contrast to a view of a classic urn and Kentish barn.

opposite By cantilevering an extension of this modern house, it sits like a butterfly in its garden which then runs on down to the river. The planting by Geoffrey Smith moves from subjects suitable for a riverside, up the hill, to plants for a hot bank.

below A view at Denmans is contained by sophora on the left and *Genista aetnensis* in front. On the right the blue flower of *Solanum crispum* offsets the grey spire of *Verbascum bombyciferum*.

a The seemingly random planting of Great Dixter, Sussex, by Christopher Lloyd conceals great art.

b A garden planted with perennials, mostly of daisy-like form. Key shrubs are essential to maintain some form throughout the year.

c A traditional spring border originally planned by Gertrude Jekyll at West Dean. In her day gardeners would have added and subtracted plants in pots to maintain the interest.

d and opposite Mixed borders at Knightshayes, by Graham Thomas for the National Trust. Within them are a variety of plant forms which bosom out into the path. Colours are soft, not strident, and the total effect is restful.

a

b

c

d

e How not to plant a border. Colour, even of the same range, is not used in a progressive way, and the boundary is all too hard.

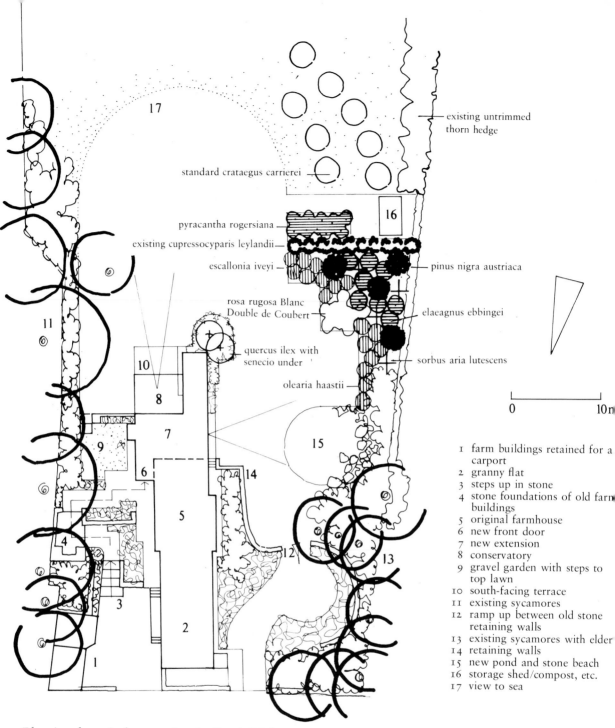

17

existing untrimmed thorn hedge

standard crataegus carrierei

pyracantha rogersiana

existing cupressocyparis leylandii

escallonia iveyi

16

pinus nigra austriaca

rosa rugosa Blanc Double de Coubert

elaeagnus ebbingei

quercus ilex with senecio under

sorbus aria lutescens

olearia haastii

11

10

8

9

7

6

5

4

3

2

1

14

15

12

13

0   10m

1 farm buildings retained for a carport
2 granny flat
3 steps up in stone
4 stone foundations of old farm buildings
5 original farmhouse
6 new front door
7 new extension
8 conservatory
9 gravel garden with steps to top lawn
10 south-facing terrace
11 existing sycamores
12 ramp up between old stone retaining walls
13 existing sycamores with elder
14 retaining walls
15 new pond and stone beach
16 storage shed/compost, etc.
17 view to sea

Planting for wind protection in South Wales

So often the orientation of a site for a view coincides with a prevailing wind, as at this old farm complex on an exposed headland in South Wales.

The original house was added to for retirement while leaving a granny flat with direct access to the road. The extension (7) provided a new front door (6), and the entrance is now gradually up through old stone farm buildings, foundations and walls (3, 4).

The new extension looks southward to the sea, but is blasted by a heavily salt-laden wind from the south-west. And while this needed a tough block, the view west is up a mountainside, so this could not be totally screened.

A conservatory (8) allows winter shelter at the southern end of the house with some terracing beyond screened by two *Quercus ilex* with a planting of senecio underneath. An existing Leyland cypress hedge running across the garden has been reduced, and will be removed when screen planting in the south-west corner is established. Due west of the house a 'natural' pool has been created, with a far shoreline composed of stone present on site. The remainder of the garden is surrounded by large wind-blasted sycamores, with an underplanting of established elder in the main. Much of this might eventually be replaced with gorse.

. . . and on the Berkshire Downs

An early block plan indicating how an exposed cottage might be sheltered. Existing sycamore and elder scrub has to be cut out, and evergreens planted to encompass the site. On the perimeter the toughest, mainly native, species will be used; as they establish themselves, a more refined selection of material will be used towards the house.

As work proceeds, the removal of only a small run of hedge opens up a panoramic view southward from the house, without letting in the wind.

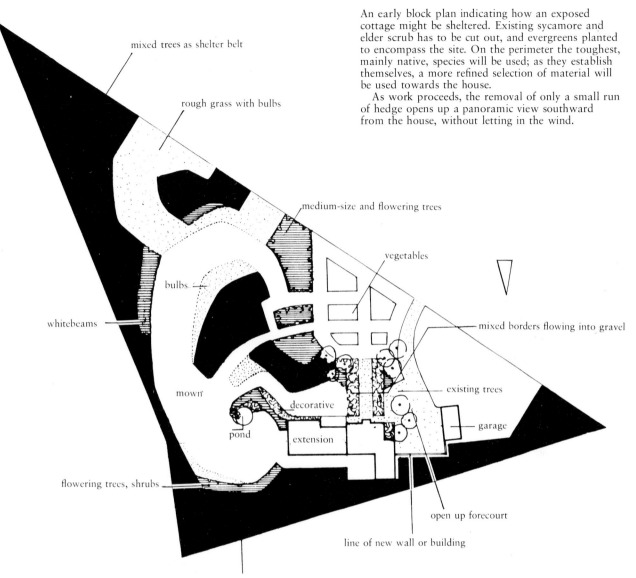

mixed trees as shelter belt

rough grass with bulbs

medium-size and flowering trees

vegetables

bulbs

whitebeams

mixed borders flowing into gravel

mown

existing trees

decorative

garage

pond

extension

flowering trees, shrubs

open up forecourt

line of new wall or building

thicken shelter planting

An enclosed Hampshire garden

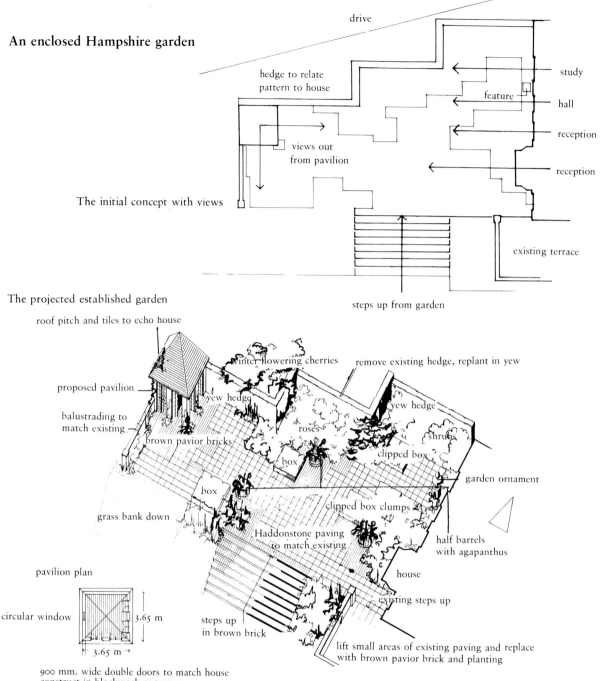

The initial concept with views

drive

hedge to relate pattern to house

study

feature

hall

reception

reception

views out from pavilion

existing terrace

steps up from garden

The projected established garden

roof pitch and tiles to echo house

winter flowering cherries

remove existing hedge, replant in yew

proposed pavilion

yew hedge

yew hedge

balustrading to match existing

roses

shrubs

brown pavior bricks

box

clipped box

box

garden ornament

grass bank down

clipped box clumps

half barrels with agapanthus

Haddonstone paving to match existing

house

existing steps up

pavilion plan

circular window

3.65 m

3.65 m

steps up in brown brick

lift small areas of existing paving and replace with brown pavior brick and planting

900 mm. wide double doors to match house
construct in blockwork as terrace
brick flooring at terrace level

There are still times when a certain degree of enclosure is necessary in a country garden. In this case the only level area in which to sit to get the sun is next to the drive on the north-west (the remainder slopes away to a view and is wooded).

The house was built at the turn of the century for a fairly grand life style, and the mood of the new enclosed garden continues this, while at the same time not denying that it is contemporary.

A staggered yew hedge relates the garden's pattern to the house at one end and a proposed new pavilion at the other. Paving is a combination of plain sand-coloured precast concrete slabs (matching the stone of the buildings and of an existing terrace) and brown brick paviors.

Clumps of clipped box continue the architectural mood of the garden and contrast well with softer shrub planting.

Particular attention was paid to shrubs with autumn, winter and spring interest since the owners are often abroad in summer.

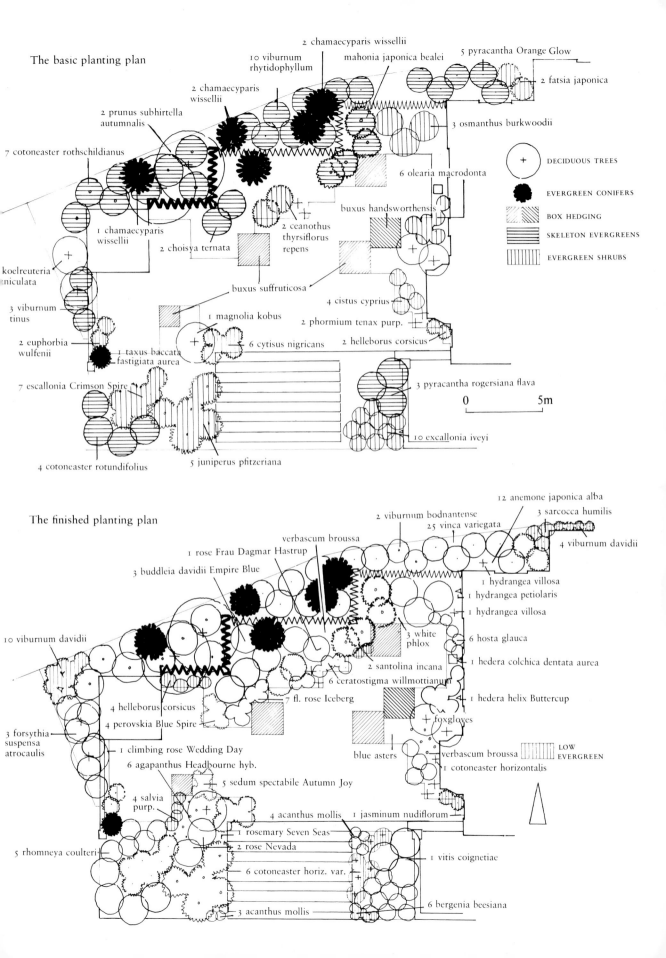

The basic planting plan

2 chamaecyparis wissellii
10 viburnum rhytidophyllum
mahonia japonica bealei
5 pyracantha Orange Glow
2 fatsia japonica
2 chamaecyparis wissellii
2 prunus subhirtella autumnalis
3 osmanthus burkwoodii
7 cotoneaster rothschildianus
6 olearia macrodonta
buxus handsworthensis
1 chamaecyparis wissellii
2 ceanothus thyrsiflorus repens
2 choisya ternata
koelreuteria niculata
buxus suffruticosa
4 cistus cyprius
2 phormium tenax purp.
3 viburnum tinus
1 magnolia kobus
2 euphorbia wulfenii
1 taxus baccata fastigiata aurea
6 cytisus nigricans
2 helleborus corsicus
7 escallonia Crimson Spire
3 pyracantha rogersiana flava
0   5m
4 cotoneaster rotundifolius
5 juniperus pfitzeriana
10 excallonia iveyi

⊕ DECIDUOUS TREES
● EVERGREEN CONIFERS
▨ BOX HEDGING
☰ SKELETON EVERGREENS
▥ EVERGREEN SHRUBS

The finished planting plan

12 anemone japonica alba
3 sarcocca humilis
2 viburnum bodnantense
25 vinca variegata
4 viburnum davidii
verbascum broussa
1 rose Frau Dagmar Hastrup
1 hydrangea villosa
3 buddleia davidii Empire Blue
1 hydrangea petiolaris
1 hydrangea villosa
3 white phlox
6 hosta glauca
10 viburnum davidii
1 hedera colchica dentata aurea
2 santolina incana
6 ceratostigma willmottianum
1 hedera helix Buttercup
4 helleborus corsicus
7 fl. rose Iceberg
4 perovskia Blue Spire
3 forsythia suspensa atrocaulis
1 climbing rose Wedding Day
foxgloves
blue asters
verbascum broussa
LOW EVERGREEN
1 cotoneaster horizontalis
6 agapanthus Headbourne hyb.
5 sedum spectabile Autumn Joy
4 salvia purp.
4 acanthus mollis
1 jasminum nudiflorum
5 rhomneya coulteri
1 rosemary Seven Seas
2 rose Nevada
1 vitis coignetiae
6 cotoneaster horiz. var.
3 acanthus mollis
6 bergenia beesiana

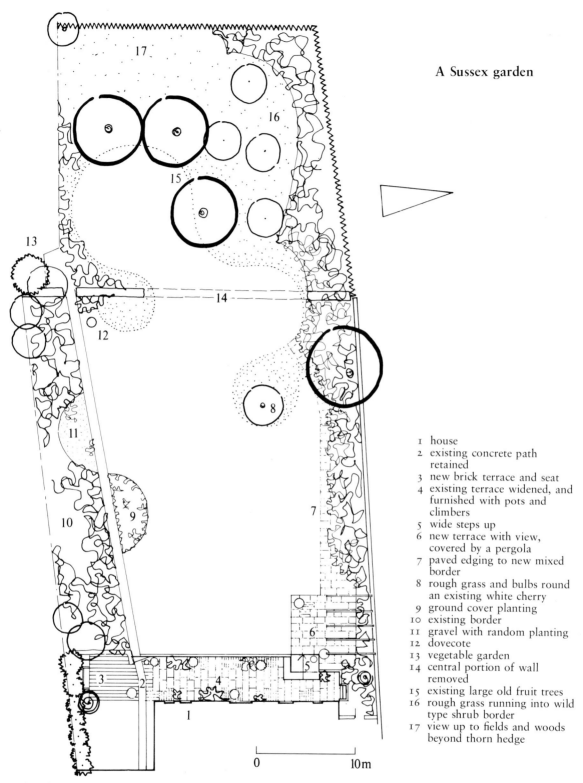

A Sussex garden

1 house
2 existing concrete path retained
3 new brick terrace and seat
4 existing terrace widened, and furnished with pots and climbers
5 wide steps up
6 new terrace with view, covered by a pergola
7 paved edging to new mixed border
8 rough grass and bulbs round an existing white cherry
9 ground cover planting
10 existing border
11 gravel with random planting
12 dovecote
13 vegetable garden
14 central portion of wall removed
15 existing large old fruit trees
16 rough grass running into wild type shrub border
17 view up to fields and woods beyond thorn hedge

0   10m

The garden of this house made from a pair of cottages was 500 mm. above the level of the narrow rear terrace (4). The ground rises gently through an old walled orchard to a view of fields and woods beyond. By taking down some of the wall, a view was opened up and a new terrace and pergola created at a higher level (6) to enjoy it. The low area adjacent to the house was widened as well, and bricks matching the house were used as part of the paving pattern infill.

Existing planting was reshaped on the left-hand side of the garden, while a new mixed border was created on the right-hand side, its paved edging being a continuation of the new terrace.

The main lawn is mown, but areas of rough grass needing only a monthly cut form part of the pattern and bring some flavour of the surrounding countryside into the orchard.

Shaping and planting a terrace in Cambridgeshire

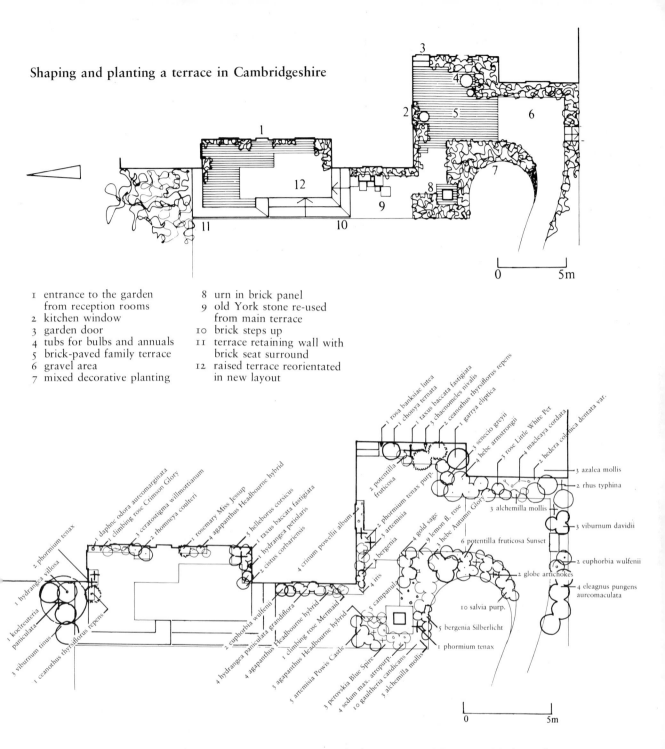

1 entrance to the garden
  from reception rooms
2 kitchen window
3 garden door
4 tubs for bulbs and annuals
5 brick-paved family terrace
6 gravel area
7 mixed decorative planting
8 urn in brick panel
9 old York stone re-used
  from main terrace
10 brick steps up
11 terrace retaining wall with
  brick seat surround
12 raised terrace reorientated
  in new layout

The house which this terrace surrounds was built at the turn of the century. It was designed to have a grand reception area (1), with a formal terrace outside and steps leading down to the garden. Times have changed, and what was the servants' quarters is now the family kitchen (2), and the servants' entrance is now the garden door.

With this change of family use the garden must change too. The grand terrace, while still leading to the main reception rooms, is now more relaxed, with a wide parapet on which to sit with a drink (11). The central steps now lead down and sideways to the new family outside area (5), where meals are taken and

sunbathing goes on. A large urn (8) sits on the corner acting as a visual pivot.

Areas of York stone on the original raised terrace have been lifted and replaced with brick. The old paving now forms an edging to abundant planting at the base of the house (9). Brick forms the floor of the outside living area, with gravel beyond (6).

Planting of the terraces is relaxed though full. Hot, stronger colours prevail near the family terrace, to simulate sun and warmth through summer.

A good proportion of the planting – shown in heavier outline – is evergreen, for it is important that the concept work sculpturally throughout the full year.

Filling the Voids

GROUND COVER

This type of detailing needs to be chosen with care, and takes time to establish, but once established it represents a great saving in maintenance which will be particularly appreciated by the weekend gardener.

The more rampant ground covers, which work most quickly, will need to be clipped over occasionally to keep them within bounds. They will in time smother most annual weeds, but they will also make it almost impossible to root out such pernicious weeds as couch grass and ground elder, so these should be eliminated before planting begins.

For full effect, choose an evergreen species. Gardening the natural way, in woodland conditions you might consider ivy, and on an acid moorland type of soil heather. On the Continent, various types of non-lawn grasses are used as well, which will stand extremes of hot and cold. Within the mass, you can then place the occasional flowering species, or bulbs. Another technique which seems to be of Continental origin is the growing of sculptural plants amid ground cover – miscanthus grass through low junipers, for instance, or acanthus through gaultheria. Commonly seen in nature, as when a birch group grows up through bilberry, the effect is equally strong and interesting in cultivation.

Ground-cover planting is becoming increasingly popular in Britain, particularly with local authorities, and much can be learnt from their methods. Nurseries are beginning to specialize, offering bundles of rooted slips rather than well formed plants, which of course cuts down on the cost of establishing a bed. Alternatively, you can buy a fully grown plant and pull it to pieces to make your own slips. Trailing plants, such as ivies, can be spread out with the branches weighted or pinned down, and the parts of the plant touching the ground will root.

Climbers like *Hydrangea petiolaris* and rambler roses can also be trained as ground-cover, though they are not evergreen.

GRASS LAWNS

Of all ground covers, the best is grass. It allows the space it occupies to be used as well; it is one of the cheapest mediums to lay, whether seeded or turfed; it takes little effort to establish, and is relatively simple and cheap to maintain; it can be cut to different heights, to create differing textured effects; any part worn or damaged can easily be replaced; and it is adaptable to all manner of situations except heavy shade and constant wet. We in Britain are almost unique in the world in being able to enjoy a lush greensward the year round. Surprising as it may seem, it is not really a natural ground cover in most parts

A Victorian pattern realized in rough and mown grass. The differing texture may be used to create all sorts of designs, as well as saving on maintenance.

'An Englishman's home . . .' – many people's ideal of the greensward mown in stripes. (This example is in Sussex.)

of the country: unless grassland is nibbled by rabbits or sheep, as on the open downs, it will gradually be colonized by herbs, then shrubs, and finally trees.

The first detailed directions for growing a lawn appear in John Rea's *Flora* of 1665: he advises laying turfs cut from 'a hungry common . . . where the grass is thick and short'. What now passes for lawn depends very much on the eye of the beholder. To many the ideal is the tailored, striped sward, weed-free and emerald green from liberal nitrogenous feeds; to others it is the carpet effect of daisies and other low-growing species which can stand mowing. In garden planning terms, the function of both is the same: to cover the voids which serve as foils to masses of structural or decorative planting. For the garden is really like a huge piece of moulded sculpture, and it is the relationship between its solids and voids, its levels, textures and surfaces which makes it satisfactory or not. If the masses are too thin, the house and viewer feel 'unheld', something we have all experienced in a new garden. In open landscape terms, too, it is the juxtaposition of mass and void that gives a region its distinctive character – the little fields between high hedges of Devon, the sweep and fold of northern uplands, or the fields carved from native woodland in Sussex and Kent. Just as one seeks to sit outside with some protection behind, so one feels exposed in flat bare countryside.

Our lawn is the domestic version of open areas of cultivation within an otherwise closed landscape. Those are the portions on which the farmer works, and this is the piece where the gardener labours too, if he allows himself too much area, or demands too high a standard. It is natural that weeds should regenerate within the unnaturally weed-free lawn, and in a country lawn areas of daisies and speedwell look charming. Moss, however, should not be encouraged, since it is not a good surface for use; moss-killer provides temporary relief, but where there are large areas of moss the drainage is insufficient.

Even a flowery lawn will still need mowing, and it makes good sense to design an area which will be practical to mow, depending on the type of machine you use. The small mower, powered by hand or motor, will negotiate awkward corners quite well, but sharp bends should still be smoothed out to more natural organic curves. The larger the machine you use, the simpler the layout should be, particularly in the sweep where a return is necessary. Gradients, too, should be natural and safely mowable if children are to use the machine at all. Steeper gradients can be cut with a rotary mower, but the operation can be dangerous for young or elderly operators.

When laying out the garden, try to make life easier for yourself by siting the compost or rubbish heap near the lawn – screened, of course, but with easy mower access to it, so you do not have to make a long trek every time the box is full of cuttings. Do not rely on dumping the cuttings on adjacent planted areas, for while a shallow layer of grass can provide a temporary mulch, too thick a layer encourages disease.

In an existing garden with an over-large lawn, consider reducing the chore of mowing by allowing areas of the grass to become rough, that is to grow 75 or 100 mm. high between monthly cuts with a rotary machine. This coarser texture of grass can be juxtaposed to mown areas, or can have mown paths cut through it, producing an attractive effect. It is amusing to feature trees in an island of long grass, or, more formally, to create a chequerboard pattern round geometrically positioned fruit trees.

A regular monthly mow does not allow many wild species to establish themselves, as you cut off the flower, and hence the seed heads, before they ripen and disperse. You can, however, deliberately encourage crops of wild flowers to establish themselves and grow to a considerable height before mowing the rough grass at very precise times of the year, though the technique is fairly complicated, and, as anyone with spring bulbs in grass knows, it is easy to allow the grass to become too long for easy cutting. The process will be described when we turn to the 'wild' garden, in the next chapter.

If you are prepared to cope with rough grass cut only two or three times a year, you can naturalize narcissus bulbs – the more robust trumpet type, or the white forms of *Narcissus poeticus*. The leaves should be allowed to die back naturally before the first cutting of the grass, for they are feeding next year's flowers in embryo. This means some untidiness, but much will be concealed by the long grass if its shape is part of the overall pattern of your garden. In shorter grass plant the older varieties of smaller daffodil, and large-flowered crocus. For interest late in the season, consider planting colchicums and autumn crocus, well away from grazing cattle.

The most common way to start a lawn is by seeding it. A good lawn from seed depends on the right choice of species, correct proportions in the mix, and seed in good condition. Of the vast range of grass species that grow naturally, only a small proportion are used commercially in seed mixtures, and of these six are used in the main for leisure and recreational purposes:

Agrostis	=	bent
Festuca	=	fescue
Poa	=	meadowgrass
Phleum	=	timothy
Cynosurus	=	dogstail
Lolium	=	rye grass

Seed mixtures fall into two groups, those which contain rye grass and those which do not. The non-rye group can be further subdivided into mixes of fescues and bents, and those containing timothy and dogstail. Rye is quick to germinate and of vigorous growth, and ultimately takes hard wear, but its seed heads are devils to mow off. To make a good lawn it needs to be supplemented by bottom grasses from any of the other species, which produce finer, more attractive grass that is easier to look after. Seed should be bought from a reliable source, and should be plump, clean and bright in colour, with no musty smell.

Some grasses are able to thrive on a variety of soil types, while others will only stand particular conditions; so your choice will be determined by the soil, its condition, and the use you have in mind for the lawn. Good preparation is essential: the ground must be thoroughly cultivated to provide a fine tilth with the correct crumb structure to assist in germination, and organic fertilizers, if needed, will be included in the final tilth. Since germination depends upon the warmth of the soil, sowing in late summer will probably be more successful than in spring, though this will vary with soils and locations.

a

b

c

a A stream of white arabis
meanders through iris and bold
juniper clumps.
b Grey rocks and boulders are
contrasted texturally with ground
covering plants.
c A bee garden: broad masses
mainly of herbs, planted to create a
dense ground cover which, when in
flower, is alive with the murmur of
worker bees.
d Irish ivy, *Hedera hibernica*,
makes an ideal ground cover,
through which little else will grow.
It should be pulled off trees,
however.
e Prostrate junipers used as ground
cover on an acid soil under a high
tree canopy, at Knightshayes,
Devon.
f Gravel with planting through it.
Use bold masses of planting to
create drifts, rather than spot-
planting individual subjects.

d

e

f

Clay soil, being cold, wet, and generally lacking aeration, is the hardest to seed. Drainage is essential, so you may need to open up the surface by incorporating coarse sand or gypsum into the top 50 mm. of earth with a harrow or a rotary cultivator. Species of grass that do well on heavy clay soils are the fine-leaved bent (which prefer acid soil) and the coarse-leaved annual meadowgrass, rough-stalked meadowgrass, and timothy.

Sandy soils containing a proportion of clay are those most favoured for finer lawns. Without clay, drainage will be excessive and the ground will dry out quickly: incorporate a top dressing of peat or compost in the top 25 mm. of earth before seeding. All fine-leaved grasses, sheep's fescue, New Zealand browntop and coarse-leaved fescue will thrive.

Chalk soils are also light and drain freely, and may also need an organic addition prior to seeding. Where clay is present, apply dressings as for it. Fine-leaved Chewings fescue, coarse-leaved hard fescue and crested dogstail are the most suitable seed mixes.

Heath and moorland soils, which are often poorly drained but which are thin, light and infertile, need a dressing of lime to reduce acidity to a pH reading of 6–6.5. Then sow browntop bent grass and Chewings fescue, together with coarse-leaved wavy hairgrass.

In shaded areas tolerant species may be used singly or in a mix (see p. 228). Near trees the soil is often dry and starved of nutrients, and acidified by lichen and leaf deposits. Under conifers sow wavy hairgrass; under trees which cast a particularly dense shade and have a heavy drip, such as chestnut and beech, do not attempt a lawn at all.

The alternative to sowing grass is to turf. Over a large area it will be more expensive, but it has the advantage of allowing one to use the ground almost immediately. It is also preferable for use on banks with any but the gentlest slopes, since rain is liable to form gullies and wash seedlings away.

Preparation of the ground for turf is similar to that for seeding, though a coarser final tilth is acceptable. Establish the quality of the turf you are buying: see the field from which it will be cut, or at least approve a sample, for it can vary enormously, from rough old meadow turf to the most refined sea marsh turf. Whatever the source, the selected sods should be carefully cut to a standard thickness for smooth laying, and they should be checked for the presence of weeds, pests, and disease. They should be laid not more than three days after receipt.

Of the various types of turf available, Cumberland or sea-washed turf, used mostly for bowling greens, is too refined for the country garden. A better choice is turf grown on thin soil over chalk, which consists chiefly of sheep's fescue, bent, and crested dogstail. Turf from the upland heath and sheep pastures, particularly in the west of the country, is composed mainly of fescues and bent, and produces a good weed-free sward.

Poor soils, on which fescue and bent flourish, tend to be acid, and it is therefore important when using fertilizers to maintain some degree of acidity and not over-enrich the soil.

ALTERNATIVE LAWNS

On a large scale grass is the only choice, but on a smaller scale you might consider a lawn of thyme or chamomile.

Creeping thymes grow naturally on open downland, and require similar conditions in a garden to succeed: without an open, well-drained position they will rot. They will do excellently on a sunny bank that is seldom walked on, where they will attract bees. Weeding them is a nuisance, but they do not need mowing, unless you do not wish them to flower.

Chamomile was until the seventeenth century the most common lawn plant. 'Like a chamomile bed – the more it is trodden the more it will spread', runs the saying, and the plant does make a hard-wearing, drought-resistant small lawn in the summer, particularly suitable perhaps in association with an area of herbs, though in winter it can look pretty miserable. Use either double-flowered chamomile or, for a better 'lawn' effect, the non-flowering *Chamomile nobile* 'Treneague'. Sow the seed on a bed prepared as for grass, then thin so the seedlings are about 150 m. apart. When established roll and weed well. Cut if necessary with shears, or with a mower set high.

PLANTING IN GRAVEL

Certain species grow better in this medium than others, and certain soils need less basic preparation to take the gravel, but once the system is understood and worked it can provide an extremely attractive and labour-saving gardening solution, ideally suited to larger areas which would need regular mowing.

Gravel can be laid over large areas and have, say, a path down the centre with planting on either side, or be a planted extension to the terrace. It can form a transition between cultivated areas and the wild garden, and need less maintenance and management than either. Once you have established a very strong planting pattern – and this is important – within the gravel medium, the species are allowed to become rampant, sucker or self-seed at will, needing control rather than encouragement. Yes, of course, it will require weeding, but a light hoeing at the right time can cut down on that too; and if you are prepared to spray or to spread a granular weedkiller (perhaps only on the areas that are walked on), the gravel can be kept quite clean.

When it comes to preparation, as for ground cover it is essential first to clear all pernicious weeds. What you do next will depend on the soil. On gravelly or flinty soil you can lay the gravel directly, in a layer about 25 mm. thick. More spongy soils will need a preliminary layer of ash or coarser gravel up to 75 mm. thick, consolidated, before the final dressing. The gravel can be laid around existing shrubs; for new planting, make a hole through the surface layers so the plant can root in the soil below.

Feed when necessary in autumn, spreading chopped manure or compost through the plants, to be carried down by worms through the winter. In spring, after any thinning, the surface gravel is raked and freshened.

Any plants that are suitable for your particular site and conditions will also be suitable for gravel planting; but those plants with a stronger form and those which like hot, dry situations tend to do better, such as cistus, helianthemum, iris, kniphofia, potentilla and sissyrinchium.

Part of a garden on the edge of Dartmoor
designed by Kenneth Ashburner which is truly
a continuation of the surrounding landscape.
A wild pool disguises the boundary. The
planting (*opposite*) is of indigenous species of
gaultheria, heaths, heathers and grasses, with
alders, birches and some pine.

The Modern Wild Garden

One kind of 'wild' garden is that planted specifically to attract wildlife, using horticultural species as well as native ones. But it is perhaps even more interesting to plant only native species, if not everywhere in the garden, at least on the periphery. Since many of us choose to live in the country to appreciate its wildness (the weekend visit being a great restorative), it seems paradoxical in a country garden to battle away against strongly growing indigenous plants and foster alien ones. Visually, one can achieve a blurring of the boundary by blending what is without and what is planted within; and native species should be easier to establish and grow in their natural habitat. Further, our native trees and shrubs, though attacked by leaf-eating insects, rot-forming fungi and the like, are adapted to resist these attackers and rarely succumb unless previously weakened by old age or physical damage. Beyond these purely selfish advantages is the bonus of replenishing our native plant material, under attack from modern forms of agriculture and industrial and housing developments, and at the same time of perpetuating the habitat of myriad forms of birds and insects (see pp.228–29).

When evolving a plan for a 'wild' garden, the same rules of design and culture apply in selecting native species as in choosing exotic ones, though the range is more limited. The arrangement will have a more random appeal, and the management will be a little different, on the whole easier: you may shape a plant, but you will seldom prune it, and instead of a smooth lawn you will have a mown path running through rougher areas, in open glades, possibly including wild flowers in the grass. Those forms of shrub which swoop to the ground will be allowed to do so, and you may permit nettles and weeds to grow at their base, completing a habitat for wild life. The total effect will thus be woolly around the edges, and altogether more relaxed.

When choosing trees, remember that the coniferous landscape of many of our commercially afforested areas has little or no wildlife at ground level, and imported trees host far fewer species of bird-attracting insects than native oaks and hawthorns (see p.228). The degree to which you encourage wildlife will of course be up to you, but naturalists and ecologists have in recent years shown how narrow the decorative gardener's view has been of the whole cycle of nature, categorizing it chiefly under the heading of 'pests and diseases', to be eradicated at all costs.

With trees, and to a greater extent with shrubs, what you will often be looking for is the non-horticultural variety of an otherwise well-known plant. It is important to find a source of supply where the plants have been grown locally in your region or county, from British stock (for throughout the nursery trade much is imported from Holland and other parts of the Continent), and to ensure that they are true native species and not horticultural varieties. Native trees and shrubs, with their characteristics and requirements, are listed on pp.222–23. You will need to exercise some caution in making your choice, for given the conditions they require certain plants become rampant, or form dense thickets without the competition they would have in nature – wild privet, for instance, or sea buckthorn.

TO GROW A FLOWERY MEAD

It was the flowery alpine meadow that inspired William Robinson to advocate growing herbaceous perennials in grass; and though his method was not completely successful, his aim – that look of wild flowers sprinkled through grass, as in an Impressionist painting – is very appealing today. Until quite recently, the technique was untried scientifically and hardly documented at all, but lately there has been considerable research into growing wild flowers.

The motive behind that research was primarily conservation, since changes in landscape use and the widespread application of selective herbicides have destroyed the habitats of many of our most attractive broad-leaved plants, or even the plants themselves. Less than thirty years ago, pastures and meadows were full of buttercups and cowslips, making a feature of lowland Britain, and grassed areas by the roadside were a flowering mass which further housed a wealth of independent wildlife. Now, even upland areas, once thought too steep for cultivation, have in many cases been ploughed, banishing the local flora and fauna.

A lawn incorporating wild flowers is a picturesque alternative to mown lawn or to rough grass, and, once you have understood the technique and got the combination established, it needs little maintenance. Another virtue is that it will do well on poor or thin soil – indeed better than on rich soil, which tends to encourage the natural progression from grass to taller species. Most gardening consists in forcing alien plants to grow in an unnatural way under foreign conditions, whereas with wild flower gardening you are attempting to preserve one natural stage.

What one seeks to achieve is an unbroken sequence of flower colour throughout the season. There are several mixtures possible, for different soils and to give different effects, but a good mix might include the following, which flower in succession from April to October: cowslips, oxeye daisies, ragged robin, meadow cranesbill, and lady's bedstraw. It is important that the species you select should be native to the location and soil, and to ensure this the enthusiast might collect seed locally. The method and timing of seed collection and the cleaning and mixing of the seeds are somewhat specialized processes, well described in a booklet published by the Nature Conservancy Council entitled *Creating Attractive Grassland using Native Plant Species*.

A more usual way to procure seed is to buy the mix of wild flower seeds suitable for your particular soil. The seed house will advise on the grass mix to accompany it and the rate at which it might be sown. Typical seed collections available are designed to create a relatively open grass cover of slow-growing species with which perennial, and to a lesser extent annual and biennial, wild flowers can develop, producing within three years a reasonably stable yet diverse vegetation. It is not possible to create a carpet of flowers in less time. (Three different mixtures of wild flower seeds are given on pp.230–31.)

On fertile clays or alluvial soil, you can sow the mix by itself, but on poorer soil where your final grassland will take longer to get established, or on banks where erosion must be prevented, it will be necessary to sow a quick-growing 'nurse' crop which will germinate fast and then die back. Westerwolds rye grass is used for this purpose, especially on low-fertility chalk and clay soils; on richer soils it will grow too lushly and swamp the other species. Sown in spring, it will provide an open though protective canopy within six weeks. Within ten weeks, or before growth exceeds 250 mm., it must be cut back or it will overwhelm the grasses and flowers you want to encourage. This mowing will also prevent the rye grass seeding itself back into the sward and returning for a second season.

The preparation of the site is in general similar to that for a lawn. It is very important to eliminate as much persistent weed as possible, since the slow-growing young mixed sward will be vulnerable, and you will not be able to use a herbicide against broad-leaved weeds once the sown species have germinated. If necessary, use herbicides in addition to cultivation. Do not include fertilizer in the final tilth, as this would only encourage the more rapid growth of weeds.

In the formative years of your 'meadow', you may need to mow it up to two or three times in a growing season to prevent grass and unsown vigorous annuals gaining ascendancy over the wild flowers – particularly where the topsoil is thick, or rich in nitrogen. Spring mowing in April and early May will be followed by another cutting in late August and a final one in November. The flowers will not be affected if the vegetation is cut no shorter than 100 mm. Use a flail or rotary mower, which handles long, dense vegetation better than a cylinder mower, or use an Allen scythe, and rake the site afterwards.

Once the sward is established, management consists of maintaining a balance, with one or two cuts in late July or August, when most species have finished flowering and set seed, followed by a final cut in November to control the species which might become dominant during the winter months. Large areas of 'meadow' might be divided into two sections, to be cut at different times in alternate years – say in late July one year and in September the next – thereby allowing later flowering species to set seed, and encouraging a more diverse flora.

For those with existing lawns who wish to establish wild flowers, it is not enough merely to let the grass grow, for wild grasses will take over instead. Cut the existing grass and wire rake the surface in October, then sow an appropriate wild flower mixture, or better still introduce drifts of established wild flower plants, grown in the garden from seed planted the previous autumn. These will flower the following spring, even if sparsely. To date, plants which have been successfully introduced into a sward include cowslip, oxeye daisy, scabious, harebell, lady's smock, lady's bedstraw and a variety of vetches.

a

b

c

d

a Yarrow, cornflowers, poppies and mullein growing wild in uncut grass during June, the wild flower month.
b Grasses make wonderful wild planting. Included here are *Arundo donaz*, miscanthus species, and fluffy, green *Stipa gigantea*.
c Hawkweed and ox-eye daisies growing in ancient meadowland on the Chiltern Hills.
d Open birch and oak woodland with natural underplanting of bluebells.
e Garden varieties of meadow flowers, with myosotis, fennel and *Eryngium giganteum* Miss Wilmot's Ghost, at Denmans.
f Narcissus as they should be grown, naturalized under apple trees in bold drifts.

e

f

Vegetables, Herbs and Fruit

VEGETABLES

The popularity of vegetable gardening has waxed and waned, but is usually at its peak during times of war or economic stress, so it is not surprising that there is greater enthusiasm now for a supply of home-grown vegetables. It is in the country that one is most able to indulge this interest, and indeed the thought of bringing up their families with the benefit of fresh produce can be a major factor encouraging many young couples to leave the town. If you value your time, however, consider carefully the extent of your vegetable garden, for what seemed initially an economic virtue can become a time-consuming vice. The same applies to weekenders, who dream of taking back crates of goodies for midweek urban dinner parties.

When planning a vegetable garden, think hard about the wisdom of growing the most common crops in season, which can easily be got from supermarkets or greengrocers – for though your own will always taste better (do they really, or are we justifying all that work?), do you want a garden full of simultaneous rows of cabbages or acres of sprouts? and does the shop price of mid-season or late potatoes really warrant the work involved in producing them? The wider the range of vegetables you grow, the wider the range of skills needed; but the average household now tends to need smaller amounts of a wider variety of vegetables, for one of the great spurs to home vegetable production is the increased interest in cooking, and the amazing range of foreign recipes which call for odd bits of this and that which the modern cook cannot buy and must therefore grow.

Some vegetables may be included in the flower garden as decorative, for example globe artichokes, asparagus and pickling cabbages. (Many herbs, too, if you are not interested in growing the whole range.) Once your selection is made and you have decided how much vegetable garden you want, decide next where to put it – if you are not lucky enough to have inherited an existing spot. Vegetable gardens need an open position, deep cultivation and an adequate supply of organic feed to establish them. An old site might well have had a hundred years and more of cultivation, and should not be sneezed at, even if it seems to be in the wrong place.

Previous generations tended to position their vegetable gardens at a distance from the house, wishing not to see anything so mundane, and having staff to trudge through rain to cut some cabbage or collect mint for the kitchen. In 1629 John Parkinson wrote, 'your herbe [vegetable] garden should be on the one or other side of the house . . . for the different scents that arise from the herbs, as cabbages, onions, etc., are scarce well pleasing to perfume the lodging of any house'. We are no longer so fastidious, and prefer convenience: it would make sense to have your vegetables as near the service entrance as possible, reached by a path that will be firm in wet weather. Besides, a well managed vegetable garden on the scale we anticipate is not unsightly, and if designed with herbal edgings, trained fruit trees or even annual hedges of peas or runner beans, can be extremely pleasant to look at.

160

You will need to be able to divide up your vegetable garden into at least three areas, for it is good husbandry to move the particular types of vegetable (leguminous, root, etc.) about, so that each grows in a fresh area annually, reducing the range of bugs which the soil might harbour. By then sub-dividing these areas in turn, you will get a satisfactory chequerboard pattern in which to grow a limited number of as many kinds of produce as you wish. For the essence of good management is not to have 100 lettuces, all going to seed at once, but 25, planted and thinned out at two- or three-week intervals throughout the summer to ensure a constant supply.

It makes sense, too, for your vegetable plot to be planned in relation to any features that serve it – a tool shed, for instance, cold frames or a greenhouse, the compost heap, and so on. Avoid the old allotment look of potting shed and noddy greenhouses dotted about a sea of rotting sprout tops. Remember that the siting of outbuildings should be in sympathy with the vegetable garden and also with the soft fruit growing area and its related caging.

An attractive way to grow a small amount of vegetables is to raise the beds slightly, using railway sleepers or concrete blocks to retain them. Picking is made easier, and – if the beds are not too wide – so is maintenance.

In an effort to make your vegetable garden decorative, do not be wooed into a fancy knot arrangement, for maintenance and cultivation depend on simple straight rows.

For a cropping plan, lists of easy and difficult vegetables, and a full guide to vegetable cultivation, see pp.232 and 234–35.

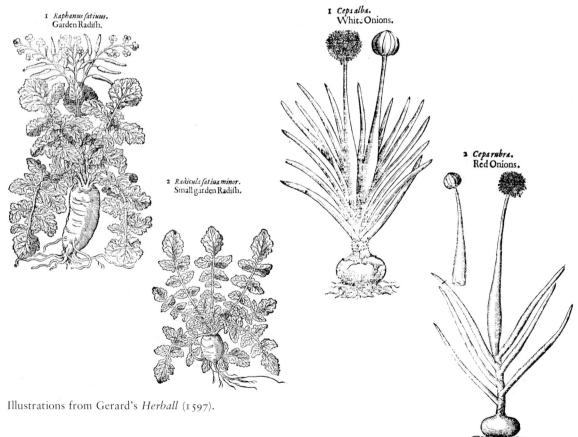

1 *Raphanus satiuus.*
Garden Radish.

2 *Radicula satiua minor.*
Small garden Radish.

1 *Cepa alba.*
White Onions.

2 *Cepa rubra.*
Red Onions.

Illustrations from Gerard's *Herball* (1597).

a

opposite An immaculate cottage vegetable garden at Bibury in Gloucestershire.

a A vegetable garden *orné* at Villandry in France, showing how vegetables, grown with roses and herbs and edged with box, can be both interesting and attractive.

b The vegetable garden at Barnsley House, Gloucestershire, is a scaled-down Villandry – a charming mixture of fruit trees trained in the French manner, of herbs, vegetables and flowers for cutting, served by brick pathways.

c Decorative cabbages with French beans and sweet peas. These glamorous autumnal vegetables will liven up any end-of-season border.

b

c

The organic way to grow vegetables

Another popular reason for growing your own produce is that you can do so organically, feeding your plants only on natural foods, and thus avoid stuffing your family with the chemicals which must linger in vegetables treated with inorganic fertilizers and sprays.

We have described the making of compost to feed the garden (p. 118). You might extend the process by growing nitrogen-rich green stuff with which to feed the compost itself. 'Biodynamic' compost activators include yarrow, chamomile, valerian, dandelion and stinging nettle, of which only small quantities are necessary. For bulk fill, you might use a crop of sunflowers, which produce a mass of greenery quickly, or grow comfrey, whose long leaves provide a good green composting material and can be harvested as many as four times a year.

Having established a naturally balanced medium in which to grow vegetables, you should establish a balanced growing programme as well. Commonsense and experience will help you to achieve this. It must be obvious, for instance, that a row of shallow-rooting shade-tolerant plants will grow well between rows of tall deep-rooting plants, as the former will take their food from the surface of the soil, while benefiting from the shade of the latter.

Another sensible step in organic cultivation is to use a plant that seems impervious to insect pests as a protection beside another that is prone to attack. Aromatic herbs play an important role in this 'companion planting', being seldom attacked by either pests or diseases (mint rust is the exception). This technique, known in old gardening lore, is increasingly being proved to have a basis in scientific fact, although it is difficult to quantify, and there is still much work to be done on the effect of plant exhalations, scents and root excretions on their surroundings. Try growing rosemary and sage, thyme and mint on this principle through your vegetables to repel insect pests. Nasturtium keeps woolly aphis at bay. Garlic and other members of the allium family protect most garden plants, while also (it is said) intensifying the scent of roses, but they inhibit the growth of peas and beans. Bitter wormwood and rue discourage insects, slugs and moles. Stinging nettles and foxgloves are both preservation plants and seem to protect others around them from fungal attack. In the orchard, chives deter apple scab, and southern wood and tansy are said to repel moths.

THE HERB GARDEN

Herbs have a strange romantic association; from earliest times, especially in Persia, the small formal herb garden was enclosed as a 'paradise' with a central feature, and sometimes the corners were said to represent the four corners of the world. This same sort of layout still prevails, seemingly descended through various knotted Tudor versions. In 1728 the architect and garden designer Batty Langley, in his *New Principles of Gardening*, lists herbs as 'absolutely necessary for the service of all Gentlemen, and other Families in general', and his design for the kitchen garden includes a herb garden and a physic garden. In the nineteenth century herbs were somewhat neglected: horticulturally they

Rose geranium
(*Pelargonium graveolens*)

were not considered suitable for the attention of hybridizers, and gastronomically they were overshadowed by imported spices. Nevertheless, they almost certainly continued to be grown in the old walled vegetable garden. Municipal bodies used them too, clipped, to form patterned edges to their crazy floral displays. At the turn of the century their decorative value was again appreciated, and there was a rebirth of herb gardening, the layout often still in the squared or circular form of earlier times, with concentric areas arranged around a central feature. Herbs are now appreciated for their decorative qualities, their culinary usage – in foreign dishes, and to pep up some of our rather bland convenience foods – and, to an increasing degree, their medicinal value as well.

Many herbs are evergreen or grey and look neat and tidy throughout the year. Others are more rampant and need to be restrained. This variance of growth pattern may account for their traditional cultivation in small beds which together make up a pattern. There is no reason, however, why that pattern has to be traditional: it could just as well be asymmetrical or free-form, if that suited the location.

Fennel (*Foeniculum vulgare*)

Whatever the style of the herb garden, it must be easily reached, with adequate dry access to the beds. Richard Bardley, writing in 1726, had the correct idea: herbs should be planted 'in some place near the House, for the Conveniency of gathering with little Trouble'. Part of the garden at least should have a southerly aspect, as the majority of herbs prefer full sun, many being Mediterranean in origin; though some – mainly medicinal – will grow in light shade. Tender herbs such as tarragon and southern wood, tall rosemary and even taller mullion, will need some protection from wind. Most herbs will need a light, well drained soil: where you have a heavy clay one, you might consider raising the beds and filling them with a prepared compost. A few herbs, like mint, prefer a moist soil.

If your herb garden is to be a formal hedged one, peg out the pattern and plant up the hedges. Make the design clean and open without too many tight corners, for nothing will grow there without smothering the pattern. Then follow the technique of planting design as described in Chapter 8: first site your specimen herbs, for instance angelica, followed by the taller shrub and evergreen ones, like rosemary and rue, to make up the bones of the pattern. Then work down in scale to smaller deciduous herbs, considering their foliage colour more than their flower; and lastly leave areas for sowing the annual types, bearing in mind the size that they will reach even annually.

Chamomile (*Matricaria chamomila*)

The informal herb garden will be much more random in feel, perhaps an incident within a flower garden, into which you move quite gradually. In such an area you might walk over thyme paths, and you will allow mullion, foxgloves, angelica and fennel to seed and romp dramatically about, contrasting them with sprawling nasturtium and flopping lavender. A herb garden of this type might be larger than a formal one, and will lack its pinched neatness, being a seemingly (though not really) uncontrolled feast of foliages, scents and flowers, through which summer bees buzz merrily. Control the garden by rigorous thinning of emergent seedlings.

Herbs with special characteristics – shade-tolerant, tall, and with distinctive leaf-colour – are listed on p.233.

Pennyroyal (*Mentha pulegium*)

A weekend cottage in Hampshire with a herb garden

1 original drive entrance
2 house
3 covered area
4 garage
5 new conservatory
6 herb garden (see detail)
7 brick terrace
8 screen planting of shrubs
9 mixed border backed by yew hedge
10 excavated new drive entrance
11 existing beech trees
12 pond
13 contoured mound with planting
14 rubbish area
15 view opened to paddock
16 existing rough grass with wild flowers
17 beech trees lining original drive
18 wild white cherries
19 circular pavilion
20 woodland backing

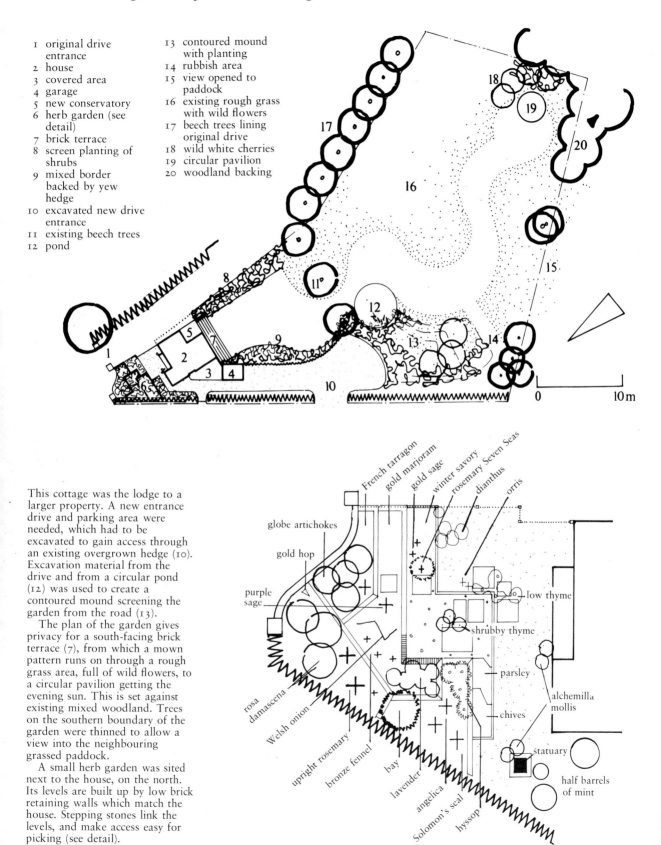

This cottage was the lodge to a larger property. A new entrance drive and parking area were needed, which had to be excavated to gain access through an existing overgrown hedge (10). Excavation material from the drive and from a circular pond (12) was used to create a contoured mound screening the garden from the road (13).

The plan of the garden gives privacy for a south-facing brick terrace (7), from which a mown pattern runs on through a rough grass area, full of wild flowers, to a circular pavilion getting the evening sun. This is set against existing mixed woodland. Trees on the southern boundary of the garden were thinned to allow a view into the neighbouring grassed paddock.

A small herb garden was sited next to the house, on the north. Its levels are built up by low brick retaining walls which match the house. Stepping stones link the levels, and make access easy for picking (see detail).

Labels on herb garden detail: globe artichokes, gold hop, purple sage, rosa damascena, Welsh onion, upright rosemary, bronze fennel, bay, lavender, angelica, Solomon's seal, hyssop, French tarragon, gold marjoram, gold sage, winter savory, rosemary Seven Seas, dianthus, orris, low thyme, shrubby thyme, parsley, alchemilla mollis, chives, statuary, half barrels of mint

right A herb garden in a medieval setting at Singleton, Sussex. It seems likely that herbs were grown traditionally in this random way rather than restrained in miniscule clipped patterns.

below A small formal area in which herbs, a few flowers and special vegetables are all grown together. The box edging gives some shape during less decorative winter months.

bottom Herbs at Denmans, grouped for their form and colour. Paving stones facilitate picking; the pot is useful for dead heads and weeds.

Where you have the space, growing soft fruit is one of the joys of country living, particularly since many forms now have an extended fruiting period so that not everything ripens at the same time. The fruit may be eaten fresh, bottled, or very easily preserved by deep freezing.

The soft fruit area, particularly when enclosed in a cage of netting against birds, is not particularly sightly; luckily it does not need to be readily accessible, and it may be sited at a distance from the house. The position should ideally be open and unshaded, although most berries will stand some shade, and the soil should be well drained, moist and loamy. Raspberries are exceptional in preferring a slightly acid soil.

The protective cage may be either a permanent structure, of posts and metal or plastic netting, or a temporary structure over which nets are thrown as the fruit ripens. Either way, it must be high enough for you to get in and hoe between the rows and pick the fruit comfortably.

The seasons given in the following lists indicate the time when the fruit is eaten.

Blackcurrants

Plant two-year-old bushes, 1.5–1.8 m. apart in rows 1.8–2.5 m. distant. Set them in deeply, so that new growth will come from below ground level. Choose several varieties to ensure a succession of fruit. The bushes will produce up to ten crops, although reversion often reduces cropping before then. Recommended:

early	Mendip Cross
mid-season	Wellington XXX
late	Westwick Choice

Red and white currants

Plant two-year-old bushes and space them as for blackcurrants. Cordon forms should be planted 460–600 mm. apart in rows 1.5–1.8 m. distant. The fruit appears on spurs on established branches, like apples and unlike blackcurrants, which fruit on the previous year's wood. The varieties of each are few, because the fruits have a limited use. Recommended:

early (red)	Laxton's No.1
(white)	White Versailles

Blackberries, loganberries and hybrid berries

Plant one-year-old blackberries 3.5–4.5 m. apart in rows 2.5–3 m. distant; the other berries should be planted with intervals of 3.5–4.5 m. between both plants and rows. Growth is fairly vigorous, though one allows only part of the fruited wood to remain each autumn, when the new growth is trained in. Loganberries are more suited to restricted space. If your rows are freestanding, place strong posts at the ends of each row and tie wires between them, the top line being about 1.5 m. above the ground; then tie new growths to the wires at intervals of 300 mm. Alternatively, you may grow your fruit against a wall or a fence. Recommended:

blackberry	August–September	Merton Early
loganberry	July–August	LY59 Clone
hybrid berries	July–August	boysenberry
	—	nectarberry

Raspberries

Plant one-year-old canes 450 mm. apart in rows 1.5–2.5 m. distant. When established the canes produce suckers and new canes each year, and by planting close together you ensure a continuous succession of new canes. Support the plants by tying each cane individually to wires, as for blackberries. The life of raspberry beds tends to be limited by disease and weed invasion. Plant a number of varieties for a longer fruiting period. Recommended:

early	Malling Exploit
mid-season	Malling Jewel
mid-season and late	Lloyd George
late	September

Strawberries

A strawberry bed is established by planting rooted runners. The plants are then restricted, either by removing the runners as they form or by allowing the runners to root down the row to form a matted bed of plants. Single plants will produce a large high-quality fruit, while rows produce a greater volume of usually smaller fruit. Plant strawberries 450 mm. apart in rows about 750 mm. distant, with the crowns exactly level with the surface of the soil. They grow best in soil rich with humus. The normal life of a bed is three crops. Recommended:

early	Cambridge Prizewinner
—	Cambridge Rival
mid-season	Red Gauntlet (for northern districts)
—	Royal Sovereign
—	Templar
mid-season to late	Gehro

Gooseberries

Plant two-year-old bushes (usually), 1.5–1.8 m. apart in rows 1.8–2.5 m. distant. Cordon forms should be planted 300–500 mm. apart in rows 1.5–1.8 m. distant. Gooseberries are normally grown with their stems clear for about 300 mm. above ground level. Recommended:

mid-season	Green Gem (dessert)
—	Langley Gage
—	Leveller
late	White Smith (dessert)

left The orchard at Sissinghurst Castle, Kent, culminates in a piece of statuary between two lombardy poplars whose scale relates to the fruit trees rather than the statuary itself. Mown grass paths articulate a pattern through rougher grass squares surrounding the fruit trees.

below A fan-trained peach tree grows against a warm brick wall.

For many years, fruit trees have tended to be banished along with vegetables to some far point of the garden, and yet they are attractive in both spring and autumn and there is no reason why they should not be more widely used for decoration.

Those inheriting older gardens are lucky if they acquire old fruit trees too. Some will still fruit regularly after years of neglect, and that's a bonus; others fruit seldom, but have a wonderfully gnarled profile and, all else failing, can be used to host tumbling plants. Pruning will sometimes revive the fruiting of such a tree, but one tends to lose on character. Newly planted trees, well manicured and spurred, have another feel altogether – and their prim neatness can be incorporated quite formally within a layout, either as specimens on a lawn, or in flower beds. Orchard plantings should be distanced so that the crop can be gathered with ease and the grass maintained between the trees.

Fruit trees need protection from north and east winds and should not be in a frost pocket; pear blossom is more subject to frost than that of apple. Most species prefer soils that are well drained and loamy, but not too rich, or they will produce foliage at the expense of fruit.

Trees which you might consider include apples and pears, cherries, plums and damsons, and, if you live in a favoured situation, peaches and nectarines. You might also use, as perimeter screening, cobnuts or filberts. Less commonly grown subjects of great decorative value are walnut, mulberry, fig, medlar and quince.

The shape and height of the fruit trees you select are purely for your convenience in cropping its fruit. Apples, pears, cherries and plums are available, like other trees, in standard, half standard, or bush size (pp.122–23). For the smaller kitchen garden area, choose rigorously trained trees, grafted on to dwarf root stocks. The dwarf pyramid will take up little room, needs no support and crops heavily. Trained specimens, used originally for planting against a wall in a kitchen garden, but which may now be incorporated into your scheme decoratively, can be espaliered in cordoned form, U-trained, feathered or fan shaped, although they may still need some support on wire.

You might consider orchard planting of fruit trees through a pony paddock (provided that the trees are protected), or converting to a more profitable purpose any large expanse of lawn, which would then only need rough cutting as opposed to regular mowing. In such situations for the first few years the trees should be kept weed-free around their base.

If you are contemplating an orchard of any size, even if it is not to be commercial, you would be wise to seek specialist advice on the spacing and siting of individual trees within it, for the permutations of correct pollinators and fruiting times are legion. It is possible to get this advice from your county horticultural adviser, who is usually located at the county agricultural or horticultural station. He will also advise on local varieties which will flourish in your particular weather and soil.

In the following tables, as for soft fruits, the season given indicates when the fruit is normally eaten.

Apples

When selecting varieties, choose at least two which blossom at the same time, so that they will pollinate each other. If your garden or orchard is susceptible to frost, although you have been careful not to site the trees in a frost pocket, pick varieties which flower late, or whose blossom can tolerate some frost. Many older varieties of apple have been forgotten or neglected by commercial growers, who are responding to the demands of marketing and large-scale production, and who can, after all, select the correct soil and situation for their orchards. But some of these older varieties have quirks of personality that make them suitable for a particular region or situation; and for his orchard the amateur, who must grow his trees where he lives, often in unsuitable soil and a difficult climate, with only time for a minimal spraying programme, needs trees which will as much as possible look after themselves.

Apple varieties fall into the following categories, of which the best known are listed.

(a) **dessert**

late summer	Beauty of Bath
early autumn	James Grieve
—	Ellisons Orange
late autumn	Charles Ross
—	Egremont Russet
mid-winter	Blenheim Orange
—	Cox's Orange Pippin
new year	Laxton Superb
spring	Tydeman's Late Orange

(b) **cooking**

September–November	Rev. Wilks
November–March	Bramley Seedling
January onwards	Newton Wonder

If you live in the West Country, and have inherited a beautiful orchard of seemingly inedible and uncookable little apples, they are cider apples. And while they may not have been picked for ages, they still will make delicious cider, even on the domestic scale.

Pears

Like many of our other fruit trees, pears originated in the warmer, drier, less windy climate of the Mediterranean, so to attain perfection they need sun and shelter from wind, and should be planted in the warmest part of the garden. To make matters more complicated, their flowers open a fortnight ahead of apple blossom: they are thus more susceptible to frost, and in the cold weather find fewer insects around to pollinate them, so that pollinators (of which more below) should not be too far apart.

The wild pear tree is a tall, hardy, long-lived tree, slow to mature but deeply rooted, and able to stand most soils unsuitable for other fruit trees. Specimens grafted onto this seedling pear stock possess the same characteristics, and they too grow into large handsome ornamental trees, with strong upright branches.

For general garden and orchard planting, the pear is grafted onto a 'quince A' rootstock, which restricts its size while speeding up the flowering process. Quince roots are shallower than the native stocks and will only do well in good soil with ample moisture, sufficient nitrogen and humus and not too much lime. If the tree becomes dry or starved, growth falls off, blossom may fail to set, and the fruit does not mature properly. In chalky soils trees may be helped with sequestrene.

When planting any grafted species, it is essential to keep the scion – in this case the pear part of the tree – well above ground level, for if it is buried it will form roots, and the good effect of the stock will be lost. The upright growth habit of many varieties of pear makes them easier to manage in pyramidal than in bush form.

The pollination needs of pears are vital and complicated. Most varieties are 'diploid' (that is, they have cells which contain two matching sets of chromosomes), so they need to be cross-pollinated by another variety; some are 'triploid', and need two other pollinators, which will also pollinate each other. The following varieties can be pollinated by one other variety within the same group:

Group A
March–April	Easter Beurré
October	Louis Bonne of Jersey

Group B
September	Williams Bon Chrétien
October	Beurré Hardy
October–November	Conference

Group C
November	Doyenné du Comice
December–January	Glou Monceau

Plums

Prolific fruiters in locations that suit them, plums are often disappointingly barren in the more westerly counties, for they like a continental climate of hard winters, short springs, and long hot summers. They are most successful in countries away from the Atlantic, and in years which have a late, hard spring. An early spring brings out the blossom before the air is warm and dry. Plums need a position that is sheltered from wind and high enough to avoid frost pockets, and a fairly light fertile soil, rich in lime, potash and nitrogen. Very careful pruning is necessary, since wounds can let in canker, a common ailment. Among the more common plums, the following may be recommended:

(a) dessert
early	Early Laxton
—	Victoria
—	Purple Pershore
late summer	Jefferson
early autumn	Severn Cross

top and above A vine growing decoratively (and edibly) under the eaves of a poolhouse in Kent.

right Vines in a Kentish vineyard grown along posts and wires. Quite a small piece of ground, at the bottom of a garden, has been utilized to produce a considerable crop.

(b) cooking

early	Black Prince
—	Czar
late summer	Warwickshire Drooper
early autumn	Marjorie's Seedling

Less familiar types of plum are damsons and quetsches, with small, late-ripening black fruit, which are descended from the sour Bullace, notable for its hardiness. Good damsons include Farleigh, which also makes an effective windbreak, and Merryweather. Quetsche (of which the fruit may be bought imported from Germany and Austria) forms a neat tree. Another type of plum that can be used as a windbreak is the cherry plum or myrobolan, which is a fast-growing tree, excellent for shade.

Sweet cherries

These tall trees quickly reach a height of 10 m. or more, so they are best suited to orchard culture, though given enough space they can be effectively grown against a high wall. They will only fruit well in certain districts, when the climate is warm and dry enough and when the blossom is not spoiled by late spring frosts. Soil should be rich, yet well drained. As with plums, careful pruning is essential to avoid canker. Cherries need to be netted against birds when they ripen.

Morello cherries are popular, since they can be fan-trained and will grow on a north-facing wall. Pollinating variances of cherries are particularly complicated: seek expert advice as to varieties.

Apricots, nectarines and peaches

Natives of China, these prunus species are also grown in the Near East and in Eastern and Southern Europe, locations which give some insight into their requirements: they need a sunny spring to ensure safe pollination of their early blossom, and hot summer weather to ripen their fruit. A dry autumn matures the shoots for next season, after which they prefer a short, cold winter rest, with just enough rain for thrifty growth. In these islands, the nearest to their home climate is to be found in East Anglia and the London area. There and in a few other favoured places, it is possible to grow peaches as bush trees, or even standards. Further west and north, heavier rainfall and uncertain seasons make culture more difficult, so the protection of a south- or west-facing wall will be necessary. The success of all trained fruit lies in their pruning, and these are usually fan-trained. Recommended:

apricots	summer	Moor Park
nectarines	—	Lord Napier
peaches	—	Lord Peregrine
—	late summer	Royal George

Brown Turkey fig

The fig is not grown as a standard in this country: it needs a sheltered and sunny wall to ripen the fruit, which hangs on to the previous season's wood throughout the winter. Growth is rampant in the south—too much so, although figs make a handsome freestanding bush – unless the roots are restrained by a shallow soil. To make them fruit, grow them in concrete tubs, or over a stone base, 70–100 mm. below ground. Alternatively, pave over the roots to restrict and divert surface water from them.

Medlar (*Mespilus germanica*)

Not planted enough, this is a rather handsome, round-topped shade tree, though slow growing. The fruit, not to everyone's taste, is pleasant to eat and can be used for jam and in cooking.

Quince (*Cydonia oblonga*)

Another very decorative tree in flower, in leaf and especially when hung with huge golden fruit, the quince likes moisture, warmth and a deep, rich soil without too much lime. It is self-fertile, but usually takes about six years to start cropping. The fruit is used in jams and for cooking.

Walnut (*Juglans regia*)

This is a most spectacular deciduous tree in maturity, but one taking a number of years to fruit. Several walnuts should be planted together, as they are not self-fertile.

Black mulberry (*Morus nigra*)

Along with the walnut, the mulberry is an admirable decorative as well as fruiting specimen. The trees become gnarled and picturesque after as little as ten years. Their only disadvantage is that the black fleshy berries can make a mess when they drop on paved areas.

Cobnuts and filberts

These are cultivated forms of the wild southern nut. Cobs are rounder, with a short husk, while filberts are longer and thinner shelled. Both are quick-growing small trees, which succeed best in deep, moist, limestone soils. They will make an excellent shelter tree for other more tender forms of fruit.

Vines

Vines have been grown in England since Roman times and the tradition of wine-making only ceased with the Dissolution of the Monasteries and the introduction of more and cheaper wines from the Continent. Vine growing survived in isolated pockets, and in coldhouses, of which that at Hampton Court, with its 'Great Vine', is probably the best known.

Today there is an enormous interest again, and hundreds if not thousands of people are making their own wine from their own grapes. The growing of grapes outdoors in England has become much more attractive and potentially rewarding since the introduction of new strains of vine which are better suited to cropping in northern latitudes. These are mainly of the Riesling type, which produces a wine similar to German hock.

Grapes can be grown out of doors as far north as a line running between the Wash and Mid-Wales, but their position is important. The vineyard should not be above 150 m. altitude or at the top or bottom of a slope. Vines like a warm well-drained site, and they should be reasonably well sheltered from high winds. South, south-west or south-east aspects are best: north-facing slopes or walls should never be used, since grapes need as much sun as they can get in this country. Vines planted against a south-facing wall will do especially well, as latent heat in the wall and reflected sun will give earlier ripening.

As far as soil goes, vines are adaptable to a wide range, all of which will be helped by a fairly generous amount of compost, although rich soils will require little feeding. Even clay soils can be successful, provided that they are broken up to facilitate the good drainage which is so essential.

Plant vines in spring, unless the site is particularly sheltered, in the same way that you would shrubs, but before planting trim the roots to about 130 mm., and the main tap root (if there is one) to about 75 mm. If the vine has not been pruned before delivery it should be cut back to two buds. It should then not be allowed to fruit in its first season. For normal garden cultivation vines are planted in rows in much the same way as raspberries. Strong-growing varieties should be at least 1.25 m. apart, in rows no closer together than 1 m., oriented north-south. When planting your vines as a little vineyard remember to leave enough room between the rows and between the plants for the passage of a small cultivator. Spraying is crucial throughout the year. After the first year pruning is a skilled business – there are several systems – and so too is cropping: at this stage seek specialist advice.

Considerable crops of grapes for home wine-making can also be produced from vines trained as decorative climbers. Vitis Brandt is one of the most popular hardy fruiting vines: it is vigorous (reaching a height of 9 m. on a suitable support) and yields masses of bunches of sweet aromatic grapes, which are dark purple in colour. An additional feature is that the leaves of the plant turn dark red and purple in autumn. Other clones of *Vitis vinifera*, the common grape vine, can be grown out of doors to produce fruit for eating.

The vines listed in the table on p.236 will all fruit in a normal summer, as long as the site is well chosen and not too high. In more northern areas or less favoured positions it is important to select the earliest ripening varieties, while in the south the later varieties will be more successful.

Water in the Country Garden

Glamorous millraces and tranquil lakes mirroring classical temples come to mind when one thinks of water in a country garden, and lucky are they that have them: the great majority make do with less, but there are many sites which offer enormous scope for using water, however daunting the prospect of its introduction.

The many moods of water give it life, and the natural forms of life which it supports further activate it and give it added interest. It always becomes a focal point in a landscape, for there is usually something happening in it or around it, and because it lies at the lowest point landform too directs the eye towards its broad mass. What actually catches and holds the eye is the way light affects water – during the day the sun moving round and glinting on it, and at night the moon's tranquillity reflected in it; rain and clouds create another mood; in winter, ice and frost evoke a painting by Bruegel. These are visual effects: the chatter of a stream adds a further resonance, as does a gentle lap on a gravelly shoreline.

STREAMS

Water in a landscape is either flowing or still, and each form has its own character. Narrow streams have a busy directional pull quite different from the calm sense of place which broader, stiller water creates. This directional pull may be interrupted by a rapid of waterfall which will punctuate the flow and produce a tranquil stretch for contrast. In general, allow water its natural course and pace. Digging it out at intervals to form pools affects the swell and pattern of the landscape in a way that can be disruptive – for while we may not be able to read a natural terrain, we are acutely aware of a violation of it. Earth-moving to reveal a stretch of water, rather than to change the water itself, is a more gentle operation with a higher success rate, and one can always modify the result with clever planting.

BRIDGES

Bridges and stepping stones allow one to enjoy water in a different way from merely standing on the bank – but both need tact, if they are not to become a dinky Japanese pastiche. It is interesting how often gardeners trying for an effect of wildness lapse into a would-be Japanese manner: it is never successful here, but from it there are lessons to be learnt, of which the most important is to work whenever possible in the idiom of your own area: see the granite clapper bridges of Devon, for instance, the slate bridges of Borrowdale and the Yorkshire stone bridges of the Dales. When there is no obvious local idiom, or

when you cannot adopt it because of cost or because local materials are not available, the alternative is to make a bold statement in another simple material. Wood works in most settings. Use elm with water, for it will not rot, and make the detailing chunky rather than decorative. Where the bridge itself is needed to complete the composition, consider its outline only, and do not clutter up the detail. Concrete is even more hard-wearing than wood in conjunction with water; but whether your bridge is to be cast in position, with reinforcements and even stressing, or cast off site and then brought in, you will need expert advice for its design and construction.

LAKES AND POOLS

In a rural situation, removed from the house, a body of still water will need to be fairly large if it is not to appear piddling. It must relate in scale to its setting, and it must look natural. Beyond that, its character will be determined in detail by the treatment of the shoreline – a sharp transition from grass to water, a transition softened by planting, or a pebbled 'beach'. Decide which look you are after. Is it the dreamy Monet lily pool, fringed with willows, or a more vigorous pond for ducks? The two can seldom be combined, for ducks will paddle about, messing the shoreline, and their feeding destroys underwater plants. If you want a fish pond, it may have to be specially deep to deter marauding herons.

When creating a 'natural' body of water, carefully scrutinize your site and its contours, making sure that your proposed location is at the lowest point of the land, and that it is near any existing source of water such as a spring or stream. If the latter is impossible, you may be able to excavate down to the level of the natural water table. Decide on the depth according to the pool's function, remembering that while a large, shallow stretch of water gives you more for your money visually, it will be more affected by evaporation in the summer than a deeper pool, and may also silt up more quickly, the process being hastened by a greater growth of weeds.

If your excavation will involve a stream, divert it temporarily if possible, or see that the digging starts upstream, so that any loosened soil which tends to flow downstream will be removed as the work proceeds and not allowed to accumulate. The excavated material may be taken away altogether, or it may be used to modify slightly the existing landform.

Where the topography allows it, you may be able to create a pool by damming a stream. You will need a site survey first, to determine the fall of the land and the quality of the foundation subsoil, and for any dam larger than 1.5 m. from base to top you must have specialist advice, since a fault could cause serious flooding. The height of the dam will be dictated by the conditions of the site, but the structure must obey three obvious rules: it must withstand pressure without moving at all, it must be higher than the overspill point (from which water is channelled back into the original stream), so that water does not flow over unprotected areas, and it must not leak. Depending on the height and thickness, dams can be constructed of earth, masonry or concrete. Earth dams are suitable only where you have a lot of space, since they must be considerably thicker at the base than they are high.

opposite Weeping willows, bamboo and the giant *Gunnera manicata* epitomize waterside planting.

a

b

c

d

a A simple timber bridge which might well be of railway sleepers.
b Stepping stones cut to match in length and placed in line have an appealing order about them.
c A traditional Devon 'clapper' bridge on Dartmoor.
d The rustic look in timber, if sound, can be very charming in the correct setting.
e A cast concrete dam in the garden of Athelhampton House, Dorset, which has a strength and scale belying the name of the river which it satisfactorily punctuates – the Piddle.
f A smaller, wilder version of the same type of dam, in Jersey. Concrete looks admirable in such a tough setting. Its detailing and construction, however, should be undertaken by an expert. Dam structures which burst may be extremely dangerous.

f

Spillways relieve the pressure of water on a dam when the downflow becomes excessive, for instance after a thunderstorm. The drawing shows a spillway constructed at a slight distance, to the right; the photograph shows one built as part of the dam itself.

When it comes to lining the pool to make it watertight, the traditional method is to use puddled clay, which has a plastic consistency. It is applied in layers 100–150 mm. thick, each of which is firmly trodden and then cut with long spades to bind it into the layer below. That laborious technique has now been largely superseded by the use of a lining made of plastic or (preferably) butyl rubber sheeting. For a large pool, several sheets can be welded together in position. It is essential that a heavy grade of sheeting be used, and that it be laid with care, for a hole once made is very difficult to locate. Puncturing can occur from below as well as above, so the lining should be laid on a smooth surface, which is usually covered with sand. Where the area is not too great, the liner is placed across the excavation and stretched taut between weights: as the pool is filled the liner sinks, and when the edges have been secured the weights can be removed.

The tricky part of finishing a sheet-lined pool is to hide the edges of the liner. One possibility is a shallow gradient cobbled or shingled to look like a beach. Where you want a sharper profile, or want to have plants growing down to the water's edge, the sheeting can be laid against a retaining wall of concrete block and folded over the top, then finished off by a coping which will weight it down and form a narrow border to the water.

The planted pool

One of the pleasures of working with water is that it allows one to make use of a different range of plant material. 'Aquatics', non-woody plants which grow in or under water, may be categorized in three main groups: those which are rooted in the soil base and grow entirely under water; those which are rooted, but have leaves standing above or floating on the surface of the water; and those which float, without roots in the soil.

Many aquatics are strong in leaf form and can be a dramatic element in a composition. The downward fall of a willow frond and the upward spikes of reeds and rushes will both contrast with the horizontal line of water, dotted with lily pads. Marginal planting needs shallow water, and the profile of your pond will determine what can be grown. In nature there is little demarcation between the water and the ground around it, but rather a boggy or swampy transitional zone where those moisture-loving plants known as bog plants thrive. Starting as single specimens, they grow and push out into open water which gradually becomes silted up with the accumulation of plant debris. These are the plants to mask the edges of your pool.

Bog plants
Phragmite australis (common reed)
Sparganum spp. (burr reed)
Phalaris arundinacea (reed canary-grass)
Butomus umbellatus (flowering rush)
Typha latifolia (reed mace or bulrush)
Alisma plantago-aquatica (water plantain)
Lythrum salicaria (purple loosestrife)
Lysimachia vulgaris (yellow loosestrife)
Ranunculus lingua (great spearwort)

At the water's edge these bog plants can be interspersed with moisture-loving forms of ornamental grass, bamboo and fern. Beyond that, larger shrubs and trees serve as a background screen or windbreak.

Trees at home by water
Salix babylonica (weeping willow) – unsurpassed as a specimen tree in this situation, but needs a fairly large expanse of water to give the correct scale
Acer rubrum (red or swamp maple)
Acer saccharinum (silver maple)
Alnus glutinosa (common alder)
Betula pubescens (white birch)
Betulus nigra (river or red birch)
Populus marilandica (black poplar hybrid)
Populus tremula (aspen)
Quercus bicolor (swamp white oak)
Quercus phellos (willow oak)
Salix caprea (goat willow)
Salix coerulea (cricket-bat willow)
Taxodium distichum (swamp cypress)

a

b

c

d

a A square brick pool, lined with black butyl rubber, with a simple fountain.
b A circular brick pool, with pavior brick coping tilted inward.
c A circular brick pool with a dribble fountain, worked by a submersible pump in the pool.

d A lake edged with rhododenrons, below a rocky outcrop, at Mullichope Park in Shropshire.
e A formal pool with a twist. By breaking the line of the edging with planting, the concept is softened to just the right balance (West Dean, Sussex).

e

a For a crisp junction between water and grass use a boarded edge (as here), or longer-lasting concrete.
b Iris and the Royal fern mark this water's edge.
c A cobble beach runs gently into this stream. Cobble will also disguise a butyl rubber lining to a pond or lake.
d A stream-side walk in Jersey has been simply edged with logs, restrained by angle irons set into the river bed.

Shrubs for planting near the water's edge

Azalea
Clethra alnifolia (sweet pepper bush)
Cornus alba varieties (dogwood)
Cornus sericea
Cornus florida (flowering dogwood)
Holodiscus discolor aeriaefolius
Rubus chamaemorus (cloudberry)
Salix daphnoides (violet willow)
Sorbaria aitchisonii (false spiraea)
Spiraea arguta (bridal wreath)
Spiraea canescens
Spiraea japonica
Spiraea salicifolia
Vaccinium myrtillus (bilberry or whortleberry)

Small decorative ponds

Smaller areas of water may be introduced in your design, in association with the terrace. It is best to stick to a formal outline, as little free-shaped pools of the fibreglass variety seldom look convincing. Similarly, concrete is the best material to use: its strength seems more in tune with natural surroundings than fibreglass or plastic or butyl rubber sheeting, and though the latter are cheaper to install they are more difficult to integrate at the edges and have no provision for drainage.

A formal pool near the terrace could be built on a raised level, with a wide surround, making it safer for children and giving you at the same time an extra seating area. The sound of water can be pleasant on a hot day, and mammoth waterworks are not necessary: a simple self-circulating submersible pump can provide an attractive water drip feature. Beware too grandiose a scheme: fountains, used in hotter climates to cool the air, here get blown by the wind, with the effect of emptying the pool.

SWIMMING POOLS

There are various schools of thought on the siting of a swimming pool within a larger layout: near the house, or away from it? if away, hidden or visible? The orientation of the site may dictate the answer by ruling out other possibilities.

When the pool can be near the house, it can be served from it or from adjoining outbuildings, simplifying access to food, drink, WCs and telephone (though wet feet going into the house might pose a problem). If the pool is to be heated by solar radiation, the panels can be disguised on neighbouring roofs. Aesthetically, too, pools seem to relate most comfortably to a building complex – though in such a setting their shape should probably be regular or rectilinear, to tie in with the outline of the buildings.

Where the pool is removed from the house, you will need to provide its own terrace and space under cover for changing, for storing poolside furniture and cleaning equipment, and for the pump chamber. Out of season a pool looks depressing, even if it is covered, and if it is visible all the time you will almost certainly want to keep it filled and cleaned. It can be hidden behind hedges, but children will not then be able to use it unsupervised, for anyone in trouble would not be seen. It can also be made a feature of the garden, where, used in conjunction with earth shaping, some of the bizarre shapes available will make sense.

The size of the pool, its shape and its layout will inevitably depend on its function and location and on economic considerations. For swimming, work out how many people are likely to be using it at one time, and allow roughly 2.5–3.3 square metres per person. The minimum size for a private pool is usually 8 × 5.4 m. The more bizarre the shape, the harder it is to heat and to use for swimming regular keep-fit lengths, but a shaped pool can be more fun for children.

You can soften the effect of a swimming pool by an intelligent use of materials around its edge and for its lining: the bright blue colour with which many pools are tiled or painted looks fine in the intense sun of southern California or the Algarve, but is quite out of character with the English countryside. The paved area around a pool should be generous, and should have a non-slip finish (both brick and textured concrete are suitable for this). If you then break the outline of the surround by planting, the whole complex becomes more integrated and less of an imposition; and the planting will also screen the pool somewhat in winter. While the best pools have their edging at ground level, you may decide to save a little on the cost of excavation and have a raised edge, which will need a certain amount of disguise in the form of shaping, retaining walls and decking. Some pools may have to be substantially raised because the local water table is high: this is structurally possible, but expensive.

The types of pool available on the market include poured concrete, concrete blockwork, prefabricated panels and fibreglass. Manufacturers tend to offer predetermined shapes, but it costs little more to design your own. Both types of concrete construction are used to produce standard, fully excavated pools. Prefabricated panels of steel on timber, fixed together *in situ*, can be used to make pools that stand on the surface of the ground, requiring no excavating: these are usually fairly shallow, which makes them particularly suitable for children. Fibreglass pools are restricted in size and shape by the moulding process used in their making.

In our wretched climate it would make very good sense to cover the pool for winter use – if not summer too – by some form of roofing. Plastic bubbles are available which are kept aloft by a wind pump and which cover a pool admirably, but they look somewhat incongruous, though it is arguable that if they are only used during the winter months the effect on your private landscape is of no consequence. You can also get frames with fibreglass infill panels, but it is not easy to engineer the span across the pool and its surround. A variety of more conventional structures will do the job admirably. You can choose whether or not to have a translucent roof, and, depending on the character of any neighbouring building, and your own taste, the pool building might be severe and modern, or it might take the form of an orangery or a large conservatory.

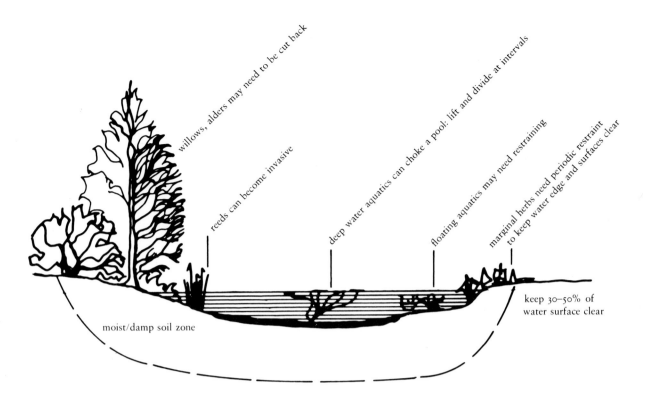

willows, alders may need to be cut back

reeds can become invasive

deep water aquatics can choke a pool: lift and divide at intervals

floating aquatics may need restraining

marginal herbs need periodic restraint to keep water edge and surfaces clear

keep 30–50% of water surface clear

moist/damp soil zone

Aspects of the maintenance of a natural pool

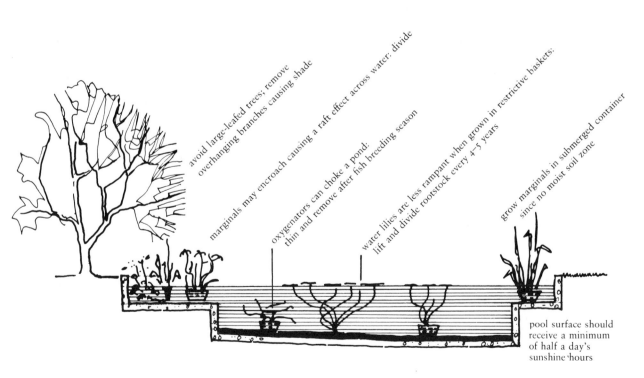

avoid large-leafed trees; remove overhanging branches causing shade

marginals may encroach causing a raft effect across water: divide

oxygenators can choke a pond: thin and remove after fish breeding season

water lilies are less rampant when grown in restrictive baskets: lift and divide rootstock every 4–5 years

grow marginals in submerged container since no moist soil zone

pool surface should receive a minimum of half a day's sunshine hours

Aspects of the maintenance of a constructed pool

above An informal West
Country swimming pool very
beautifully designed by Julian
Cooper. The edging detail is
particularly sensitive, while the
bold rock groups bring the
vigour of the house to the
pool's edge.

left The geometrical swimming
pool at St Ann's Hill (see p.49)
was devised by Christopher
Tunnard to curve round an old
clump of *Rhododendron
ponticum*.

The reconciliation of a modern swimming pool with a period house

The design for this Surrey pool is an attempt to harmonize modern summer living in the garden with the background of a Queen Anne house. There was also a need to give some logic to a gravel forecourt which connects a garage block with the rear access to the house.

The pool surround was sunk 300 mm. below the normal terrace level to provide shelter when in the pool and when sunbathing (9). The paving is of squared brick tiles. Paving connecting the house and sunken area made use of existing larger slabs on site and gravel which surrounded the east end of the house. With planting, this combination makes a focal point of a sundial (17) when seen from the main reception room – for pools, even when not lined in blue, are not the prettiest things through the winter months. A stepped concrete block wall, coloured to match the house, screens and shelters the pool from the forecourt area. A bench seat is sited in the south-facing corner (12). Mixed planting softens the wall pattern when seen from the garage forecourt on the other side.

1 main reception room
2 study window
3 rear access to house
4 solid timber gate through concrete block wall
5 swimming pool
6 pool plant and changing space
7 existing hard standing
8 garaging
9 step-up surrounding pool
10 white bench seat
11 mixed planting and climbers
12 built-in timber bench seat
13 sunbathing area
14 gravel areas
15 tubs for bulbs and annuals
16 clipped box with annuals
17 sundial
18 gravel forecourt

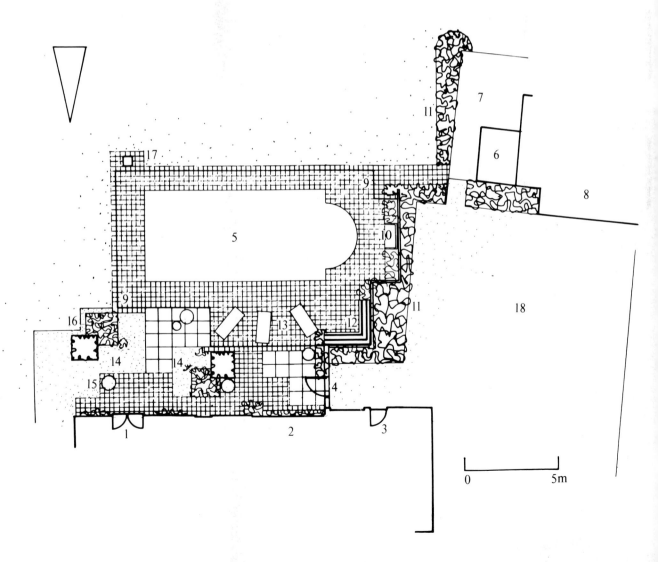

0   5m

opposite This pool is deliberately placed at a lower level than the garden, which is independent in pattern and edged by a balustrade. This means that throughout winter, when the pool might be empty, it can be ignored.

above An informal pool, with surrounding brick terrace, sits beautifully in the landscape of the Surrey hills. Like the pools on p.192, it was designed (by Michael Newberry) to fit into a particular site. Too often an abstract shape is selected for no apparent reason.

right Wide terrace areas next to the pool allow for the clutter of living out.

Some Thoughts on Garden Restoration

Much of what has been said so far is applicable to anyone restoring a garden, but there are other questions to be considered as well. To what period are you seeking to return? Is your aim to be historically accurate, or only to recapture a general mood? It is expensive in both time and money to restore a period piece totally, since we have moved on in the materials available and in the techniques used. For a re-creation you need not be so precise.

There are various schools of thought on the advisability of trying to put the clock back totally. Much of the charm of the English townscape and landscape lies in the mixture of styles, blended over the years. The immaculate period gardens of certain great country houses were not intended to accommodate the masses who now invade their original privacy, needing seating, picnic places, and ample hard surfacing if they are to enjoy the area in wet weather. And it is something of an uphill task to maintain, with expert labour, a planting idiom which is now obsolete. Nevertheless, there are situations which call for total restoration, and superbly successful examples can be seen – at Ham House near London and Plas Newydd on Anglesey, for instance, both due to the National Trust, or the Queen's House at Kew, restored by the Department of the Environment.

Once the decision has been made to carry out a full restoration, research the history of the garden thoroughly. Greater houses will be fairly well documented in local libraries, but it is worth hunting further in specialist topographical bookshops. With luck you may find an old print or plan showing your garden, or at least a portion of it, and you may even find bills for plants supplied and for work completed. Failing any specific information, find out what would be suitable for the period of your house, and use as your model any other layout sited as close as possible to your own. For gardeners were not great travellers in the main, and like us they would have been influenced by what was around them. Above all else, try to put yourself in the shoes of the original owner and work through his or her eyes.

For advice on period planting, contact the Tradescant Trust Museum of Garden History, St Mary-at-Lambeth, London S.E.1. The Garden History Society is prepared to research and advise on truly historic gardens, and has regular and informative literature for members. Contact the Hon. Membership Secretary, P.O. Box 10, Dorking, Surrey. Individual counties have their own Restoration Societies, which are researching and listing noteworthy gardens within their region. They may be contacted through the Garden History Society. Any grant aid for genuine restoration work would come from them or, in the case of parks which make a contribution to the amenity of the countryside, from the Countryside Commission. Finally, you might also contact the National Council for the Preservation of Plants and Gardens, which is based at the Royal Horticultural Society garden, Wisley, nr. Ripley, Surrey.

FORMAL GARDENS

The scale of formal gardens varies enormously, from small medieval gardens of herbs through Tudor layouts and the great tracts of intricate patterns seen in the early eighteenth-century views of Jan Kip to nineteenth-century Italianate schemes. The chances are that any restoration of the formal kind will be on a small scale, since the labour to maintain anything larger is prohibitive for a private owner.

Such a restoration will take one of two forms: redesigning and planting to plan on a freshly cleared area, or cutting away to reveal an original scheme. Where that scheme relied on planting, little will be apparent; but a structure, a sundial, or the pattern of earlier paths may tell something of the story, blurred by subsequent layers of development.

Many of our older formal gardens which escaped the eighteenth-century 'improvers' were revamped in the nineteenth century, and the scale of that planting will have outgrown the initial intention. Much of it, too, will be inappropriate. Take out or fell what does not belong to the original period, and cut back any hedges – which should be box or yew – to an acceptable size. The National Trust have made some bold cutbacks (literally) in their formal hedging, reducing a 7 m. wide overgrown hedge right back to the trunk. While the result looks alarming at first, after a few years a neat tight green hedge has regenerated that is in character with the original design. Such an undertaking calls for great courage and patience, but if the alternative is to grub out the overgrown specimens and buy new hedging, it will be seen that economics dictate the former course.

Box hedging is less successfully cut back than yew, since its shaping, however small, calls for the strength of new plants. It is often difficult to obtain in any quantity, and with some forethought one can propagate one's own.

Get the layout established with pegs and strings first, then recreate the paths, using any surviving original material. If there is not enough, you might find some elsewhere on the site when excavating for a drive, service run or foundations. Failing that, the wanted material might be found somewhere else in the neighbourhood, for transport was expensive and materials were usually of local origin: try such places as builder's yards and local sales. If you cannot find the old brick or stone that you want, you will have to use a modern equivalent or else another medium incorporating the original. The result will be a pastiche rather than a full restoration, but it may be perfectly acceptable.

Once the pattern has been set, it is time to think of infilling the beds. Many old formal gardens made use for colour not of flowers but of coloured grits. Herbs as an infill are sometimes suggested, but anyone who has grown them for culinary use knows that many are extremely invasive and rampant. Lavender, rosemary and santolina can be clipped, it is true – but a herb garden as such needs far greater variety. Where planting is desirable within your bedded areas, research will show you that the range of plants available at the time you are aiming for was probably extremely limited. You may well have to accept modern forms of the plants, for while various bodies have been concerned to establish the original forms of our current species, the results are not commercially available.

Stages in the thinning and renovation of a yew hedge:
1 the overgrown hedge, reducing path width and smothering border plants
2 one side cut back hard to main trunk. Follow with organic fertilizer and mulch
3 repeat the process on the other side one or two years later
4 the hedge after four or five years, restored to its original dimensions

197

When it comes to larger plants, trained topiary specimens can be bought, though they are mostly importations from the Continent. Trees trained or pleached to form shaded walks will need to be started from scratch (see p. 128). Hornbeam was used in the earliest gardens, beech not until the seventeenth century. Fruit trees trained as fans or espaliered are probably of late sixteenth- or early seventeenth-century French origin. Those flowery tunnels composed of fruit trees, wisteria or laburnum trained across expensive metal arches are Victorian features which demand a high degree of maintenance.

Lastly, the furnishings. The form and detailing of your house may give the key to the ornamentation of the garden. Antique finials, urns and vases of lead or stone can still be had, at a price, and extremely good copies are also available made of reconstituted stone, which is soon mellowed by weathering (encouraged by painting with liquid dung or milk). Decorative garden seats seem not to have appeared until quite late. Before that, benches made of logs, or constructed of sawn timber filled with earth and 'upholstered' with herbs, were more usual. Medieval gardens did not contain Gothic seats like those delightful Victorian creations of cast iron!

Another type of formal garden is the traditional walled one, which was to be found at almost any country house and at many farmhouses too, usually for the growing of fruit, vegetables and flowers for cutting. Early gardens were walled for shelter, and to keep vermin at bay; later in the eighteenth century walls concealed utilitarian cultivation from a contrived pastoral landscape; and in the nineteenth century horticulturists exploited their possibilities to the full, even heating the walls to encourage out-of-season exotic fruit.

The layout of such gardens was usually simple: paths traversed the area at right angles, and in the middle there might be a circular pool, originally for carp. The central paths were flanked by borders of flowers, backed after the seventeenth century by trained fruit trees. Three of the four quarters of the garden were used for standard crop rotations, while the fourth would contain soft fruit in cages or specialist crops such as asparagus and sea kale. A further path ran round the perimeter walls to service the fruit trees trained on them. Starting in the eighteenth century, the warmer of the walls had glasshouses built against them for the growing of more exotic fruit. Next to the greenhouses there was often a potting shed, backed by a bothy in which the young apprentice gardeners lived. Also as part of the walled garden complex there would be stove houses and propagating ranges serviced by glass frames.

The demise of these walled gardens came about through a shortage of labour and a lack of informed knowledge about their management. The walls and structures of many still remain intact, though the majority are half used at best. To recreate such a garden would be a monumental task, and its upkeep a further one, but it is possible to modify the original scheme, for instance by greatly reducing the area of intensive vegetable production and increasing the area for soft fruit. There is, however, one further problem: unless the household the garden serves is enormous, or there is a commercial outlet for its produce, the sheer volume of fruit and vegetables could be an embarrassment.

To help evoke the period feel, consider incorporating within your formal layout a dovecote for ornamental pigeons or doves (not on the scale of historic dovecotes, which housed the landowner's winter diet), and some beehives.

opposite The formal garden at Canons Ashby, Northampton- shire, on its way to recovery. The stepped and compartmented layout, designed about 1710, is shown as illustrated by Inigo Triggs in his *Formal Gardens in England and Scotland* (1902).

The upper photograph shows the view from the house along the axis to the 'fruit garden' in 1980, when the garden was both bare and overgrown. The lower photograph shows the same scene in 1983, after some two years' work by the National Trust. The yews are being re- trained; beds can eventually be re-created with permanent planting rather than bedding-out. The lower level is again to be largely an orchard

THE LANDSCAPED PARK

The restoration of an idealized park-type landscape, whatever its scale, could become a mammoth operation, for the chief effect is provided by tree planting – and what with the natural aging of the trees, and the ravages of Dutch elm disease, many eighteenth-century parks look very sad indeed. Where the planting has not deteriorated too far, however, it is possible over a period of five years or so to bring even a reduced part of such a park back to life.

Many parks are as well documented as the houses which they surround, and their plans may appear in the records of the local authority, or in books (for instance biographies of famous inhabitants of the house). Few modern owners, however, would aspire to – or indeed wish to – return such an estate to its pristine condition, but some of the original quality might be recaptured by clearing scrub and such intruders as groups of rhododendrons taking over where they were never intended; and if you are not prepared to fell and replant large areas, you can at least selectively remove specimens that are decayed and interplant with younger trees, which may, on the periphery at least, be more up-to-date (and perhaps faster-growing) species than the fairly small range of long-established trees used by the great 'improvers'. But do not let the overall effect appear merely decorative.

From the famous 'Red Books' in which Humphry Repton used flaps to illustrate estates before and after his improvements, one can see that planting was by no means all that went to making a landscaped park: streams were dammed to form lakes, and the surrounding landform shaped to hold them. Buildings or statuary were erected at focal points within the layout to enhance the picturesque effect of the composition.

A major undertaking in restoring this type of landscape is often the rehabilitation of the lake. A build-up of silt is the common problem, combined with excessive growth of vegetation and marginal reeds. Access may be difficult, and it will probably be necessary to clear or at least thin the surrounding banks before starting. If the stretch of water is narrow enough and access is adequate, a lake can be cleared by using a drag line manipulated from the banks. If not . . . handcutting of reeds from a boat is a slow process, and only relieves the problem for a short period: the real solution is dredging or excavation, to remove roots and deepen the water to discourage growth.

Silt is a soft organic mud deposit which both clouds the water and reduces its depth. Its removal is a tedious and expensive business, to be undertaken by specialist firms. The lake is first drained and the silt allowed to dry out. This process can be assisted by hand-ditching, though this is never a pleasant operation; the mud continuously flows back into the trench, so the cuts should at first be shallow, and gradually deepened as the area drains. The excavation work itself is done by bulldozers (which will need an access ramp), and it is normal practice for them to take out more than just the mud, deepening the pond by removing a further 150 mm. of native soil.

The disposal of the cleared mud is your next problem, for it is not readily usable on agricultural land when freshly dug. Cured for a year and mixed with sharp sand – with lime added to correct excess acidity when you have checked its pH value – it makes an excellent topsoil.

opposite Work in progress to restore eighteenth-century parkland at Hatfield Peverel, Essex. The owners found the original design of 1765, by the landscape gardener Richard Woods, in the county record office. They set to work to clear later scrub and clean out the lake (top, in the plan), and will eventually replant the layout with species known to have been available in the eighteenth century.

The photographs show part of the land before, during and after clearing. The subtly moulded landscape reflects Woods's advice to his workmen at another estate, Cusworth in Yorkshire, to 'use all your enginenowitty to give the ground as much variety and life as possible by rowling and waveing it about . . .'

201

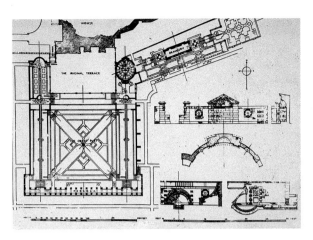

Hestercombe, at Taunton in Somerset, was planted up by Gertrude Jekyll to Lutyens's plan (*above*). So far as possible, her planting has been faithfully restored by the Somerset Fire Brigade.

opposite Mixed borders below the original terrace have been replanted with a predominance of grey foliage material and white flowers. Note the bold masses of individual species.

right Lutyens's water channels on either side of the Great Plat (*below*) are enclosed by fine borders.

below The Great Plat, a sort of parterre planted with roses, to be seen from surrounding walks, and a magnificent pergola in oak overlooking the surrounding countryside on the other side.

The draining and excavation will have exposed the banks, which should be examined. Any that have eroded may be consolidated with excavated earth. Now too is the time to reinstate any tiled edgings which have rotted.

VICTORIAN AND EDWARDIAN GARDENS

After the landscape movement came something of a reaction: fired with enthusiasm by the great variety of plants being brought back from all parts of the world, gardeners became plantsmen, and their gardens were conceived as collections of specimens. There has been some debate as to whether plant collections of this type can be called 'historic' for purposes of restoration, since their design is not their primary feature; but they cannot be overlooked, for the introduction of new ranges of plants from abroad has been one of the major formative influences in the development of garden style. Original plants surviving in such gardens are likely to be unusual, and should at all costs be safeguarded, for their replacement might be difficult.

As the century progressed, a number of designers whose techniques are well documented worked in the domestic field. They include William Andrews Nesfield, William Robinson and Gertrude Jekyll, Harold Peto, Thomas Mawson and Percy Cane. The work of certain nursery firms was also distinctive, among them J. Cheal and Son of Crawley in Surrey, George G. Whitelegg of Sevenoaks in Kent, Harry Veitch and Sons of Chelsea, London, and William Wood and Sons of Taplow, Buckinghamshire. It should be possible to find illustrations of their work, for instance in old *Country Life* magazines, which would give you an idea of the original effect of their gardens.

Within these larger layouts were areas of specific interest, such as water gardens and rock or alpine gardens – the latter a new development in the history of gardening, posing its own problems for the restorer. Rockeries are essentially reconstructions of natural outcrops, many of them made from massive boulders shipped half way across the country. A firm which specialized in these often magnificent constructions was Gavin Jones of Letchworth, Hertfordshire, whose exhibits were a highlight of the Chelsea Flower Show. Rockeries were expensive to maintain even at the time, and when left unattended soon become enveloped in moss, weeds and grass. Trees initially planted as a background have outgrown that use and now cast the rockery in shade. They should be cut back to allow in air and sunlight, for most alpine plants need an open airy situation. The cleaning of what can sometimes be miniature mountain ranges is a painstaking job, but once cleared they can appear spectacular if replanted with more permanent woody species of shrub or low-growing conifers.

Work has recently been done on restoring some of the gardens designed by Lutyens and planted out by Gertrude Jekyll. Detailed plans of their semi-formal layouts survive, and from them it has been found that many of the plant varieties originally used are not now readily available. The task is not impossible, however, and an exemplary restoration using the correct plants can be seen at Hestercombe in Somerset.

Beyond the Pale 14

This chapter is dedicated to those with a field or two, or a paddock, beyond the perimeter of the area they designate as garden. One hundred years ago it might have been called a small estate; today it is land for ponies, for a few head of cattle, perhaps a decoy pond or a small game covert, and trees on a scale you could not afford in the garden itself.

WOODLANDS AND SHELTER BELTS

Landowners have been active for over two hundred years in planting and tending their trees for shelter. They have thrown a network of shelter belts over many of our bleaker uplands, enabling profitable stock-raising and arable farming to be carried on at heights unthinkable in a treeless landscape, and across the lowland counties innumerable hedgerow trees, linked to small woodlands, provide another shelter pattern. Estate owners have also put to good use for forestry the winding glens, cloughs and dingles that thread the uplands of Scotland, northern England and Wales. Under trees, such rough and often steep land can give both a timber crop and shelter, while soil erosion and silting of the streams is checked. Game too is fostered by a well-managed woodland.

Woodlands

Before 1919, when the Forestry Commission was formed, nearly all the woodlands in Britain were privately owned. Over half still are, giving woodland owners an important share of the forestry industry: indeed, because the indirect advantages of scenery, shelter and sport are so widely appreciated, private woodlands often occupy rather better land than is available to the Forestry Commission, and have an accordingly higher rate of timber production. They form our main source of the hardwoods oak, ash, elm, beech and sycamore, and also provide much good Scots pine, larch and spruce. This happy situation is the result of decades of conscious management.

During the First World War much of the better timber was felled, and between the wars replanting did little more than keep pace with demand. The Second World War used up many of the surviving stands. The Forestry Commission's financial and technical help to private owners gained momentum with the launching in 1947 of the Dedication Scheme, under which owners, in return for financial assistance, covenant to use their woodlands for timber production and manage them according to an approved Plan of Operation. Owners whose woodlands are too small or too scattered to fit into this scheme may receive a Small Woods planting grant. Besides giving financial aid, the Commission has helped in the formation of forestry co-operatives and has made available to owners the results of its research and

a Wattle hurdles stop sheep from rubbing themselves against newly planted trees.
b Traditional cleft oak or chestnut fencing, mortice-jointed with hardwood verticals.
c Sawn softwood horizontals fixed to hardwood verticals. Metal link netting is lamb- (or dog-) proof.
d A tree guard high enough to prevent cattle, horses or deer from browsing, and tough enough to withstand their efforts to do so!

experience. Because trees take so long to mature, special arrangements apply for income tax and estate duty, and also for Selective Employment and Capital Gains taxes, all of which helps to promote long-term investment.

Complementary to this encouragement of planting there is control of felling. Originally a wartime measure, felling by licence continued under the Forestry Act (1967), which was designed to conserve our limited stocks of growing timber. (On Dedicated estates, control is through the Plan of Operation.) This ensures the replacement of felled woodland, because replanting conditions are attached to licences whenever it is desirable and practical for the land to be restocked.

The interests of private owners are looked after by the Timber Growers' Association in England and Wales, and by the Scottish Woodland Owners' Association. For more information, see *Grants for Woodland Owners*, published by the Forestry Commission (25 Savile Row, London W.1).

Shelter belts

Most estate plantations were established between 1760 and 1820, during the great landscape movement. Such planting continued rather longer in Scotland, stimulated by the introduction of conifers from North America: not only was the treeless landscape of southern Scotland transformed into one of wood-lands (who, looking now at the region celebrated by Sir Walter Scott, would recognize the 'cold, naked country of Tweeddale' that depressed a traveller in 1746?), but many farms colonized the wet and windswept moors, protected by shelter belts whose mature presence is a feature of the scenery today – as are the rows of Scots pine in the windy East Anglian Breckland. Shelter belts on this scale do not affect the climate, as huge forests do, but their significance for farm management was great, and their effects are well shown by land which has enjoyed wind protection for over a hundred years.

A comparatively new landscape pattern of forestry and shelter belts in the Scottish Border country. Planting has regard to contours, to avoid a too obviously man-made look.

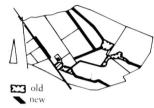

Linking isolated blocks and clumps by new shelter belts increases overall shelter.

In many areas, the agricultural depression of the late nineteenth and early twentieth centuries led to the neglect of woodland and shelter belt planting, and this has sometimes been compounded by the more recent grubbing up of hedgerows, which can result in wind-erosion. The gains from planting belts of trees are, as we have seen, not only the shelter itself, but possibly timber and game. Many now mature shelter belts, carefully built up with tall trees for wind protection and ground cover to prevent wind sweeping round the trunks, owe their composition and frequently their efficiency to the influence of a gamekeeper; and narrower windbreaks, though little use for nesting, make excellent rises for game. A final point in favour of such planting is more general: trees and wildlife habitats are constantly being lost to urban development, and one might do what one can to redress the balance. An obvious deterrent to planting on any scale is the sacrifice of arable or grazing land, but seen in a longer perspective this is outweighed by the gains; and as long as land prices continue to rise, permanent improvements must be a safe investment.

While being functional a shelter belt may still be ornamental, for there is a great variety of trees to choose from, the choice narrowing only as the situation becomes higher or more exposed to the sea, or the soil poorer. (In such conditions you will seldom get timber of any value, but the shelter itself is all the more valuable.) As was the rule for windbreaks, be guided by what grows naturally in the surrounding country. Hardwood forest is the natural climax vegetation of most of the British Isles, but among evergreens the Scots pine, yew and juniper are indigenous: there is thus a place for both types of tree, the emphasis varying according to location and site. Broad-leaved trees, particularly those that yield good timber, are mainly suited to deeper and more fertile lowland soils and lower hill slopes. When cut back they throw up coppice shoots, allowing their density to be regulated and giving better shelter near the ground. A drawback is that they lose their leaves in winter, making them less protective then; but the bare branches allow the wet ground below them to dry out more quickly in spring. Conifers, on the other hand, seem generally more tolerant of exposed hill ground and its poorer, more acid soil (though there are exceptions). Shelter belts made up entirely of conifers of the same age and height, while excessively dense in youth, eventually thin out up the stems and are difficult to regenerate without heavy felling. A mixture would therefore seem best – hardy, wind-firm, broad-leaved species adding strength and stability and forming a background to later generations of shelter trees, and conifers for better winter protection.

As with garden windbreaks, think carefully of your aim before starting to plant: it is pointless to choose major forest trees for cramped quarters, where less lofty species would grow as quickly and last longer. Check the tolerance of your proposed species to such things as wind, frost, salt spray and general exposure, and their requirements as to soil type and drainage. Rate of growth will be important, too, if you are interested in the future value of the trees or their thinnings for timber.

For lists of native trees, see p.222, and for species suitable for windbreak and shelter belt planting, see pp.224–25.

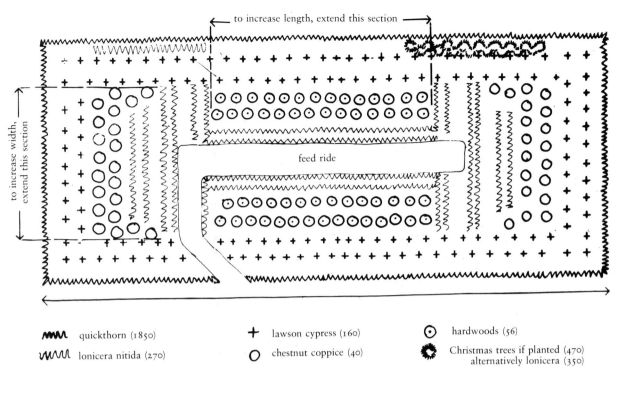

An ideal plan for a game
spinney

ENCOURAGING GAME

To create a game spinney

Game birds such as pheasants and partridges have been under threat from a number of the techniques of modern farming: the removal of hedgerows, which provided their natural habitat; strip grazing, where feeding stock are concentrated and trample nests; and lethal burning of stubble and straw after the harvest. Yet all is not lost, for our landscape is increasingly being replanned to accommodate larger fields punctuated by shelter belts, and odd corners are being converted into coverts for wildlife. This is possible on a smaller scale as well, and anyone with up to an acre of land to spare might consider using part of it as a game spinney, where birds may be nested, reared and held in bitter weather, and which in the long term will yield commercially valuable timber.

The plan shown here represents just half an acre, about 30 × 76 m. It could be extended in length and/or breadth to suit individual sites. The spinney can provide nesting cover suitable for both pheasants and partridges, and also, in the central area, within a shelter belt of Lawson cypress, a release pen for two to three hundred young pheasants, which can be freed for a shoot by rolling up the bottom 460 mm. of the netting. In that event gates must be allowed at both ends, giving access for beaters and allowing drives all ways. If the adjoining ground is sown with a cover crop such as kale or mustard, breed birds may be run from the spinney into it, and then flushed from it, for it is generally easier to show the birds well from woodland. Towards the end of the shooting season, the spinney will provide good warm holding cover, even when the adjoining fields are ploughed, for the numbers of birds will by then be reduced.

It is essential to understand the principles of planting such a spinney, and where for cultural reasons it is necessary to use different trees and shrubs from those suggested, make sure that the alterations will serve the same purpose.

The spinney in the plan is surrounded by a hedge of *Lonicera nitida*, a plant rarely eaten by rabbits or hares, which is readily available, provides ground shelter for birds, and is not invasive. Within the hedge is an outer row of trees, which should be of medium size and fairly slow-growing, not affording too much shade to the surrounding land and yet berrying well as pheasant food. Within these trees, in turn, are hardwood species which are also selected for their value as sources of food – oak and beech and sweet chestnut (where suitable) for long-term returns, and alder and birch for more rapid growth. Between the lines of trees three rows of Jerusalem artichokes are planted to provide cover for birds. These should be at least 1.5 m. apart, and may be planted mechanically in a trench. When after two or three seasons they have become too dense and the crops too low, it is best to spin them out mechanically and replant. The spaces between the rows are grassed over as marginal nesting cover for both pheasant and partridge. The grass may be cut each year to keep down the weeds.

The same planting scheme can be used for odd corners left over in arable farming, and it will also work on stock land, though some fencing will then be necessary. It can obviously double as a shelter belt or a windbreak where necessary, with only some slight modification of the tree species within its layout. Such a spinney needs informed management, but once the system is understood this should not be excessive.

Rising areas: bad, better, and best

To create a flight pond for duck

More than just a sheet of water is needed to keep ducks happy, for they also want nesting and brood cover, food supplies, safe resting areas, and so on. Further, the habitat and the ducks themselves have to be protected and managed rather than left entirely to nature, if the birds are to multiply and produce a shooting surplus. As with the practical management of pheasants and partridges, this is a specialized subject on which you will need separate information.

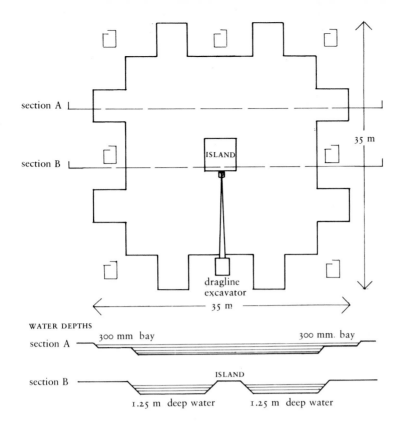

section A

section B ISLAND

35 m

dragline
excavator

35 m

WATER DEPTHS

300 mm bay   300 mm. bay
section A

ISLAND
section B

1.25 m deep water   1.25 m deep water

Schematic layout for a
wildfowl breeding and
flight pond

To attract ducks, your pond will need to be sited near an existing waterfowl
feeding or roosting area, or a flight path – a route, often following the course
of a river, along which ducks fly sometimes quite considerable distances at
dusk to feeding areas, returning to their resting areas at dawn. With careful
management birds can be lured a long way from their previous haunts. If you
have an old farm pond which ducks are seen to visit you can feed and develop
it. Otherwise, it is easy enough to create a pond on the lines already described
in Chapter 12. A quiet location screened by mature trees is ideal, for you want
some protection from wind and disturbance, but not absolute shelter, for with
a slight circulation of air ice is less likely to form in winter.

The pond itself should have a low central island, kept clear of growth,
which the ducks use for loafing, sleeping or preening, safe from predators
except when the water is frozen over. Around the edge are bays planted with
reeds and sedges to create private brood territories for breeding, and between
the bays are areas to be used for hides. The depth required will depend on the
species of duck that you expect to attract: 150 mm. is enough for mallard and
teal, but diving ducks need considerably more. The pool may be excavated
mechanically and lined throughout with 1,000 g. polythene or butyl sheeting
(the edges buried at least 1 m. beneath the banks, so that ducks will not expose
them by their dibbling around the shore); or you might be able to excavate
down to the water table, or – if the subsoil is impervious – create a pool by
damming and flooding. The accompanying diagram can of course be
considerably modified to suit particular locations, eliminating bays to
accommodate large trees or land irregularities, for instance, but the principle
will remain the same.

The excavated soil can be used to help shelter the pond, and might be planted as a wind baffle. In choosing species for the banks, be guided by what grows along local watercourses. Different plants will have different uses in a flight pond – providing food directly by their seeds, or indirectly from the animals that live on them; affording cover in winter or only in summer, sheltering broods or moulting birds. All will help prevent bank erosion. For the types of native plants that would be suitable, see pp.185 and 189.

GRAZING YOUR LAND

For those with large areas of grass, the odd piece of paddock or unkempt orchard, the relentless necessity to keep the grass mown, even if only rough cut, often seems a pointless exercise; and yet one cannot let one's property go literally to seed.

If such a piece of ground adjoins a field you own, you might adjust the boundary to allow it to be grazed along with the field. Failing that, you might come to an arrangement with the neighbouring farmer to graze it; but while you may charge for grazing rights, before the cash tills start tinkling in your mind's ear remember that you will probably be expected to maintain the boundaries of the land. You are then exchanging one problem for another. A better arrangement, on a more friendly basis, would be to allow the farmer access for a legally stated number of days in the year, rent free, in return for which he maintains the boundaries. Have a word with your solicitor before embarking on such a project, and have a simple document drawn up to formalize matters.

Other possibilities include grazing the field with your own sheep or beef cattle (of which the management can be contracted out if you choose), or on a smaller scale getting a donkey, some geese, or a goat or two to keep the grass down. The geese and the goats might be productive, too. But before launching out, think long and hard and read up as much as you can on the care that would be needed, for livestock are undoubtedly a tie, and can prove enormously expensive and worrying if you cannot cope.

Donkeys

The dear old donkey is perhaps one of the easiest animals to keep. Donkeys are extremely economical and make very intelligent pets – if you can stand the noise. It is perhaps kinder to keep a couple of animals, each of which will need half an acre of pasture, with hay and greenstuff in winter supplemented by a handful of concentrate per day. They require no shoeing, though they must be groomed, and can live outside the whole year round, needing only a covered shelter open at one side to protect them from the worst weather.

Goats

Unlike donkeys, goats cannot be left untended even for a day, and must have cover every night and during bad weather. They require more land than donkeys, too, about $\frac{2}{3}$ acre each, and if you want a regular supply of milk you will need two nannies, which are mated in alternate years and then yield milk uninterruptedly for two years after kidding, at an average rate of about three pints a day each.

Goats are browsers, and will eat clean rough stuff that cows would not touch. If your boundaries are very stock-proof you can allow your goats free range; otherwise they may be tethered, but they then need to be moved at least twice a day. In their pens they should not be tied up, and horned specimens should not be penned together.

A code of practice for the keeping of goats has been drawn up by the British Goat Society (Rougham, Bury St Edmunds, Suffolk), who should be approached for detailed guidance on maintenance, on the type of breed common in your locality, and on the proximity of a suitable breeding buck or billy. Possible breeds include the British Toggenberg, British Alpine, British Saanen and Anglo-Nubian.

Geese

If plenty of grazing is available, geese are one of the cheapest poultry birds to keep: they will thrive on rough grass, weeds and garden stuff, with one meal a day of scraps and mash to improve egg production. They live considerably longer than most poultry, and keep up the same rate of egg and gosling production throughout their lives. Geese are easy to house and may be kept in a rough open-fronted structure of turf sods roofed with thatch; indeed, if there is no danger of predators, they need no shelter at all. They do not need water in which to swim, but they must have adequate drinking water at all times. Geese kept in an open situation are liable to stretch their wings in a high wind and take off: to prevent this, clip the flight feathers on one wing from time to time with shears.

A breeding pen of three geese and one gander will produce about 100 eggs in a year. A hen will hatch about 4 goose eggs, but a goose will sit on 13 or 14. Goslings need cossetting with chopped hardboiled eggs and meal for three or four days before going on to more adult feeding.

Rare breeds

In the late eighteenth and early nineteenth centuries parks were enlivened by grazing herds of deer. Today, you might consider using a rare breed of cattle or sheep – as long as you are prepared to look after the animals, of course. You would not only be turning your grass into some profit, in the form of beef or milk, lamb and wool, but also helping to perpetuate some of our fast-disappearing variety of breeds. For as a particular vegetation, crop, and type of building developed according to a particular location, so the early farming improvers bred stock to suit a particular region as well. These specialized breeds of cattle have gradually been replaced by the ubiquitous Friesian, and a similar process has occurred with sheep. While the older breeds might not prove economic on a large scale, the smaller holding can help to ensure their survival and preserve their distinctive characteristics for future generations.

For information on the stock suitable for your area and the size of your holding, contact the Rare Breeds Survival Trust (4th Street, National Agricultural Centre, Kenilworth, Warwickshire).

above This timber loose-box stabling fits beautifully next to an old Welsh stone barn. *above right* Orchard grazing in Devon. A traditional stone wall and pier works well with a tough utilitarian metal gate, strong and high enough to withstand horse pressure.

Horses

Volumes are written on horse management, and this book can in no way describe the detailed day-to-day work which keeping a horse or pony entails, but some pointers can help you to decide whether your land and your talents are suitable.

Where you have a choice of location, horses prefer a good range, rather than a small field. Kept in a restricted space over a hot summer, they tend to come in for the winter season soft and fat. Horses are gregarious creatures, too, and prefer company: a donkey will do. The field should have good shade within it, and at least one spot, protected by a hedge on the windward side, where the horse can shelter from wind and rain during summer storms. Good fences are essential, preferably of the post-and-rail type, free from any loose strands of wire. Ensure that the field has no other hazards, such as old machinery which may have become hidden in long grass.

There must be a plentiful supply of fresh water in the field, for a horse will drink between six and ten gallons a day. A running stream with a gravel bottom, and a good approach to it, is ideal; ponds are generally not satisfactory, as they become stagnant. Most people will have to provide a trough which is kept filled by piped water. Site the trough on well-drained land, clear of trees, so the area does not become muddy and clogged with leaves. The container itself should be 1–2 m. long and 500 mm. deep. It can be filled by a tap, which should be at ground level, and the pipe leading to the tap should be fitted close to the side of the trough as anything that projects can be dangerous for the horse. Much the best way of keeping a trough filled is to fit an enclosed ballcock system at one end. The trough should be attended twice a day in frost or snow.

When it comes to housing your animal, whether you are proposing to build an individual loose box or a range of stabling, bear the following points in mind. Since frequent attention will be necessary in all weathers, day and night throughout the year, it is essential to have hard dry surfacing, preferably well lit. Access must be easy and turning space adequate for wheeled vehicles, such as a loose box or tractor and trailer. The structure should be sheltered as much as possible from severe prevailing winds, but not overshadowed, as it needs sunlight and the free circulation of air. If you are building a range of stabling, with tack room, store room, etc., a cluster or square formation looks well but increases the risk of contagion when any form of sickness is present.

The building itself should be of sound construction, with solid foundations, and fully damp-proofed. The floor, which should be raised above ground level, should be non-slippery and impervious to moisture, so that the horse does not feel a chill when it lies down. Ideal flooring materials are stable bricks or the composition called 'Tartan'. To ensure drainage, the floor should slope up slightly from front to rear of the stall or loose box. Any structure for a horse needs to be at least 4 m. high at the springing of the roof. In ground area, loose boxes for hunters should be no less than 3.5 × 4.25 m.; loose boxes for ponies no less than 3 × 3.5 m.; and stalls 1.6 × 3.3 m. from wall to heel post.

Whatever sort of stabling you propose, you will need a manure pit. If it is to be limited in size and close to the stable, it must be emptied frequently. If the manure is to be stacked and left to rot, the site should be well away from the stabling so that flies do not trouble the horses. Ideally you need three heaps: the oldest, well-rotted pile ready for the garden; a pile in the process of rotting away; and a pile in current use. Close pack the muck heap, beating it well down and squaring it off as you go to aid decomposition and heat generation, and inhibit flies.

Shavings, sawdust or peat moss used for bedding should be stacked separately, for although they make equally good compost they take longer to decompose.

Electric fencing

Electric fences can be a great help when animals are to be confined on a fairly temporary basis (when you do not want the trouble and expense of a permanent fence) or when an existing hedge is inadequate. They are light and easy to move, and use current only when an animal touches them. A six-volt motorcycle battery will power an unlimited length of fence for several months, or you can use mains electricity. Horses or cattle need only one wire to control them, pigs and sheep need two, and goats three, though the bottom one need not be electrified. Stock are made aware of the fence initially by baiting the wire with green fodder, so that on taking it they get a shock. As the current is only intermittent, at some forty impulses a minute, it does them no harm.

Maintenance and Protection

MAINTENANCE

Thanks to the taste for simplicity and naturalness, the modern country garden is considerably more labour-saving than its predecessors, but there are still regular jobs to be done, and they will be made easier not only by good machinery (of which more presently) but by good planning in your initial layout – in broad terms designing to suit the character of the site and any peculiarities it may have, and in detail eradicating small areas that cannot be mown or planted, paths that are too narrow, paving patterns that are too complicated, and so on.

A tightly designed complex will save time on all the necessary little trips for logs, for herbs or vegetables, and to the garage. The layout should be logically arranged, with those things most often needed closest to hand. Try always to simplify. Good paths are crucial, too: the extra expense of laying paths and paving to a high standard, using the best materials, well jointed and on sound foundations, will be repaid many times over. Get the falls right, so water runs off quickly to open ground where it should disappear, Or take the water to a drain run and soak away. (Icy or slippery paths in winter can be dangerous, particularly where they service a main entrance.) Where there are any changes in level, make them generous and not too steep. Consider carefully the junction between a step and the adjacent earth, for that too can be tricky. Provide adequate lighting for paths and working areas of the garden.

Moving outward to the soft landscape, do not over-reach yourself in areas which will need regular cultivation and/or mowing. Work out how much vegetable produce you will need, and don't grow any more than that: remember that when you have a main crop so does everyone else, and so do the shops. Maintain only the minimum of grass that demands a once-weekly cutting: allow some areas to become rough, and make a deliberate design juxtaposition between the two. Within mown areas, avoid introducing plants which you would have to navigate round. Contour the layout so that whatever kind of mower you use can be easily turned. It is worth laying paved edges, which simplify mowing and allow plants more freedom. Have a place for grass cuttings conveniently close.

Where you have grass banks, make their gradient both safe and manageable.

As an alternative to mown lawn, consider using areas of ground cover, or planting in gravel.

Do not be wooed into having too much 'decorative' garden, unless that sort of horticulture really interests you. Cut down on ornamental borders, particularly high-maintenance herbaceous ones. Plant wild hedges in preference to formal ones that need regular clipping, or choose shrubs that will keep their shape without too frequent attention.

216

Lastly, work with your site: grow only what likes your soil, and select species that are correct for the situation. Do not feel bound to 'garden' every inch, but allow some to become wild, planting there what grows naturally.

Most maintenance jobs in the garden can now be done by some form of machine. Many of these are highly dangerous, however: closely follow the manufacturer's instructions, dress sensibly (no bare feet when mowing lawns), and never entrust them to children or those infirm in any way.

Cultivators

With tines driven by rotary action, these machines cut into and mince up the soil, incorporating as they go any organic material on the surface. Models vary in power, in number of tines and in the width of the strip they cultivate. The strongest have power-driven tines, in front of or beneath the engine. Those with power-driven wheels, which have tines at the rear, are easier to operate and produce fine seedbeds, but do not dig so well. Even a small machine, whose tines go no deeper than hand cultivation, will ease the work of light digging and inter-row cultivation.

Some models can be fitted with attachments for row cropping that include hoeing blades, cultivating feet and tines for making furrows, and some will tow equipment such as tipping trucks, seed and fertilizer distributors and shredders for compost, turf, etc. A cultivator can also be used to produce the power for hedge trimmers and grass cutters.

Power mowers

Power mowers are of two distinct types, each of which has particular talents and gives a particular character to the grass it has cut. Cylinder mowers – like the old traditional hand-pushed variety – give a closer cut to the grass and leave a better finish, but will not cut anything longer than about 65 mm. Rotary mowers will cope with grass that is considerably longer, and powered side-wheel mowers are useful for really heavy work, such as clearing old orchards.

Cylinder mowers can be powered by petrol, by mains electricity, or by battery (usually with a built-in charger). Mains-powered models are inevitably restricted in range, so either of the other types has the advantage on more extensive ground. All three types have cutting widths of 300 mm. upwards, and all pick up the grass. To the larger machines it is possible to fix a ride-on attachment, which sits on an additional roller.

Rotary mowers, most of which are petrol-powered, vary from relatively light-weight machines, for lawn use, through to heavy-duty models capable of cutting tall, dense growth and weed. Some have a mulching device, which leaves the grass finely cut and gives a superior finish; coarser grass needs raking if it is not to become hay.

A variant on the rotary mower is the airborne mower, useful for problem banks, areas under low bushes, and damp or boggy ground where a wheeled machine would leave marks. Several sizes are available: the largest has a cutting width of 480 mm.

Moving up the scale of rotary mowers, the ride-on lawn tractor, a comparative newcomer, is a godsend for people with a lot of grass to cut. These invaluable little machines, which come in various horsepowers, have rubber wheels and are easy to manoeuvre. Some have a floating cutting head for use over uneven ground, devices are included for grass collection, and the tractors can also be used to roll or sweep the lawn, or to pull a small dumper truck. Models are available which have tiller blade attachments, grading blades and blades for snow removal. The permutations are legion, and the range on the market is steadily increasing.

For those with really large areas to mow, there is a minigang mower which has a cutting width of about 1.5 m.

Trimmers

Hand-operated trimmers are useful for edging lawns and working round the base of trees, and also for getting into awkward corners (which in a properly designed garden shouldn't exist!). More sophisticated models are now power-driven, and among these a really heavy-weight version exists for cutting brush. Such machines are ideal for clearing new sites that are not quite level and are too small for some of the rougher-cutting rotary mowers.

Leaf sweepers

Designed primarily for collecting fallen leaves in autumn, and invaluable to anyone with an abundance of trees, these machines can also be used to collect mowings left by a rotary grass cutter and to clear paths and drives. Rotary brushes sweep as the machine moves forward, and throw material into a container at the rear. Various widths are available.

Hedge trimmers

These come in a variety of types – powered by electricity or by petrol, with built-in motors, with leads, or worked off a mower or cultivator. For mature hedges, the longer the blade the better, though the machine will be heavier to manage. In general, be careful to choose a machine whose weight is comfortable for you, for as you get tired it could become highly dangerous.

Of the trimmers with integral motors, those powered by a battery are the lightest and easiest to use. Petrol-powered machines are heavier and more costly, but they are better for cutting in the rough, when the job is too long for a battery to cope and too far from a power point to use mains electricity.

Machines with an external source of power are all lighter in weight. Those run off the mains are fine unless you get careless with the flex. Trimmers operated from a mower or cultivator are powered by means of a drive shaft, available in lengths of about 3–5 m., which may be inconvenient if your hedge lies on the far side of a border or other planted area.

It is vital to realize that any of these machines will only *trim* a hedge, not give it the correct structure. To become impenetrable, a hedge needs to be properly laid.

Power saws

Chain saws, driven electrically or by two-stroke single-cylinder engines, take the hard work out of winter tree-clearing and logging, although all are fairly heavy to use. They are dangerous gadgets, to be kept well away from children.

Sprinklers

In this country there are not many areas, or indeed many summers, in which an irrigation system is warranted; but if you find that frequent summer watering is necessary, a permanent installation consisting of underground pipes connecting a number of sprinklers to the mains can save a great deal of time. Conventional types of sprinkler, or perforated hosepipe, can be used, and there is the sophisticated pop-up type, which rises from its mounting when the water pressure is turned on, and sinks down out of sight when it is turned off. All may be controlled by a time clock. Oscillating sprinklers are also available which work more simply from the water pressure of a connecting hose.

Sprayers

Syringes of all-brass construction, with easily cleaned, non-corroding plastic containers for the liquid, are excellent for general spraying. Some hand sprayers are pressurized by pumping before use, while others have to be activated continuously by a plunger or trigger. More elaborate ones have a constant double action, the spray being expelled when the plunger is pushed and when it is pulled. For any use more extensive than greenhouse or small-scale spraying, for instance for fruit trees, there are sprayers which are carried like a knapsack or are free-standing.

DEALING WITH PREDATORS

What is and what is not a predator will depend on what you grow in your garden. Considering my previous advice on cultivating plants to encourage birds and animals, the reader could be forgiven for thinking that I want to have my cake and to eat it – but even the most ardent conservationists will not want sparrows or finches to dig up their newly planted seeds, or the surviving plants stripped by rabbits or marauding woodpigeons. Nor do they wish jays to rip beans and peas from their pods, or blackbirds to eat ripe cherries and raspberries. It is also probably fair to assume that mice do not nibble the seedlings in their greenhouses, or rats make free with the grain stored in their barns. In many country areas, deer become a hazard in winter and will gladly make a meal of roses; sheep or the local dairy herd, if they can get in, will demolish herbaceous borders and wreak havoc on the lawn; grazing ponies may strip young trees, and goats or donkeys will eat almost anything, given half a chance. On all fronts, seemingly, the country gardener is threatened if he does not take measures to fend off these predators – though he has some friends, too, which are to be encouraged: the hedgehog, the frog, and the toad; and among insects the ladybird, hoverfly, lacewing, ichneumon fly, centipede (not millipede), and ground beetle.

The best way to protect at least the cultivated part of your garden is to fence it securely, though remember that a fence, like a chain, is no stronger than its weakest part. If you live in the middle of a wood and the odds seem too great, rethink the layout of your garden to reduce its cultivated area so that you can protect even a small part of it really thoroughly. Hosts of different bird-scarers and bits of thread hung with foil or rattling pins are altogether too nerve-racking. To deter marauders at your boundary, hedgerows should be kept close at their base by occasional laying. Fences need to be stout and of the correct height: a deer fence, for instance, needs to be 3 m. high!

Where rabbits abound, extremely firm measures are needed to keep them out. Ideally, your garden should be enclosed by galvanized mesh or netting of 25 mm. gauge, extending at least 1 m. above ground level and 150 mm. below to prevent tunnelling. A good wooden fence need have netting only at its foot: using a band of mesh 500 mm. wide, bury 150 mm. of it in the ground and staple the rest to the wood on the outside of the fence. To rabbit-proof a hedge, the mesh should be fixed independently on the inner (garden) side, with the top edge bent over outwards and fixed with brackets to prevent rabbits from scrambling over. It is also said that rabbits hate onions, and that a border of them or any other member of the onion family planted all round the area will keep them off.

Young trees are very susceptible to attack from predators, particularly specimen trees or groups in an open paddock or parkland, and fruit trees in an orchard. One way of protecting them is to use pieces of galvanized or plastic-coated wire mesh, 1.5 m. high by 760 mm. wide, rolled round the stem to form a cylinder 230–300 mm. in diameter and secured to the tree stakes by means of galvanized wire staples. Where several trees are planted together, it may be simpler or cheaper to put up a rabbit-proof fence round the whole group. If animals will be grazing in the area, a further protective guard is necessary to stop them stripping leaves or bark: use three stout posts to form a triangle, and fix stout horizontal rails to them. Metal guards are also available, some of them rather sophisticated and suburban in appearance, but including a good simple type of guard for more mature trees which comes in various sizes, 1–1.37 m. high and from 1.2 m. in diameter.

Despite good fencing, a gun may be the only way to deal with rabbits, rats and woodpigeons when they have become serious pests. Guns used are the air rifle (which is not always effective), the .22 rifle, and the double-barrelled 12-bore shotgun. No licence is needed for an air rifle on one's own property, but for a rifle or shotgun, no matter where it is to be used, a Firearms Certificate must be obtained from the local police. The bullet from a .22 is too dangerous used inside a mile range, leaving the shotgun, which for shooting in a garden can be the smaller .410 calibre, known as the 'four ten'. Killing pests is not a form of sport: sitting targets should be chosen, for to shoot a bird or animal in movement may mean wounding it so that it dies a lingering death elsewhere. Rabbits are elusive, dodging under the cover in the vegetable patch, but you are likely to catch them sitting still in the early morning or just before dusk.

Before undertaking any large-scale extermination of predators, you might check that you are not breaking any law – for our native vermin do have their role in the great ecological cycle. The following could all be helpful: the Royal Society for the Protection of Birds, the Council for Environmental Conservation, the Ministry of Agriculture, Fisheries and Food's Infestation Control Laboratory at Slough, local authority Environmental Health departments, Rentokil and the British Pest Control Association.

Tables

Native wild tree species

	site			soil				average ultimate height			features				
	wet	exposed	shady	light, dry	heavy	acid	alkaline	up to 5 m.	5–15 m.	over 15 m.	flowers	fruit/berries	autumn colour	evergreen	good for hedging
alder (Alnus glutinosa)	●						●		●						
ash (Fraxinus excelsior)	●	●		●	●					●					
aspen (Populus tremula)		●		●	●	●				●					
beech (Fagus sylvatica)				●		●	●			●			●		●
birch, downy (Betula pubescens)	●		●				●			●			●		
birch, silver (Betula pendula)			●	●		●				●			●		
cherry, bird (Prunus padus)	●					●	●		●		●	●			
cherrt, wild/gean (Prunus avium)					●	●			●		●	●	●		
crab apple (Malus sylvestris)				●	●		●		●		●				●
elm, wych (Ulmus glabra)			●		●	●	●			●					
hawthorn (Crataegus monogyna)		●		●	●	●	●	●			●	●	●		●
hazel (Corylus avellana)			●		●		●								
holly (Ilex aquifolium)				●	●	●	●		●		●	●		●	
hornbeam (Carpinus betulus)					●		●			●			●		●
lime, small-leafed (Tilia cordata)					●		●		●				●		
maple, field (Acer campestre)			●		●		●		●				●		
oak, common or pedunculate (Quercus robur)		●			●		●			●					
oak, sessile (Quercus petraea)		●						●							
pear, wild (Pyrus pyraster)				●	●				●		●				
pine, Scots (Pinus sylvestris)		●		●		●				●				●	
poplar, black (Populus nigra var. betulifolia)	●			●	●		●			●					●
rowan/mountain ash (Sorbus aucuparia)		●		●		●			●		●	●	●		
service-tree (Sorbus torminalis)			●		●		●	●			●				
wayfaring tree (Viburnum lantana)					●		●	●			●		●		
whitebeam, common (Sorbus aria)		●		●	●		●		●						●
willow, goat (Salix caprea)	●	●	●						●						
willow, white (Salix alba)	●	●								●					
yew (Taxus baccata)			●	●		●							●	●	●
willow, crack (Salix fragilis)	●	●							●						

Native wild shrub species

Native wild shrub species	site			soil				features						
	wet	exposed	shady	light	heavy	acid	alkaline	climbing	evergreen	autumn colour	flowers	fruit/berries	good for hedging	invasive
bilberry/blackberry (*Vaccinium myrtillus*)		•	•			•						•		
blackthorn/sloe (*Prunus spinosa*)				•	•	•	•				•	•	•	•
bog myrtle (*Myrica gale*)	•					•								
bramble (*Rubus fruticosus*)	•		•	•	•	•	•				•	•		•
broom (*Cytisus scoparius*)		•		•		•					•			
buckthorn, alder (*Frangula alnus*)	•						•							
buckthorn, purging (*Rhamnus catharticus*)					•		•							
buckthorn, sea (*Hippophae rhamnoides*)		•		•								•		•
butcher's-broom (*Ruscus aculeatus*)			•				•		•					
dogwood (*Cornus sanguinea*)				•	•		•			•	•	•	•	
elder (*Sambucus nigra*)				•	•		•				•	•		•
gorse/furze/whin (*Ulex europaeus*)		•		•		•					•		•	•
guelder rose (*Viburnum opulus*)	•		•		•		•			•	•	•		
hawthorn, Midland (*Crataegus laevigata*)			•		•		•							
heath, cross-leaved (*Erica tetralix*)	•	•				•			•		•			
heather/ling (*Calluna vulgaris*)		•				•			•		•			
heather, bell (*Erica cinerea*)		•		•		•			•		•			
honeysuckle (*Lonicera periclymenum*)			•	•	•	•		•			•	•	•	
ivy (*Hedera helix*)		•	•	•	•	•	•	•	•					
juniper (*Juniperus communis*)		•	•	•		•	•		•					
osier (*Salix viminalis*)	•									•				
privet, wild (*Ligustrum vulgare*)			•	•			•				•	•		•
rose, dog (*Rosa canina*)		•		•	•						•	•		
rose, field (*Rosa arvensis*)			•		•						•	•		
spurge-laurel (*Daphne laureola*)			•	•			•				•	•		
traveller's joy/old man's beard (*Clematis vitalba*)			•	•	•		•	•			•	•		
tutsan (*Hypericum androsaemum*)					•						•			
willow, grey (*Salix cinerea*)	•	•	•										•	
willow, purple (*Salix purpurea*)	•	•												

Tree species for windbreak and shelter belt planting

FERTILE SITES

Wet	deep, rich, very moist alluvium and fenland, mostly cultivated	hybrid poplars, common alder, common cricket-bat and crack willows, Norway spruce (with nurse)
	heavy, wet compacted silts, limestone clays, low-lying fertile calcareous soils in damp districts	alder, ash, grey poplar, Norway and Sitka spruce, western red cedar
	wet clay patches on fertile hill ground	alder, willow, Norway spruce, western red cedar (with nurse)
	loose peat in wet hollows	alder, poplars, Norway spruce or Sitka spruce (if exposed)
Moist	fertile valley soils, which are good farmland	ash, sycamore, grey poplar, alder, horse chestnut, hornbeam, lime, field maple, walnut (if not cold), western red cedar, Lawson cypress
	heavy loams and clays of central England	common oak, Turkey oak, horse chestnut, hornbeam, lime, scarlet oak, Norway maple, Japanese larch, Norway and Sitka spruce, Scots pine (in the east), Corsican pine (in dry districts)
	steep, fertile rocky slopes, deep fertile non-alkaline soils, loose sand and gravel in valleys	European larch, Scots pine, Douglas fir, Norway spruce, Lawson cypress, western hemlock, silver fir, beech, hazel, alder, birch, pine, wild cherry
	fertile rocky slopes too high for oak and ash, perhaps covered with bracken	Sitka and Norway spruce, European larch
Dry	chalk downs, limestone hills in areas of low rainfall	Austrian, Corsican and Scots pine, birch, lime, wych elm, whitebeam, horse chestnut, beech (with nurse), European larch (as nurse planting)
	shallow calcareous soils	Japanese larch, Corsican pine, wych elm, birch, beech, ash (as nurse), Norway maple, Turkey oak, hawthorn, prunus spp.
	sands over chalk and limestone in south and east	Corsican and Austrian pine (latter for shallower soils), western red cedar

MODERATELY FERTILE SITES

Wet	rich flushes with shallow peat	Norway spruce, alder, sallow
	shallow peat, usually over heavy clay soil	Norway and Sitka spruce, western red cedar, alder, aspen, sallow
Moist	heavy, slightly impervious acid soils	sessile oak (with nurse), alder, birch, Sitka and Norway spruce, Scots pine, western red cedar with western hemlock for underplanting
Dry	well drained loams, light sands and gravels in south-eastern England and eastern Scotland with low rainfall; well drained rocky slopes in higher rainfall areas; dry oakwood areas; dry porous soils of moderate fertility	Japanese and European larch, Douglas fir, Scots pine, Corsican pine (on light soils in south and east)

Wet	leached soils, and limestone hills	Sitka spruce (on turf), common alder, common birch
	fibrous peat	Sitka spruce (on turf, with lodgepole pine as nurse)
Moist	shallow acid peaty areas	Sitka spruce, Norway spruce, Scots pine, western red cedar
	birch scrub areas, western districts	Sitka spruce, Douglas fir (in hollows), Scots pine (on mounds)
	bare exposed moorland over heavy impervious soils	lodgepole, mountain and Scots pines, common birch
Dry	dry heathland	Scots pine (in the north), Corsican pine (in the south)
	sandy, acid or gravelly ground of low fertility	Scots and Austrian pines, maritime pine (on deep sands in south and west), western hemlock, birch, red oak

Shrubs to form an impenetrable barrier

	deciduous	evergreen	planting intervals (mm.)
Crataegus spp. (hawthorn)	•		230
Ilex aquifolium (holly)		•	460
Prunus spinosa (blackthorn)	•		300
Pyracantha spp. (firethorn)		•	600
Rosa rugosa (Ramanas rose)	•		600
Ulex europaeus (gorse)		•	460

Shrubs for formal hedging

	deciduous	evergreen	planting intervals (mm.)
Buxus sempervirens (box)		•	460
Carpinus betulus (hornbeam)	•		300
Cupressocyparis leylandii (Leyland cypress)		•	460
Fagus sylvatica (beech)	•		300
Ligustrum (privet)		•	300
Lonicera nitida (Chinese honeysuckle)		•	300
Prunus lusitanica (Portugal laurel)		•	600
Rosmarinus officinalis (rosemary)		•	460
Taxus baccata (yew)		•	460
Thuja plicata (western red cedar)		•	600

The management of formal hedges

Trim once a year (usually in autumn)	*Aucuba japonica variegata* (variegated spotted laurel) *Berberis darwinii* (barberry): trim in spring after flowering *Berberis stenophylla* (barberry): trim in spring after flowering *Elaeagnus pungens* (oleaster/wild olive) *Laurus nobilis* (bay laurel) *Prunus lusitanica* (Portugal laurel)
Trim twice a year (July/August and October). Some may need a second trim only to remove any secondary growth made since the first trim.	*Berberis buxifolia* Nana (dwarf barberry) *Buxus* spp. (box) *Carpinus betulus* (hornbeam) *Chamaecyparis lawsonii* (Lawson cypress) *Corylus avellana* (hazel) *Cotoneaster simonsii* (cotoneaster) *Cupressocyparis leylandii* (Leyland cypress) *Cupressus* spp. (cypress) *Escallonia* spp. (Chilean gum box) *Euonymus japonica* and vars. (spindle tree) *Fagus sylvatica* and var. *purpurea* (beech and purple beech) *Ilex aquifolium* and vars. (holly) *Juniperus* spp. (juniper) *Pyracantha* spp. (firethorn) *Rosmarinus officinalis* (rosemary) *Symphoricarpus* spp. (snowberry) *Taxus baccata* and vars. (yew) *Thuja plicata* (western red cedar) *Viburnum tinus* (laurustinus)
Trim several times a year to retain formal shape	*Crataegus oxycantha* and vars. (hawthorn/quick) *Ligustrum ovalifolium* and vars. (privet) *Lonicera nitida* (Chinese honeysuckle) *Prunus cerasifera* (myrobolan) *Prunus spinosa* (blackthorn/sloe) *Ulex europaeus* (gorse/furze)

The management of established informal hedges

Cut flowering shoots back to two or three buds in late winter/ early spring	*Acer negundo* (box elder) *Buddleia davidii* and vars. (buddleia) *Fuchsia* spp. (fuchsia) *Hydrangea arborescens* (hydrangea) *Hypericum patulum* and vars. (hypericum) *Lavandula* spp. (lavender) *Olearia haastii* (daisy bush) *Potentilla fruticosa* (shrubby cinquefoil) *Rosa pimpinellifolia* (Scotch or burnet rose) *Rosa rubiginosa* (sweet briar) *Rosa rugosa* (Ramanas rose) *Sambucus nigra* (elder) *Santolina chamaecyparissus* (cotton lavender) *Spiraea japonica* and vars. (spiraea)
After flowering, cut back shoots to within 150–200 mm. of their base and thin as necessary	*Amelanchier canadensis* (snowy mespilus) *Berberis darwinii* (barberry) *Berberis stenophylla* (barberry) *Buddleia alternifolia* (buddleia) *Ceanothus dentatus* (Californian lilac) *Chaenomeles japonica* (quince) *Cytisus* spp. (broom) *Deutzia* spp. (deutzia) *Forsythia* spp. (forsythia) *Hippophae rhamnoides* (sea buckthorn) *Kerria japonica* (jew's mallow) *Mahonia aquifolium* (Oregon grape) *Osmanthus delavayi* (osmanthus) *Philadelphus* spp. (mock orange) *Prunus blireana* (purple-leaved flowering plum) *Prunus cerasifera pissardii* (copper-leaved flowering plum) *Ribes sanguineum* and vars. (flowering currant) *Rosa moyesii* (rose) *Spiraea thunbergii* (spiraea) *Viburnum opulus sterile* (Guelder rose or snowball bush) *Weigelia* spp. (weigelia)
Little or no trimming, except for cutting back long untidy growth in autumn or spring	*Arundinaria japonica* (bamboo) *Berberis thunbergii atropurpurea* (purple barberry) *Cotoneaster franchetti* (cotoneaster) *Cotoneaster frigida* (cotoneaster) *Cotoneaster microphylla* (cotoneaster) *Hebe traversii* (veronica) *Kalmia latifolia* (calico bush) *Lonicera fragrantissima* (bush honeysuckle) *Phillyraea decora* (mock privet) *Rhododendron* spp. and vars. (rhododendron and azalea) *Rosa* spp. (rose species and musk roses) *Skimmia japonica* (skimmia)

Grass species and seed mixtures for shaded areas

type of soil		species of grass	% of seeds in mix
heavy, moist	rye	*Lolium perenne* S.23 (perennial)	50
	meadowgrass	*Poa trivialia* (rough-stalked)	30
	bent	*Agrostis stolonifera* (creeping)	20
medium	rye	*Lolium perenne* S. 23 (perennial)	25
	meadowgrass	*Poa pratensis* (smooth-stalked)	50
	dogstail or	*Cynosurus cristatus* (crested)	25 (med.-light)
	fescue	*Festuca ovina* (sheep's)	25 (med.)
light	bent	*Agrostis tenuis* (browntop)	30
	fescue	*Festuca ovina* (sheep's) *Festuca tenuifolia* (fine-leaved) *Festuca rubra* S. 59 (creeping red)	40 20 10
peaty heathland	fescue	*Festuca tenuifolia* (fine-leaved) *Festuca rubra* S. 59 (creeping red)	30 30
	hairgrass	*Deschampsia flexuosa* (wavy)	40

Planting to attract birds

Native trees and shrubs	*Garden trees and shrubs*	*Some wild plants*	*Some garden flowers*
bilberry	barberry varieties	grasses	antirrhinum
bramble	cherries	knapweed	cosmos
buckthorn, sea	cotoneasters	nettles	Michaelmas daisies
crab apple	elaeagnus	poppies	scabious
elder	guelder rose	ragwort	sunflowers
hawthorn	honeysuckle	teasels	
holly	Japanese laurel	thistles	
poplar, black	pyracantha		
rose, field	pernettyas		
rowan	roses		
spindle tree	snowberry		
wayfaring tree			
willow, white			
yew			

Numbers of insect species on various forest trees (C = coniferous)

oak	284	pine (C)	91	lime	31
willow	266	alder	90	hornbeam	28
birch	229	elm	82	larch	17
hawthorn	149	hazel	73	fir (C)	16
blackthorn	109	beech	64	holly	7
poplar	97	ash	41		
apple	93	spruce (C)	37		

Some native trees and shrubs attractive to insects

alder
bilberry
birch, downy
crab apple
elm, wych
hawthorn
hazel
pear, wild
pine, Scots
whitebeam, common
willows, crack, goat,
   grey, purple

Some garden plants which attract and support butterflies

alyssum
aubretia
bird's foot trefoil
bramble
buckthorn
buddleia
candytuft
catmint
coltsfoot
cornflower
dame's violet
forget-me-not
golden rod
hawthorn
heliotrope
hemp agrimony
honesty
honeysuckle
hyssop
ice plant
lady's smock
lavender
lilac
marjoram
Michaelmas daisy
mignonette
petunia
pinks
polyanthus
primrose
purple loosestrife
ragged robin
scabious
sea thrift
sweet rocket
sweet violet
stinging nettle
thyme
verbena
veronica

Some night-scented plants which attract and support moths

alpine violet
bladder campion
Californian primrose
evening primrose
everlasting pea
honeysuckle
jasmine, white
night-scented catchfly
night-scented stock
petunia
soapwort
sweet rocket
tobacco plant
valerian
verbena

Some food plants for bees

alyssum
barberry
bladder senna
bluebell
candytuft
catmint
celandine, lesser
chives
clarkia
coreopsis
cornflower
cotoneaster
crocus
delphinium
dogwood
foxglove
French marigold
godetia
globe thistle
ice plant
Japanese quince
larkspur
lavender
lemon balm
lobelia
lungwort
lupin
Michaelmas daisy
monkshood
narcissus
nasturtium
rock rose
sage, common
scabious
sea holly
sea lavender
snowy mespilus
teasel, common
thyme
veronica
Virginian cowslip
wallflower
yellow archangel

Wild flower mixture for a wide range of soils and situations

SPECIES	COLOUR	HEIGHT	FLOWERING PERIOD											
			Jan	Feb	Mar	Apr	May	Jun	Jul	Aug	Sep	Oct	Nov	Dec
red campion (*Silene dioica*)	red	tall			■	■	■	■	■	■	■	■	■	
kidney vetch (*Anthyllis vulneraria*)	yellow	short					■	■	■	■	■			
black medick (*Medicago lupulina*)	yellow	low					■	■	■	■	■			
field forget-me-not (*Myosotis arvensis*)	blue	low					■	■	■	■	■			
ragged robin (*Lychnis flos-cuculi*)	pink	tall					■	■						
oxeye daisy (*Chrysanthemum leucanthemum*)	white	tall					■	■	■	■	■			
white campion (*Silene alba*)	white	tall					■	■	■	■	■			
lady's bedstraw (*Galium verum*)	yellow	short						■	■	■				
hedge woundwort (*Stachys sylvatica*)	purple	medium						■	■	■				
self heal (*Prunella vulgaris*)	violet	low						■	■	■	■			
common teasel (*Dipsacus fullonum*)	blue	tall							■	■				
common St John's wort (*Hypericum perforatum*)	yellow	tall							■	■	■			
hairy St John's wort (*Hypericum hirsutum*)	yellow	tall							■	■	■			
slender St John's wort (*Hypericum pulchrum*)	yellow	short							■	■	■			
square St John's wort (*Hypericum tetrapterum*)	yellow	medium							■	■	■			
harebell (*Campanulata rotundifolia*)	blue	short							■	■	■			

Wild flower mixture for use with native grasses, suitable for a wide range of soils and situations

SPECIES	COLOUR	HEIGHT	FLOWERING PERIOD											
			Jan	Feb	Mar	Apr	May	Jun	Jul	Aug	Sep	Oct	Nov	Dec
kidney vetch (*Anthyllis vulneraria*)	yellow	short				■	■	■	■	■	■			
field forget-me-not (*Myosotis arvensis*)	blue	low				■	■	■	■	■	■	■		
ribwort plantain (*Plantago lanceolata*)	brown	medium			■	■	■	■	■	■	■			
birdsfoot trefoil (*Lotus corniculatus*)	yellow	low					■	■	■	■	■			
oxeye daisy (*Chrysanthemum leucanthemum*)	white	medium					■	■	■	■	■			
salad burnet (*Sanguisorba minor*)	green	short					■	■	■	■	■			
caraway (*Carum carvi*)	white	medium						■	■					
chicory (*Chicorium intybus*)	blue	tall					■	■	■	■	■			
foxglove (*Digitalis purpurea*)	pink	tall					■	■	■	■	■			
yarrow (*Achillea millefolium*)	white	medium					■	■	■	■	■	■		
sheep's parsley (*Petroselinum sativum*)	white	medium							■	■	■			

Old corn field mixture, to be sown with grasses or as a supplement

A mix of annuals characteristic of traditional corn fields, producing over many weeks a mass of blooms in a wide range of colours

SPECIES	COLOUR	HEIGHT	FLOWERING PERIOD											
			Jan	Feb	Mar	Apr	May	Jun	Jul	Aug	Sep	Oct	Nov	Dec
field forget-me-not (*Myosotis arvensis*)	blue	low				■	■	■	■	■	■	■		
corn cockle (*Agrostemme githago*)	pink	tall					■	■	■	■	■			
white campion (*Silene alba*)	white	tall					■	■	■	■	■			
cornflower (*Centaurea cyanus*)	blue	medium						■	■	■	■			
corn marigold (*Chrysanthemum segetum*)	yellow	medium						■	■	■	■	■		
corn poppy (*Papaver rhoeas*)	red	medium						■	■	■	■			

Easy and difficult vegetables

VERY EASY
(simple to grow, need no heat or glass in early stages, suffer from few diseases)

salads:	radishes, spring onions, lettuce (all kinds)
roots:	Jerusalem artichokes, beetroot, parsnips, potatoes, salsify, swedes
stems and bulbs:	garlic, kohlrabi, leeks, onions (from sets), rhubarb, shallots
legumes:	broad beans, haricot beans
leaves:	cabbage (all kinds), kale, purple sprouting broccoli, spinach, all herbs

LESS EASY

roots:	carrots, turnips
stems and bulbs:	onions from seed
legumes:	peas, runner beans (need staking)
leaves:	Brussels sprouts, spinach, cauliflower
various:	vegetable marrow, globe artichokes, pumpkins, watercress

MORE DIFFICULT
(need to be raised under glass in compost, are selective in their soil needs, and require special treatment in their cultivation)

celery, ridge cucumbers, squash, sweet corn, asparagus, outdoor tomatoes

TO BE GROWN UNDER GLASS THROUGHOUT

aubergines, melons, cucumbers, indoor tomatoes

Cropping plan for a garden of about 20 square metres
providing vegetables for a family of four to five people
(* = successive sowings required)

vegetable	quantity needed	number of 10-m. rows needed
artichokes, Jerusalem	50 kg	4
*beans, broad	54 kg	4
beans, runner	65 kg	4
*beetroot	25 kg	2
*cabbage (all kinds)	200 heads	10
*carrots	38 kg	4
kale	18 kg	2
kohlrabi	4.5 kg	1
leeks	32 kg	4
onions	102 kg	6
parsnips	25 kg	2
potatoes	152 kg	8
*peas	50 kg	4
shallots	19 kg	2
swedes	50 kg	4

Herbs for dappled shade positions

alkanet (*Alkanna tinctoria*)
angelica (*Angelica archangelica*)
bistort (*Polygonum bistorta*)
boneset (*Eupatorium perfoliatum*)
burdock (*Arctium lappa*)
celery (*Apium graveolens var. dulce*)
chervil (*Anthriscus cerefolium*)
garden sorrel (*Rumex acetosa*)
lady's mantle (*Alchemilla vulgaris*)
lungwort (*Pulmonaria officinalis*)
marsh mallow (*Althaea officinalis*)
sweet cicely (*Myrrhis odorata*)
valerian (*Valeriana officinalis*)
wintergreen (*Gaultheria procumbens*)

Herbs that will thrive in deep shade

ramsons/wild garlic (*Allium ursinum*)
Solomon's seal (*Polygonatum multiflorum*)
woodruff (*Galium odoratum*)

Herbs that grow over 1.25 m. high

American senna (*Cassia marilandica*)
angelica (*Angelica archangelica*)
chicory (*Cichorium intybus*)
elecampane (*Inula helenium*)
evening primrose (*Oenothera biennis*)
fennel (*Foeniculum vulgare*)
hop (*Humulus lupulus*)
lemon verbena (*Lippia triphylla*)
lovage (*Levisticum officinale*)
mullein (*Verbascum thapsus*)
rose (*Rosa canina, R.damascena*)
rosemary (*Rosmarinus officinalis*)
sunflower (*Helianthus annuus*)

Small trees and shrubs

bay (*Laurus nobilis*)
broom (*Cytisus scoparius*)
juniper (*Juniperus communis*)
myrtle (*Myrtus communis*)
witch hazel (*Hamamelis virginiana*)

Herbs with distinctively coloured leaves

Dark leaves

basil, purple (*Ocimum basilicum* Dark Opal)
bay (*Laurus nobilis*)
fennel, bronze (*Foeniculum vulgare*)
geranium, peppermint-scented (*Pelargonium tomentosum*)
ground ivy (*Glechoma hederacea*)
horehound, black (*Ballota nigra*)
juniper (*Juniperus communis*)
mints: black peppermint (*Mentha piperita*)
     Eau-de-Cologne mint (*M. piperita citrara*)
myrtle (*Myrtus communis*)
sage, red (*Salvia officinalis Purpurescens*)
tansy (*Tanacetum vulgare*)
thyme (*Thymus serpyllum Coccineus*)
wall germander (*Teucrium chamaedrys*)
woad (*Isatis tinctoria*)

Variegated leaves

Plant these less-hardy herbs in sheltered places, avoiding shade as they tend to revert to green without sunlight

lemon balm, variegated (*Melissa officinalis Aurea*)
lungwort (*Pulmonaria officinalis*)
meadowsweet, variegated (*Filipendula ulmaria Variegata*)
mints: pineapple mint (*Mentha suaveolens Variegata*)
     ginger mint (*M. gentilis Variegata*)
pelargoniums: many scented geraniums have variegated leaves
rue, variegated (*Ruta graveolens Variegata*)
sage (*Salvia officinalis Icterina*)
—, golden (*S. officinalis Tricolor*)
thymes

Pale and silver leaves

artemisia/southernwood (*A. abroanum* (wormwood), *A. absinthium, A. canescens, A. pedemontana, A. stelleriana*)
camphor plant (*Balsamita major*)
clove carnation (*Dianthus caryophyllus*)
costmary (*Balsamita major*)
dittany of Crete (*Origanum dictamnus*)
donkey's ears (*Stachys byzantina*)
eucalyptus (*E. globulus*)
horehound, white (*Marrubium vulgare*)
lavender (*Lavandula angustifolia*)
marsh mallow (*Althaea officinalis*)
mints: apple mint (*Mentha suaveolens*)
     horse mint (*M. longifolia*)
mullein (*Verbascum thapsis*)
rue (*Ruta graveolens* Jackman's Blue)
sage (*Salvia officinalis*)
santolina (*S. chamaecyparissus*)
sea holly (*Eryngium maritimum*)
thymes (woolly thyme (*Thymus pseudolanuginosus*), *T. citriodorus* Silver Queen, *T. vulgaris* Silver Posie)

Gold leaves

feverfew (*Tanacetum parthenium*)
marjoram, golden (*Origanum vulgare Aureum*)
purslane, golden (*Portulaca oleracea Sativa*)
thymes: golden lemon thyme (*Thymus citriodorus Aureus*)
     golden thyme (*T. vulgaris Aureus*)

Vegetables: a guide to cultivation, and to the space they will need

vegetable	period of use	space between rows (mm.)	space between plants (mm.)	sow	comments
artichokes, globe	July–Oct.	900	900	[plant Apr.]	decorative enough to grow amongst flowers, etc.
artichokes, Jerusalem	Nov.–Mar.	600	300	[plant tubers Feb.–Mar.]	
asparagus	Apr.–June	375	375	[plant Mar.–Apr]	weed as necessary during growing season
beans, broad	May–July	180	150	Nov., Jan., Feb.	pick when pods are finger-thick
beans, dwarf French (under cloches) (outdoors)	July–Oct.	200 600	150	Apr. May–July	pick regularly before beans become tough and stringy
beans, runner	July–Sept.	300–375	230–300	May	can provide an ornamental screen
beetroot	July onwards	230–300	100–150	Apr.–May	start using roots of globe varieties when they reach tennis-ball size
beet, seakale	Aug.–Sept.	300–375	100	May	treat leaves like spinach; cook stalks separately; serve with white sauce
broccoli, heading/spring	Feb.–May	760	450	Apr.–May	
broccoli, purple sprouting	Mar.–June	760	450	Apr.–May	pick 150-mm. side shoots only
Brussels sprouts	Oct.–May	900	760	Jan., Mar., Aug.	remove only 3–4 sprouts at a time from each plant
cabbage, spring late summer winter	Apr.–June Sept.–Dec. Dec.–Feb.	600	450	Aug. Mar. Apr.	savoys and drumheads will stand hard frosts for up to two months
carrots, maincrop	Sept. onwards	375	150	Apr.	can be stored in sand after twisting off the tops
cauliflower	Sept.–Oct.	600	600	Apr.	
celery, self-blanching	Aug.–Oct.	450	300	Mar.–Apr.	weed in early stages; water often
chicory	Nov.–Mar.	375–450	300	June	

cucumbers (under glass)	July–Sept.		900	May	water frequently; cut regularly
kohlrabi	May onwards	300–375	150–300	Mar.–Apr.	
leeks	Dec.–May	300	150	Mar.	
lettuce, summer and autumn	May–Oct.	300	230	Mar.–Aug.	choose varieties suited to the time of year and method of cultivation
winter (outdoors)	May–June			Aug.–Sept.	
winter (under glass)	Apr.–May			Oct.–Nov.	
marrows, bush	July–Dec.		900	May	best cut when 200–300 mm. long; for storage leave till Oct. to pick
onions, salad	May onwards	300	230	Mar.	sow sparingly; use thinnings in salads
maincrop (sets)	Aug. onwards			[plant in spring]	
parsnips	Nov. onwards	375	230	Mar.	
peas	June–Sept.	75	50	Jan.–July	tall varieties need support
potatoes	late June onwards	600	600	Feb.–May	lift when tubers are large enough
radishes, salad	Mar.–Sept.	300	300	Mar.–July	make frequent sowings for succession
winter	Oct. onwards			July	
salsify	Dec.–Apr.	375	200	May	scrape or peel just before cooking, as flesh discolours quickly
shallots	July onwards	300	230	Mar.–May	
spinach, summer	May–July	230	150	Mar.–May	use plants when 150 mm. high
spinach beet	Aug. onwards	230–300	150	June–July	pick leaves only, and sparingly
swedes	Nov. onwards	450	230–300	June–July	water well in dry weather
sweet corn	Aug.–Nov.	450	450	May	
tomatoes	Sept. onwards	600	375–450	mid-Feb.	side-shoot regularly; pinch out top above fourth flower truss
turnips (late sown)	Oct.–Feb.	300	230	July	

Rotation of vegetable crops

Plot 1	Plot 2	Plot 3	Plot 4
beans, peas, celery	beet, carrots, parsnips	cabbage, broccoli, savoy cabbage, sprouts, cauliflower, turnips onions, leeks, shallots, lettuce, spinach	potatoes

If potatoes are not grown, a 3-plot rotation only will be needed.

A further plot, outside the rotation, is set aside for secondary and perennial crops: asparagus, horseradish, rhubarb, seakale, globe artichoke, Jerusalem artichoke, strawberry bed (3 years only), bush fruits.

Grapes

	EATING OR WINE	WINE-MAKING
Outdoor early ripening	*Siegerrebe:* good crops of large gold grapes with strong Muscat flavour *Précoce de Malingre:* prolific growth, of French origin; excellent wine and good dessert grapes *Madeleine Angevine:* masses of white grapes of medium size	*Siegerrebe* *Madeleine Sylvaner:* white grape of fine flavour *Ortega:* German vine making an excellent wine
Outdoor mid-season	*Muller-Thurgau* (Riesling Sylvaner): mainly grown for wine, but good eating *Marshal Joffre:* French hybrid black grape; very attractive vine with good leaves *Seyval blanc:* hybrid mainly grown for wine, but pleasant to eat *Perle de Czaba:* produces smallish grapes of excellent Muscat flavour	*Muller-Thurgau:* highest quality grape producing hock-type wine; widely grown *Seyve Villiard* 5/276: prolific cropper, producing high standard white wine; best on chalk soils *Siebal* 13053: hybrid black grape *Zweigeltrebe:* a recent Austrian introduction, producing promising red wine *Pinot Chardonnay:* white grape from the Champagne area
Outdoor later ripening	*Chasselas d'Or, Chasselas Rosé:* standard French eating grape, used for wine-making in Alsace; especially good on walls *White Frontignan:* magnificent white grape with Muscat flavour; only suitable for well favoured sites or under cloches	*Wrotham Pinot:* highest quality grape producing hock-type wine; grown in England since Tudor times *Traminer:* weak growth but fine wine; needs a good site *Regner:* vine susceptible to disease, but producing wine of exceptional quality

Bibliography

Armstrong, P.H., *Discovering Geology*, 1978

Battiscombe, G., *English Picnics*, 1951

Beckett, K. and G., *Planting Native Trees and Shrubs*, 1979

Caborn, J.M., *Shelter Belts and Windbreaks*, 1965

Cartner, W.C., *Fun with Geology*, n.d.

Cheatle, J.W.R., *A Guide to the British Landscape*, 1976

Church, T., *Gardens are for People*, 1983

Coles, C. (ed.), *The Complete Book of Game Conservation*, 1975

Colvin, B., *Land and Landscape*, 1948

Cook, O., *English Cottages and Farmhouses*, 1982

Drabble, M., *A Writer's Britain: Landscape in Literature*, 1979

Edlin, H.B., *Timber, Your Growing Investment*, Forestry Commission Booklet No. 23, 1969

Fairbrother, N., *New Lives, New Landscapes*, 1972

—— *The Nature of Landscape Design*, 1974

The Garden (periodical)

Garland, S., *The Herb and Spice Book*, 1979

Girouard, M., *Life in the English Country House*, 1978

Harris, J. (ed.), *The Garden: A Celebration of One Thousand Years of British Gardening*, 1979

Harvey, N., *Fields, Hedges and Ditches*, Aylesbury 1976

Hoskins, W.G., *English Landscapes*, 1973

—— *The Making of the English Landscape*, 1955

Hyams, E., *An Englishman's Garden*, 1967

Jellicoe, G., *Studies in Landscape Design*, 1960

Lamb, R., *World Without Trees*, 1979

Laurie, M., *An Introduction to Landscape Architecture*, 1976

Marlowe, O.C., *Outdoor Design*, 1977

Massingham, B., *Miss Jekyll: Portrait of a Great Gardener*, 1968

Muir, R., *The English Village*, 1980

Pevsner, N., *The Englishness of English Art*, 1964

Reader's Digest Association, *The Gardening Year*, 1974

Savage, D.S., *The Cottager's Companion*, 1975

Seddon, G., *Your Kitchen Garden*, 1975

Seymour, J., *The Countryside Explained*, 1979

Sharp, D., *Walking in the Countryside*, 1978

Stuart, D.C., *Georgian Gardens*, 1979

Tunnard, C., *Gardens in the Modern Landscape*, 1938

Waldstein, Baron, *The Diary of Baron Waldstein, A Traveller in Elizabethan England*, ed. Gordon Groos, 1981

Wells, T., Bell, S., and Frost, A., *Creating Attractive Grasslands using Native Plant Species*, 1981

Wilson, M.I., *The English Country House*, 1977

Wilson, R., *The Back Garden Wildlife Sanctuary Book*, 1979

Wright, T., *Large Gardens and Parks: Maintenance, Management and Design*, 1982

Index

Page references in *italic* indicate illustrations.